"*All Quiet on the Western Front* drives its readers to the front of World War I. *F.N.G.* helicopters its readers to a new front: Vietnam."
Bestsellers

"A powerful social document and a well-written, deeply moving first novel... highly recommended."
Library Journal

"Bodey brings back alive the particular horrors of that particular war so well that we participate in it with frightening directness. His prose is exacting, his rendering of evocative details thoroughly accomplished, and the pacing absolutely absorbing. His refusal to engage larger political or policy issues seals us into the experience perfectly and reminds us how narrow all our views of that conflict were, and what terrible waste the war effected."
Chicago

F.N.G.

Donald Bodey

BALLANTINE BOOKS • NEW YORK

Library of Congress Catalog Card Number: 85-10629

ISBN 0-345-33945-2

This edition published by arrangement with Viking Penguin Inc.

Printed in Canada

First Ballantine Books Edition: February 1987
Eighth Printing: May 1992

Dedicated to my father's memory and to my mother; to all my brothers—blood and spiritual; to each and every surrogate mother, wife, sister I've needed; and for Mike Morgan, KIA, because I could never keep the promise I made.

CONTENTS

"I can forgive, but if you ask me to forget, you ask me to give up experience."

—Louis Brandeis

F.N.G.

TWO SEATS AWAY IS A GUY WITH A HUGE ADAM'S APPLE and blue eyes like two line drives. His face is probably on a calendar; he's too young-looking to be on Uncle Sam Wants You posters, but the face is too honed to go to waste. He isn't looking right at me, but out the window behind me, and for a minute I can't look anywhere but into his eyes. I think of line drives. Say, when the mosquitoes are in off the river, last of the sixth maybe, sun down over third base behind the shabby bleachers, and I'm playing center field *when a crack like a hickory breaking brings me a shot over second and I gotta dive to even knock it down* . . . well, the guy's eyes are like two of them.

Of course I'm *trying hard* to think of something else.

Everybody looks alike in this jet that is as big as a barn-yard. I wonder where we are. From Seattle to Wake Island, where I only barely got awake because me and some little guy from Phoenix sneaked a bottle of bourbon through the fence in Seattle.

The goddamn U.S. Army locks you in a fence twenty-four hours before your flight.

Fifteen bucks for a bottle, but man, good. So I was passed out all the way to Wake Island, and when I woke up there was when I first felt this alone. So alone, even

1

though all the guys in the plane look like me. Like a box of play soldiers.

The wing of the plane points steady at a dot of light rock while we spiral lower. The seat belt feels too tight and I need to piss. The guy beside me wakes up and soon everything is almost upside down.

I like it but I don't, like swinging over the creek on a rope.

●●●●●●●●●●●

"FALL OUT!"

Some prick lieutenant screams it like his echo is the only thing he's ever heard. Okinawa is another airport. The Army world is airports—stepping-stones to some whore's door.

"Ungoddamnly hot here. I'd rather be home." He moves his mouth a lot when he talks and his whole face changes but it starts and stops in that calendar smile. His Adam's apple moves like a bobber does when a minnow is nibbling.

". . . Nowhere." Some lifer directs us to a yellow line while he is talking. "This here shit-lookin' rock is Ok-i-fucki-Nowhere," he says.

Ok-i-fucki-Nowhere is concrete checkered by red and yellow lines. The front wheels of our plane are straddling a red one. We are spilling into line on a yellow one looking west, unless the sun sets different over here.

We are jungle-green mockingbirds and, like he's the one with the cracker, there's a guy facing our line who reads the roll-call numbers through his nose:

"US five-five, niner-four, niner-seven, one, one."

"Here," one bird mocks.

"RA three fifteen, forty-six, sixty-six oh seven"—like he is pinching his nostril.

"Here."

Standing in that heat, completely Olive Drab, we don't

2

seem like men—like poultry, like a truckload of fryer hens, all so alike.

"I'm Albert Steven Saxon, answer to Ass, hail from Kansas City, and I'd rather be there instead of here," he says.

His speech is fast and even, like baseball chatter. He pops little bubbles out of his chewing gum when he isn't talking. It seems like his jaw muscles would get sore.

"I'm Gabriel Sauers, from near Cincinnati."

Our line moves toward the tropical webbing that pushes against the airport concrete. There are vines as thick as telephone poles that wind through each other and into some stubby trees that don't have tops. Above the trees is the tower of the terminal, looking out on the landing field like it was a rooster looking at us slaughter hens.

A path that is almost invisible from the runway leads to an open area where a lot of guys are sitting in red dust. No one seems to have anything to do. Here or there some guy is reading, but they are mostly grouped into fours and fives, squatting or sitting in the dust, probably talking about yesterday or a year ago.

Albert Steven Saxon sprawls into the dust and pulls his hat over his eyes. He is lanky. His legs look like they grew twice as fast as the rest of his body, and his uniform fits funny. His shirt bags out like it is full of air and his pants are about the right length but they are shaped like sausages.

"How long you reckon we'll be laying around this here hole?" he asks.

"Not long enough. The next stop is the big one, I'm sure of that."

"'The big one.' I like that, Gabriel," he tells me, from underneath his hat. He says it again, and the bill of his Army baseball hat is so low all I can see is his smile.

Another plane comes in, a military transport, camouflaged in the same colors as the jungle that this airport is hacked from. But I'm not ready for the load of guys that streams out: not in any line. One tall guy kisses the ground and gets some laughs.

Marines. Fuckin'-A filthy. Pimples galore, jags of beard, in ODs that are torn and stretched and not even olive drab but permanently rusted-looking, red, the color of the dust. The first ones that come into the clearing pass the word back to the others still on the airfield.

"Hey," one yells. "Get a load of these newby dudes!"

And as they come in with their enormous packs, every single one stands a minute and eyeballs us. They are ragged, they stink, there is almost no difference between the color of their jungle utilities and their faces. They are carrying rucksacks that are like mule packs: dirty, bulging sacks with things tied on by shoelaces; bandoliers of machine-gun ammo are strung around them like vines. They've got every weapon I've ever seen: mostly rifles, M-16s that are gouged and broken. Some are held together by tape. There are M-60 machine guns and a few shotguns. Almost all of them have grenades tied to their rucks, and everyone who has a hat on has a Boonie hat, camouflaged jobs, like duck hunters wear.

"Jesus." Ass comes off his back and pushes his Issue baseball hat back, then just sits there, eyes line-driving the other guys. A short Marine comes over our way and stands staring back at Ass, who is staring only because he can't help it. The Marine asks if anybody is from the City, and the guy next to us answers Oklahoma City.

"Oh, Jesus. A bunch o' dumb-fucker clodhoppers."

The first few minutes of conversation are like that. We are foreign and antagonistic to each other. As more Marines come and spread throughout the clearing the conversations change. One guy wants to know who is leading the American League and if the '69 Chevies will really come stock with FM radios.

"Where'd ya get those hats?" Ass asks eventually.

4

"Quang Tri. We're up near the Z. They sell 'em everywhere. You'd best get one if you go to the field."

He takes his hat off and gives it to us. It has been rolled, crammed, and wadded so often it doesn't have a shape. Like a shrunken gunnysack. The whole thing is covered with inkings that are fuzzy because they've been wet and been gone over a lot of times. It has a calendar with days x'd off and the names of places he has been. *God is my point man* is written in red ink.

"Keep your pot close by, though," he says. "You'll want to crawl up inside that fucker sometimes." He slaps his steel helmet, which hangs on the bottom of his rucksack like a mushroom broken off its stem. He lights a cigarette with matches and uses only one hand.

"Been in the field for seven months and been getting the shit kicked out of us for a solid week so they lifted us out, too many guys losing it, know what I mean?"

"Guys going crazy, huh?"

"Going, goinger, and gone—that's all there is left of us. I flipped my own damn self, couldn't have taken another day. Fuckin'-A lost it."

I wish afterward that I didn't notice his eyes that get like clear shooting marbles in the handsome red face.

∎∎∎∎∎∎∎∎∎∎

THERE IS SOMETHING SO *COMMON* TO ALL OF THEM. THINGS hang around their necks: dog tags taped together so not to rattle, rosaries, three and four strands of beads, silver crosses, crude peace medals. There is no extra flesh on the hundred of them. They are all, in fact, as skinny as Bluetick puppies.

And they're all high or getting that way. One guy pulls out a bag of dope that is as big as a softball and rolls a joint eight inches long out of C-ration toilet paper, and when I get a hit I know it ain't like any dope I've ever had.

On two hits I get ungodly high. I keep flashing between

5

these veterans and squirrel hunting back home. Today is opening day. These guys and their plastic rifles don't have much in common with the old farmers waiting in the cafe for daylight, but as I lie there too stoned to move I hallucinate and the feelings seem a lot alike. Bullets are the only thing hunting and war have in common, but I keep looking for others.

■■■■■■■■■■

FOR TWENTY-FOUR HOURS THE WAR MACHINE BREAKS down somehow, somewhere. The Marines can't leave until something changes, and we are held up by something else. Little by little we mingle with the vets, but there is a constant gap of experience that keeps hold of the conversations, the feelings, the looks, even the laughs.

I keep tripping on the differences in their hats and ours. Ours are all alike: olive-drab Army baseball hats. The tags inside all read *Cap*, *man's cotton*, *OG 107 DSA 100-65*, but all their Boonies read differently:

Fuck the Army.
Try a little tenderness.
War is hell and scary.
West by God Virginia.
Stop ugly children, sterilize LBJ.

I spend the whole night in about the exact spot where I first sat down. The air hardly changes temperature, and when I wake up in the middle of the night the sky glitters. Ass is sleeping beside me, and the sounds he makes are like practice snores, as if the voice he snores through hasn't deepened yet. On the other side of the clearing I can see a flashlight moving and a guy is calling, "Hawkins, Cecil Hawkins," in a singsong way, over and over. After I get up and take my leak and get back down I don't think I'll be able to go to sleep again, but the last thing I remember is that voice singing for Cecil Hawkins, nearer but still far away.

It is just getting light when they line us into the plane alphabetically. Saxon, Albert S., draws the seat across the aisle from mine. He is making conversation with the guy next to him while the plane is taxiing.

"Well, y'reckon the war will be over by tomorrow?" he asks me after we level off.

"I doubt it. Last I heard they couldn't decide what shape to make the peace table."

"Why don't they make it the shape of Nam, and the good guys can sit on one side and the bad guys on the other?"

I try to read but I have to keep going back. When I give up the book we are going through clouds the color of Mom's hair.

When we begin to drop he says, "Here we go," so when we land I say, "Here we are."

Cam Ranh Bay doesn't look anything like I imagined it.

And I imagined it, imagined it, imagined it.

When we were making our low approach, the village itself looked like a pile of wood chips.

We get processed through the airport and put into a bus. The compound is centered around the airport. There is nothing but buses, jeeps, and trucks on the roads. For one short distance we cross through gates and drive for five minutes through sand dunes. All along the road is concertina wire laid in three layers with guard towers every so often. There are Vietnamese walking along the road. There is a scrapped tank swarming with little naked kids. Everything seems extra noisy—the high whine of the bus's diesel engine, planes landing and taking off over the road, helicopters hovering in lines.

I can see the village now and then through the sandhills. It is very low to the ground. Nothing sticks up higher than ten feet. When we approach another part of the compound the road is flanked by sandbagged watchtowers. Men hang out of some of them as we go slower now. They yell.

"God pity Eleven Bravos."

"I'll be eating your sister's sandwich in twenty days."

"Peace, brother."

No one in the bus yells back. Eventually we stop and line into lines that line into ranks that line-drive into a mess hall, eat in twenty minutes, and line again in front of a staff sergeant.

"Men, welcome to Vietnam."

The NCO is young but wrinkled and squints into the sun behind us. He goes on in a monotone that must have been saying the same thing for a year.

"Since there are almost no VC left around here you will not be issued weapons until you get ready to go to your units. Anybody who doesn't have his dog tags go to the line over there. You must have two dog tags all the time in Vietnam. If you get blown away, somebody will shove a tag between your teeth and kick your jaw shut, so we don't ship the wrong bag of guts to your mama. Any questions?"

I think at a million miles an hour while we go from station to station: to be positive we all have two dog tags, to be given ration cards, to have explained for the tenth time why U.S. forces are in Vietnam. We get told to buy savings bonds, warned about Hanoi Hannah—"the blackest clap of 'em all"—taken to a sandbagged chapel where the chaplain is drunk, then issued a steel pot and five pair of green underwear. Mine are big enough to fit a rain barrel.

On our way to the mess hall we have to get pneumatic shots. A tobacco-spitting medic who tells the guy in front of me he was a garbage truck driver on the Outside hits my vein, and the blood runs down to my elbow and drops onto my pants. The medic waiting to shoot my other arm says, "Let it drip and put in for a Purple Heart."

●●●●●●●●●●●

EVERYBODY IS TIRED AND GROUCHY AND THERE IS SHOUT-ing in the barracks after supper. There is a two-man out-door shower, and the line moves fast because everybody in line hustles the guys under the water. I'm a little surprised that the water is lukewarm. It comes from a big tank that gets heated by the sun.

The barracks are stuffy, and after I claim a bunk below Ass I go outside to have a smoke. Ours is the last one in a row, and the distance between the barracks and the perime-ter of the compound is only two hundred meters.

The airfield is toward the center of camp. Over the roofs of the barracks buildings there are at least twenty helicop-ters heading different directions, blinking green lights. Al-most all the sound I hear comes from the helicopters: sometimes I distinctly hear the *whoosh* of their jet motors, but mostly there is the out-of-cadence *whap-wop-wop-wop-whap-whack* from the blades chopping air at different angles. The birds have red and green lights but only the green lights blink, and watching them from this distance is like seeing a pinball machine working through an arcade window. All at once I am conscious of a guy standing be-side me, and I get the feeling he is watching the exact green lights that I am.

"Howdy," he says; then, before I can answer, "You're new, huh?"

His voice is higher than I expect. He is a pretty big dude.

"Been here almost a day."

He lights a smoke in one quick motion, and when I smell it I know it's dope.

"With luck you've only got three hundred and sixty-four more. I got one." He whistles the smoke out and hands me a joint.

"What's it like to make it?"

"I didn't make it whole," he says. Now I see his arm is bandaged and strapped to his side.

9

"How bad, uh . . . ?"

"Coulda been my nuts," he says. "I've got all my hand left. . . ."

"Good, I—" I mean to fill the silence.

"One finger."

The quietness gets clumsy. Next thing I know I ask him how it happened. The dope is making me talk.

"On an ambush. A noise, and some Effengee panicked and laid a round my way. Simple."

"Effengee?"

"F, period. N, period. G, period. Effengee. Fuckin' New Guy. They're all alike. You're one. You'll see. I'm Lonesome."

"Me too, and I just got here."

"Lonesome's my nickname. I got it because I built one-man hooches when I was in the field." He stands up. "I'm done here. Goin' home, can you dig that? One more day of that fuckin' hospital and I get on my freedom bird. In a hundred hours I won't be Lonesome. I'll be Chester again. . . . Or maybe I'll get a new nickname, maybe Unfinger. I'm going shopping in the village, wanna come? Ten bucks for a pipe of opium and a blow job."

"Thanks, man, but I just got here."

"And you might get your shit blown backwards tomorrow. Think about it."

■■■■■■■■■■■■

HALFWAY ACROSS THE OPEN AREA HE TAKES HIS HAT OFF and gives it to me. The back of his head is shaved and bandaged, but I don't ask him anything about it.

"You got to get rid of that Effengee baseball hat as soon as you can. Get a Boonie, first time you go to a PX. In the field it's like a woman, can you dig that? I mean, it's something the Army doesn't give you. They give you a number and everybody else a number. But the hat is yours and you can paint it pink if you're nuts enough. Putting your name on it is enough. Like a zero—the Army doesn't like zeros. The reason I gave you mine to use is so not everybody can tell at a glance you're an Effengee, can you—"

"Dig it," I say. I can see him smile in the light from the bunker line.

Our side of the perimeter is dark, but the outside is lit up by huge spotlights mounted on top of the guard towers.

He stops us in back of Bunker 23 and hollers, "Three times twenty-three is sixty-nine."

A flashlight shines from the window and a voice comes from where it goes out. "Wanna get the clap, eh, Lonesome?"

"I got the Jones, man. Gotta get one more crossmounted pussy before I'm a gone muthafucker tomorrow at noon, buddy." He says "gone" especially loud.

"What's in it for us, my man?"

"Best they got."

"Wait one." And the spotlight on the bunker goes out.

Lonesome shows me how to get through a break in the concertina wire, and we are soon galloping down a wide path beyond the range of the spotlights. Another, smaller, trail leads through some vegetation for maybe fifty meters and suddenly to a hut. The hut is lit by a candle sitting in the middle of the dirt floor. A small woman with black teeth is sitting beside the candle smoking what looks like a cigar rolled out of banana leaves.

"Mamasan," Lonesome says, "We want opium and a blow job, one at a time."

"Only one girl," she says.

He goes into the corner and lies down on a pile of brown rags. Mamasan motions to me to sit down and pulls a rag out of her dress, which is a rag too. A girl who can't be over four feet tall comes in and goes to Lonesome. She doesn't say anything. She begins playing with Lonesome,

11

and when she kneels down I see that she only has half her right arm.

The woman looks like a squirrel. Her face is small and round and her black teeth move nervously like a squirrel's. She opens the rag on the floor beside the candle, and there is a small pipe with a long stem and a small bottle of brown liquid. She lights a piece of straw to warm the pipe, then hands it to me and fires it while I drag—just one quick sensation that makes me think of swallowing a spark. The woman sticks the tip of her brown tongue into the bowl of the pipe, then props it between her feet to refill it with one more drop.

The first rush comes and it feels like a part of my head inside is soft and woven, airy, like I've got a sock cap between my brain and my skull. The edges of everything fade too, like wearing sunglasses at night. The woman looks even more like a squirrel, and when she brings the pipe to my mouth the way she holds her arms is the way a squirrel holds a nut.

After that hit she and Lonesome help me onto the pile of rags and I just lie there and cruise. Another GI comes to the door and Mamasan goes outside to talk to him. Lonesome is sitting by the candle with his pants rolled up to his knees, scratching. His feet and ankles are black.

The girl comes to me and I want to look in her face but she keeps it turned away from me. She washes me and some of the water runs down into my new green skivvies. I eventually almost pass out, I think, and I am done and the girl is moving toward the candle when I wrestle my mind back into this hut. Lonesome is lying out flat on the dirt floor and the woman and the girl are whispering: their talk is full of high pitches and low grunts. Once again when the woman turns a certain way I think of a squirrel.

I think I am almost asleep and dreaming about hunting in Schrader's woods when the woman and Lonesome stand up. I come awake, and it feels like I am looking out of a big black umbrella that only lets me see their legs. The woman's dress is longer on one side than the other and makes her legs look like two small saplings broken off at different heights. Lonesome's pants are still rolled up, and the blood from a big picked scab dried while his leg was horizontal so, when he stands up, the scab makes me think of a mailbox flag, swung down. The girl is there too and her legs look ordinary—for a six- or eight-year-old. They all have on the sandals made out of tires, "Ho Chis," and all six feet are black around the straps.

I know this is a moment I'm going to remember.

The hike back to the bunker line seems to take hours. My sense of sound is completely fucked up and I keep seeing things move. It is all I can do to keep from yelling. I don't feel much like talking when we get back to the shadows of the barracks, even though I am not quite as high, but I say thanks when I give Lonesome his hat.

"So you're not quite the Effengee you were," he says. "Stay high, man. Keep your fuckin' head down. Good luck. Never forget there's no such thing as a coward. Look me up, only one in Odgen, Utah. Peace." And he is gone.

●●●●●●●●●●●

I MUST BE AWAKE, BECAUSE I SEE A GUY COMING UP THE two steps to our barracks floor, and I see he's got a garbage can. He throws it down the aisle, and the lid comes off and the can and the lid make unbelievable noise on the concrete floor in that small room.

When everybody jumps, not knowing what the hell to do, he says, "Breakfast is served in five minutes, and for only five minutes, in case the goddamn Chinese send troops in, so get the fuck in line." Then he goes out the door.

Breakfast doesn't even look like food. It should be biscuits and sauce but it looks like half-mixed mortar sitting in kettles the size of big washtubs. There is only one guy serving and he just pours—the guy getting the ration is the one who has to aim the plate. I move mine under the ladle in time to get about half. It's like the cook doesn't even notice. He tells the guy behind me that he is so short he can sit on a dime and swing his legs.

The next line is in front of a sergeant. He is tall and full of muscles and has his cap pulled low onto his brown forehead. Somehow he looks more kind than he sounds. He stands calmly with his hands behind his back until we all get fairly quiet. His uniform is faded but pressed.

"Name's Browser," he says. "If there is only one thing I know, I know most of you mens don't wanna be here, noway, nohow, and nomore, already. I don't neither. I don't like it here, and I don't have to go where some of you mens do. There's not much I can say will cheer you up, but that ain't my job. My job is to keep you busy while you're here in Cam Ranh. There's a chance some of you might go up north early, there may be empty planes. So anybody who ain't an Eleven fall out, get in line; you're goin' on detail. The 'Levens can hang loose because if there's any room on a plane youse grunts'll ship out today. Any questions?"

About half of us are Elevens: infantrymen. The others go to another line and we go back to the barracks. Ass asks me if I want to pitch pennies but I don't so he gets another guy. They are using a crack in the middle of the concrete floor. A couple guys are reading comic books and a couple others are writing letters. I am lying in my bunk thinking about what an odd bunch we seem to be. A great big black guy is sitting on a bunk and whittling with a big knife. He is whistling to himself. There is a pile of shavings between his legs and some on his bunk and on the floor.

I'm the first one to see an officer come through the door. In The World I would yell *Attention!* and we would all stand up until he put us at our ease. I don't really think about it much, but I decide not to do anything and see what

14

happens. He is the lowest-ranking officer there is, a second lieutenant, and he looks like he is younger than I am. But the closer he gets the more I try to look asleep. I hear him go on by my bunk and I can tell he stops at the black guy.

I turn my head enough to watch. The guy at first keeps whittling, then stops and looks up at the second lieutenant.

"What the hell do you think you're doing, Private?"

"Just passin' the mornin', waitin' for shipout order."

I can tell the lieutenant is aching to prove himself somehow, but I don't think the black guy knows it yet.

"See this?" the lieutenant asks. He points to the rank on his shoulder. He's gotta be a first-rate asshole.

"Yeah."

"Yeah?"

"Yeah, sir. I see it, sir."

"Well, you dumb black. . . . What's your name, Private?"

The black guy stands up slowly and a lot of shavings fall off his lap. Some of them land on the officer's boots.

" 'Dumb Black' is pretty close, *sir* Smart-ass White. Just call me Black."

He is going to swing when another guy grabs him. I get up and get hold of his free arm, although he has cooled a little by now. We don't know what to do and neither does the lieutenant. He knows he fucked up, though; it's all over his face, which is extra white right now. His ears are red. Everybody in the barracks has come over.

"You better learn to control your temper while you're here, Private, or you'll end up in LBJ." He walks off fast. The black guy gives him the finger.

We all sit down again, and the guy who restrained him lights a cigarette and spits the way the officer went.

"That guy was a number-one prick," he says.

"Hey, uh, Mister Callmeblack," Ass begins. "What's LBJ?"

"Long Binh Jail."

15

"I'm Ass," Ass says.

"'Callmeblack' is fine with me," the big guy says. "Fact o' matter is, I like it."

There is a guy from New York named Green who has been called Oliverdrab or OD since he's been in the Army. The littlest guy's name is Bakerson. There is a Horstman and two Smiths, one white, one black. The white one has blond hair.

"So how about you being Blacksmith and you Goldsmith? I'm Sauers."

"Everything sours over here."

I lose track of all the names but I've got a new feeling. These guys are going to go through the same thing I do, whatever it is. I feel like a teammate, the same way I have felt toward guys on my baseball teams. It's a warm feeling. I sort of want to tell them about last night but I'm afraid if I do they'll want to go tonight, and I don't.

I need to take a dump so I walk down to the latrines. There is some old woman in there who looks like the woman at the whorehouse last night. She is somewhere between the color of Callmeblack and a feed sack. She is tiny, not even five feet tall. When I come up she is dragging a fuel can that weighs more than she does over to a cut-off oil drum. The drum is a catch pit for the two-holer outhouse. Of course it is full of shit and toilet paper. Just when I get to the shithouse the woman pours some fuel into the drum and lights it: smoke blacker than barn-swallow shit. After it burns down she stirs it and it begins burning better again. I can watch her through the wall of the shithouse because there is about two inches between the boards. She doesn't act like I am around. She is chewing something and spits every so often at the burning shit.

It reminds me of a time five years ago: *Grandaddy spitting his chaw out and climbing down between the spikes of the manure spreader. "Shit is the beginning of everything," he says. I am taking a leak by the wagon and watching elementary school practice in Schrader's field across the creek.*

I wonder why I am flashing all the way back to when I was a kid.

■■■■■■■■■■

THEY COME AND GET US ABOUT NOON. OUR PLANE THIS time is Air Force. A Cargo, camouflaged like the one the Marines had landed in Okinawa. Sitting there on the landing strip, it is huge. It seems to me it would make a hell of a good target, even up in the air.

There are about thirty of us, and we squeeze into the back section. The hatch door slams shut but there is almost a foot of space between the door and the plane. It isn't sealed like an airliner. I feel like I'm in something big and alive, like a whale.

Air Force guys strap us into belts that go all the way across the plane. Five guys under each seat belt. The inside of the plane looks fragile and is crossed by steel struts that are bent and dented. The panels between the struts vibrate in the suck of the propellers while the engines warm up, and when we taxi over the bumpy runway everything shimmies like a washing machine's insides. It is far too loud to talk, but I feel like I am screaming inside myself.

When we lift, the cases of supplies in front of us slide our way. I feel plain scared. Scared this plane is junk, scared of getting shot down, scared I'll crack up before I even get to my rifle unit because I'm so scared.

I remember playing in an abandoned school bus that sat in a big sinkhole behind the school. Playing war. When it rained and thundered and the wind blew we pretended we were in a tank because that old shell rocked and its rattles got loud, like the rattles of this whale plane, which increase when we come down on another airport that looks the same as all the others but is smaller. The jungle is

17

closer and greener; we're in Kontum Province, Central Highlands, near Cambodia.

This is the Division base camp. It's as big as a lot of towns in Ohio but a lot smaller than Cam Ranh was. The buildings are mostly wooden and it reminds me a little of Fort Polk, Louisiana. There are details of men doing the same dumb-ass stuff they'd been doing in The World. I see one group painting rocks white to go alongside a pathway. There is a *Keep Off the Grass* sign in front of one company's mess hall.

At Supply we get a rucksack and a frame. The ruck looks really silly empty, like a present from an aunt that I don't know what to do with. We get issued jungle utilities too, a poncho and poncho liner, steel pot, and a Red Cross packet that has shaving cream, stationery, a pocket Bible, and a dinky package of three moist towels like at a restaurant. It's almost like somebody is playing a joke.

At the Arms Room we get our rifles and a bandolier of ammo. The rifle blows my mind. We trained mostly with M-14s and only had M-16s for three days. Now that I am holding one again, I get the same crazy feeling: it feels and looks like a toy. It doesn't even weigh four pounds but will put out eighteen rounds in less than two seconds. It's plastic, it amazes me, but the feeling I have is foreign. I won't turn this rifle back in tonight, and this bandolier of ammo isn't for target practice.

This shit is meant to kill.

We all go to the PX together. The PX is like a supermarket in The World. After the grittiness of all the Nam I've seen, the inside of the PX is weird, like being in a big plastic bag full of wrapped presents. There are aisles of cameras and stereo equipment and cigarettes—anything made in Japan. The customers are all GIs. Vietnamese are stocking shelves, and there's a long line at the cash register. I buy a ballpoint pen, a Boonie hat, and a carton of cigarettes.

Ass buys every comic they have, a hat, candy bars, and two sets of beads. He gives me one set. The beads are shaped like wisdom teeth and painted to look like ivory. I put them around my neck while we are standing in the cash-register line and he can't leave them alone. He puts my dog tags inside my shirt and puts the beads under my collar. Then he steps back and acts like he is taking a picture.

"With those on," he says, "I can see you in that ungoddamnly dark jungle we're going to."

When we get outside we have to stand around until everybody in our group is done. Ass and I read his comic books and sweat. Even though we are in the shade of the building and standing still, the windless air is skillet hot. By the time he gets to his second candy bar, it is melted to his pocket and he ends up slurping it out of the wrapper. All around his mouth and in his thin mustache are globs and smears of chocolate; he looks younger than ever. I wonder at least once what I look like in my beads and new Boonie.

No sooner have I got my carton of smokes stuffed into my rucksack than a guy comes in and tells us to pack up, then pick up C-rations at the mess hall and report to the helicopter pad because there's a chance we'll be going out to our units. Knowing we're going makes me remember my fear, and I catch myself catching my breath. Nobody says anything, but Ass is kind of singing to himself. Callmeblack is packed and asleep on his bunk. Goldsmith is popping pimples into a round mirror he holds on his knees. My legs ache and the hair under my arms feels matted.

The pad area is fenced off by extra concertina. The actual landing pad is only big enough for two helicopters and is made out of what looks like roof decking, except it's olive drab like everything else. The area is outside the main perimeter, so I get my first daytime look at the country. Along the perimeter line there are little round clouds of

19

red dust that look like giant pillows above the bunker line. They are made by helicopters landing and taking off.

The earth around the pad is red and cracked. Out on the edge of what is cleared is a detail of guys shoveling and raking gravel into the cracks. They're all in tee shirts or bare above the waist, and some of them have shorts on. They're passing a big pipe around. Beyond them is the jungle, and though I can't see it very well I can tell there are trees cut down and that it's been on fire. In the distance are the mountains covered with jungle, and one range after another steps up higher and higher into a layer of chocolate clouds of dust.

A guy with hair longer than anybody's I've seen in Nam comes over to us. His eyes look too small for the rest of his face.

"Anybody going to Bravo Company?"

Three guys are.

"Well, hey," he says, "take some beer out. Give me your ration cards and I'll go to the PX and get beer on your card. We'll bring it out to the field and I'll get your cards back to you out there. Believe me, you'll have more friends this way."

"How about Echo Company? There are three of us here going to Echo."

"Sorry to hear that," he tells me. He has his tee shirt pulled around his neck like a towel, and now he rubs it back and forth like he is drying off more than just sweat there.

"If you wanna give me your cards I'll get the beer and try to find somebody to bring it out, if you're gone before I get back."

"I wonder what he meant by 'sorry' we're going to Echo?" Callmeblack says.

"I don't want to know," Ass says. For the first time his face isn't the calendar face it should be. I guess I knew all along we were all scared, but there's no use talking about it.

The guy running things from our gate has on a headset and a torn shirt that shows a big scar across his chest. I wonder if the scar is a wound.

"Anybody here from Arizona?" He has to yell because the chopper that has just come in doesn't shut down. Nobody is.

"I can't get you on a bird for quite a while, so meantime start loading that bird with those cases of C's." He points to a stack, then goes over to talk on his radio to the pilots.

The C's are heavy. We hand the cases in to the door gunners, who stack them all around the inside of the helicopter. Before it's full the gunner signals us to stop and move back. The pilot lifts the bird up a foot or so and sets it back down and the gunner signals us to bring ten more cases.

I wonder where it goes after it passes over the first range of mountains. I know there are five companies in a battalion and I wonder if all five are together. Eight helicopters come in one right after another and we load them all with C-rations. The stack around the pad is getting small and a two-ton truck brings another load. We unload that too and by the time it's done I'm beat. There's so much dust around that Ass ties a handkerchief around his face. While we're unloading the truck the guy who took our ration cards comes back in a pickup. He's got twenty cases of beer. He gives us our cards back. He didn't get any beer on our cards but he gives us a case to drink. It's warm. We give some to the padman and he gives some to the crew on the next bird. That one takes the mail, bright red nylon bags. The sun isn't very high above the mountains now and I wonder if we'll go out after dark. He tells us to be ready, that we're going out on the next flight. My nuts draw tighter. My stomach and groin feel stitched together and I feel vaguely hungry. I chug the beer I'm drinking and open

21

another one, then put one in my ruck. I'm just going over to piss behind a water trailer when the bird comes in low and glides onto the pad. It bounces a little, then sits there, with the pilots helmeted and looking like two of a million eyes on a giant fly.

Everything seems like it takes longer than it should take once we're loaded into the bird: me, Callmeblack, Ass, an extra mail sack, and a few cases of C's. I am sitting directly behind the door gunner. I'm tense and I can't tell if I am shaking or not because the bird is throbbing as the pilot increases the speed of the rotor. The noise is ungodly. I look at Ass and Callmeblack and it is night and day. Ass looks almost excited but Callme looks like I feel like I do, wound plenty tight. It's a relief when the bird finally gets into the air.

Helicopters pop up from other pads of the big camp and spoke out in every direction: toward the setting sun, toward the fuselike river, toward the olive-drab hue that must be the Cambodian jungle. We go that way, away from the distant haze of the ocean, over rice paddies that look like cheesecloth snipped jaggedly by the rugged mountains.

Up here in the blinding wind the valleys are black and the ranges that catch the last light look like the veins of a fallen leaf, and as we step down on currents of air the ground falls closer, the jungle looks like steel wool, then pubic hair, and we are aiming for a spot that is as red as it is green and dotted by sandbagged huts that look like muskrat hills.

Our pilot sways the bird into a hole cut like a stovepipe in the jungle, and about six feet off the ground the machinegunner throws the mailbag off, then signals me to jump. The rucksack is heavy as hell from the C-rations and ammunition, and I take the shock too stiff and roll over on my back like a possum with my rifle held up while the helicopter is hovering, stirring the chopped bits of jungle that are everywhere, into my eyes. The others jump and the bird leaves without ever coming any closer to landing. There are about half a dozen guys standing around in tee shirts laughing at us, and when the bird is gone more guys come out of the sandbagged hooches to root through the mail.

"Better learn to stay on your feet, Effengee. You'll be in a hot landing zone one of these days and you don't wanna be rolling around on the ground, you know what I mean?" The dude is helping me to my feet and another one who has been through the mail already is there with a joint.

"Welcome," he says, and hands me the joint that I hit, mostly to be polite. I'm nervous as hell. I've been thinking about this moment for months, and now that it's here it doesn't seem real at all. It makes me think of walking into a strange building and finding a map with a big arrow that says YOU ARE HERE.

"OK, goddammit, let's hustle," a guy says. "It'll be dark in an hour. Get these guys underground."

Within the next hour the blackness spills out of the jungle and into that little chimney so I lose all my orientation. I meet a lot of guys: Bull Durham, Pops, Chickenfeed. But I can't tell them apart, can't remember who is which while I eat C's and bullshit in the light of a candle made from the sealing wax of an artillery canister. There are five of us in a hooch that is dug maybe four feet deep and topped by timbers as thick as wagon tongues, all covered by sandbags.

"Tomorrow, if we don't hump out, you Effengees wanna build yourself a hooch and dig it as deep as you can, can you dig it?"

We spend what is left of the day in the hooch smoking pot and listening to a cassette recorder whine some sound through the gummy red dust that is everywhere. Not much gets said because we are so loaded. Other guys wander in to share a bowl, a guard roster is got up, and I will pull from three to four thirty with Bull Durham, a big guy who sleeps in the hooch next to this one. Bed is ammo crates dug into the earth wall, and even in the dimness of the candle I can see spiders the size of quarters scurrying into holes, propping themselves at their doorway watching us.

■■■■■■■■■■■

"*INCOMING!*"

I hear the shout before I hear the thuds of the rounds. The first explodes at the edge of my hearing and the next ones come closer and closer. We are all crumpled into the aisle of the hooch and I'm not on the bottom and not on the top. My mind throbs like the flashes that pour a neon-blue light into the hooch. Two bright flashes, and the rest of the rounds land farther away.

"Goddamn, he put a couple in here that time," a deep southern accent says; then a guy unwinds himself from the top of the pile even while rounds are still landing, scrambles to the doorway, and peeks out.

"Let's go," he says.

I'm not ready for this. I am goddamn insane. My hands are shaking so bad that the clip and the rifle won't come together. I don't have any meaning for the whines I make following somebody's ass through the small doorway and crawling on my belly toward some sandbags where other guys are digging, but the insanity leaves me when somebody brings a flashlight and plays it on an arm coming out of the heap of sandbags where everybody is digging. So I know we are digging out what was a hooch, scratching and tossing burned sandbags out from around the arm. I'm pretty useless. *I don't know what to do*. A big black guy barges past me and begins working at the pile of bags.

"Rogers," somebody says.

He is alive but barely and doesn't begin to take normal breaths until he is flat on the ground. His face, which stands out like a color photo in a picture album for the moment the flashlight stays, is broken. There isn't much

24

blood but the face is bent to one side like a front fender that has bought the shape of a tree.

I am mentally paralyzed. I can only sit, shaking, near Rogers and stay out of the way. I hear some guys yelling across the clearing and into radios.

"Dustoff! Direct hit, get us a bird!"

"Anybody know where it came from? Who was on guard?"

I know a Dustoff is an ambulance helicopter although I don't know what I expect to see when it gets here, but it seems like it is taking forever. Everything is confusing.

Pops gives me a hand-held flare and leads me down the hill to where the Dustoff will land, but I don't know what exactly to do with the flare and Pops leaves before I can ask him.

Then, while I'm standing near where the bird will land and trying to see anything in the darkness that will tell me something about what is around me, I hear the bird coming, far off, rubbing its way up the long valley to us. The sound calms me down some.

The helicopter comes up in total blackness just at the time there is rifle fire a short distance off. Everybody hits the dirt and one of the wounded screams and starts crying. I feel like crying too, I'm that scared.

The downthrust of the rotor is unbelievable. It feels like somebody is pushing a hat down on my head. It is impossible to tell how far off the ground the bird is, and in the noise, the dark, the confusion the whole experience is un-goddamnly frightening. *I wish I was friends with some-body.* About fifteen feet off the ground the pilot turns on his huge landing light and comes down swiftly. The scene is Halloweenish: guys with slung rifles in skivvies and steel pots helping load the casualities. There must be half a dozen woundeds, and when they're all on Pops says, "OK, bring the KIA."

That hadn't entered my mind.

I didn't even know there was a dead guy, and it turns out his body is right behind where I am so I load him. I take hold of a foot and am surprised that the boot is so new. *Like mine*. All the other guys' boots are red like the ground is but these are green and black, like mine, like—*ASS*! A flash of light pins his face like a dime in the gutter, down to the big Adam's apple.

I want to shriek but I eat the want: I function. I load the weight that drags away that glimmer of a face I will wear like these beads he gave me that don't really shine in the dark. Nothing does. It is extra dark when the bird goes in a cold wind.

I drag my body and part of my mind back to the hooch that is now all piss-yellow in candlelight. Pops, Bull, a couple other guys are there smoking cigarettes and listening to the traffic on the radio.

"Rogers is OK, ain't he?"

"Yeah, I think so."

"Too bad about the Effengee. What a way to go out— you know, first night."

The dirt wall feels cold on my back when I lean against it and watch the spiders mosey through the shadows, hauling things, like—yes, like pallbearers.

TWO SQUAD

I LIE AWAKE LISTENING HARD TO EVERY SINGLE SOUND. I am too scared to sleep. I've never been this afraid of anything, and I really don't know what it is I'm afraid of. I keep thinking if I am going to get killed tonight I want to go fast—I want to go to sleep so that I'll die asleep and not have time to be more scared than I am now. I constantly roll over trying to get comfortable. I leave my boots on, and they make my feet feel as if they're in casts. I begin to breathe too fast and have to sit up on my ammo-crate bed to get a deep breath. It is stuffy. There are animal sounds near my head. Rats? There are big noises in the distance, sounds of big rounds landing and, once in a while, the scary little pop of hand-held illumination going up on our perimeter. I can hear the guards' voices as they walk past to get coffee at the CP tent. The other three guys in the hooch are sleeping, and whoever is sleeping in the top rack on the other side is whining and talking.

But toward the end of darkness I fall asleep. When I wake up I feel muddled, unsure of the reality of last night, not sure at first whether I dreamed it all. Not even sure that I am really where I am. All I feel is tension, fright, disbelief.

Ass got killed.

The first thing my mind registers is Ass's face, after he

was dead. The face didn't look like the calendar boy I first met on the plane. Last night the face was without distinction, and this morning the facts seem without possibility.

I've only known one guy since I got to Nam, and he's already *dead*. I don't feel like myself. All I feel is fear and disbelief. *It couldn't have happened.* There is bright light coming in through the doorway, and only one guy is still sleeping besides me. My boots still feel like casts, and when I move my feet it is like they are far beyond the end of my legs. I am super aware of small things: the wet spots under my arms, the beads Ass gave me that pull at the hair on my neck, an aching in my ankles where the tops of my boots rub, and a feeling in my stomach like a million scurry ants. I don't know who I am. I am the F.N.G.

░░░░░░░░░░░

POPS IS TWO SQUAD'S LEADER. HE IS TWENTY-FOUR. HE has small brown rabbit eyes and a face the texture of shorn sheephide. His skin has baked; it looks like a butterscotch cake. His arm muscles are long and thin but the muscles in his neck are knotty, like cauliflower heads. He is from Kentucky.

It isn't Pops asleep in the other rack. Pops is always going. He has to make meetings with the Brass, the first sergeant, and the platoon leader—he has to know more about what is going on than anybody else in the squad. I think he likes being busy. He and I are opposite kinds of soldiers this morning. Twice while I am lying in the hooch he comes in and gets something, then leaves. The first time I am still enough that he might think I'm still asleep, but the second time I've got a cigarette going.

"Sauers? Shitbird, you can't sleep all day long, even if you are brand-spanking-new here." At the same time he is talking to me he is giving the guy in the other rack a neck rub, absentmindedly maybe, but there is carefulness to what he does. "How you feelin' today, man?" He asks softly. He pats the guy's back but the guy doesn't move.

"Man," he says to me, "you gotta get under the ground. We've only been on this hill for about a week and there aren't any extra hooches so you better start digging."

"OK."

"Did you know the Effengee that got killed last night?"

"We came over together. His name was Saxon but his initials spelled Ass, and that's what he went by. I barely knew him."

"That's good. Knowing barely is lucky for you. That way you didn't have a chance to like him too much. You'll know some of these guys better than you've ever known anybody. It happened to me. I know more about some of 'em than I know about my own family. We spend *every* goddamn hour together here, can you imagine?"

He is silhouetted by the light from the doorway, and his voice seems like it is coming from higher up than where he stands. It is my way of seeing things this morning. *Nothing* seems real.

"You gotta remember last night because it tells you the whole story of this goddamn war—anybody out here can get it any-fucking-time."

Smoke comes out his nose and his mouth. It stays circling around his head, and in my cobwebbed comprehension of this morning he is blowing smoke out his ears, even his small eyes. I like him. I feel so odd at the moment, still so new and nervous. It's like telling somebody you're an only child; they react like there is a mistake and you're it.

Seemingly as absentmindedly as he rubbed the other guy's neck, Pops keeps offering me his pipe with one hand and scratching jungle rot around his raw nuts with the other. He only has OD skivvies on. The rot is two-tone sore; half black scabs, half yellow pus. His hands are dirty and he expertly scratches around the yellow pockets of pus. He moves toward the doorway to take a better look at the mess. I feel self-conscious and he seems so opposite, his nuts tenderly in his hands now. I look at the wall and the mascot spiders are there in their holes, looking at me and Pops's spotted nuts.

■■■■■■■■■■■

A HOOCH IS A HOLE. ITS UPPER SIDES AND ROOF ARE layers of sandbags. The sandbags are about half as big as a pillow and filled with the dirt from the hole, then stacked into walls, and on these walls lie timbers that are cut from the bigger trees in the jungle. There are a few chain saws to cut the trees down, but most of the time a work party goes out with their rifles and ammo, a couple axes, and some machetes. The difficulties are finding a strong tree that is straight, and getting the log back to the hole. Sometimes there are two timbers to the hooch roof, sometimes three. Smaller pieces serve as roof joists, then a piece of something waterproof, generally canvas or plastic, is laid across these smaller logs, and on top of that go sandbags. Many, many sandbags. Three layers of sandbags full of dirt is a lot of weight, and even the stoutest timbers sag.

The inside of an ordinary hooch is about as big as the inside of a Volkswagen bus. Most of the time three or four guys live in the hooch. Hooches are like clubhouses, and they are the sanctuary on a new LZ. Our platoon and especially Two Squad is at full strength; there are seven men in the squad, the fullest it has ever been. There are usually two guys on guard duty at night and at least two on various other work parties during the day. Everybody's gear is in or around the squad's hooch so there is no spare room. Another hooch has been started. Ass was sleeping in one without a full roof last night.

When I come into the daylight for the first time I have to stand a minute to clear the dizzies. When I can focus, the first thing I see is the hooch that got hit, and it doesn't surprise me. It is eerie that there are still some personal things around as if to remind me to be scared.

"If Charlie could set his mortar tubes up in the same place he was set last night, he could drop another round in almost that exact place," Pops says. "So you know it isn't much of an adjustment to put one in our hooch. But he'd have to be in the same place."

The other guys in the squad are digging a hole down the hill from the hooch that is finished. Two guys work hard and two guys rest. The black guys are resting now. Their backs are toward us, and the sun and the sweat on their muscles make their backs look like big wet rocks.

It is still early and the sun is just beginning to show over the mountains, bright red so the top of it looks like a chunk of cherry LifeSaver before it is suddenly there in the sky, whole and round. There are twice as many hooches that aren't finished as there are finished ones. Men slept everywhere last night, always near a hooch that is done, and as Pops and I sit not talking—he's stoned and I'm sleepy and scared—the noises of daytime begin. From a big transistor radio leaning between two full sandbags comes:

"Armed Forces Radio presents: The Adventures of Chi-i-i-icken-man!"

The radio seems so out of place. Fake. I wonder how far the sound carries. At the same time as the radio, three guys in separate parts of the LZ accompany the cry, one guy right below us still under his poncho liner. What catches my attention is that the show comes immediately after the introduction; no commercial, no weather or station break, no number to call for requests. The radio is constant, canned. *Unreal, like everything else.*

The ground is covered by chopped-up vegetation. Paths show clearly, and most of them lead from one finished hooch to another or to where a new one is being built. There is a wide path of trampled jungle stalks from our hooch to the hole the black guys are digging, and there are smaller trails too. These lead to personal areas, where a guy who doesn't have a hooch yet has his slit trench dug and usually a lean-to made from a shelter half. There are three lean-tos together, and in the nearest one is a guy in Issue glasses and an intricately scribed hat crumpled on his head. He's got a huge tattoo of a peacock on his chest and a dirty red rabbit's foot around his neck. He smiles quickly when he sees me.

"Morning, glad to have another leg," he says, sticking out his hand that holds a spoonful of whatever is in the can in his other hand.

He doesn't talk as fast as he does everything else. His movements are semi-jerky. He never stops spooning the stuff in while he tells me, "We split up all the extra shit that our squad humps, like the radio and batteries, machine-gun ammo, claymores. We split all that equally; therefore when the squad is light all of us carry more. Two Squad is like a caterpillar, and every guy is a leg, dig it? They call me Peacock."

"I can guess why."

"Got drunk in Hong Kong four months ago. Next morning I had this. I haven't ever seen all of it; I can't get hold of a mirror big enough. Do you like it?"

"Righteous, Peacock, goddamn righteous. How 'bout struttin' your purdy ass over here and helpin' Gabe on a hooch?"

Pops is smiling. I can't tell if he talks quite like that all the time or if he's exaggerating his drawl. Peacock is from the East somewhere and I wonder about him too, whether he's exaggerating his manners a little. He gives Pops the finger.

■■■■■■■■■■■

THE SHOVELS ARE ONLY ABOUT THREE FEET LONG. IT FEELS good to dig, just to be doing something. Peacock sits on a full sandbag, holding open empty ones, and I fill them. A shovel and a half per bag. When they're full he throws them into a pile. The way he does it all in one motion—tying them and heaving them—impresses me. He's done a lot of it.

I don't know if Peacock is naturally quiet or doesn't feel like talking to a new guy, but he doesn't say a single thing. I don't feel like talking either. It is all I can do to believe my surroundings. The mountains covered with jungle are beautiful. The air is clear.

The LZ, called Niagara, overlooks the An Loa River. The Z is a flat red scar cut into the mountain, near the top. There is one small bulldozer working on the other side of the Zone, puffing thin streams of black smoke irregularly. The operator is wearing a steel pot and a flak jacket. He is mostly making small patches of level land, pushing big piles of the jungle over the edge, working his way farther around the mountain. One of the bulldozers used to cut the LZ is lying almost on its top, out of commission with a hole seared in its side. Farther up the hill are engineers with their det cord, preparing to clear more of the tangled vegetation. They too are wearing steel helmets and flak jackets. All around them are grunts lying in the weeds with rifles and grenade launchers. At this point, the LZ is not a clear shape. There is a roughly defined circle where the jungle has been blown away, or is about to be, and a track going around the circle where the bulldozers have cleared a path of the red ground. Within the circle are the hooches and small remaining patches of jungle that isn't as green as that on the outside; it has been uprooted some and is partly burned in places. There are small fires everywhere and guys throwing jungle fuel on these fires.

Almost as if a signal started it, the whole LZ is suddenly full of movement. All work. Everybody is either digging and filling sandbags, clearing away patches of what still stands upright, or feeding the fires. The resupply pad is in an area by itself and there is a steady stream of helicopters coming in with boxes of C-rations, cases of soda and beer, artillery ammunition. The artillery section is in the center of the Z. There are five guns in the batteries and two of them have parapets built around them, but the other three sit vulnerably in their positions. The big guns are top priority, so not only are the artillerymen working to level the guns and make them operable but there are grunts from Echo Company and another company helping to build walls around the positions. In the very center of the battery of guns is the biggest hooch of the LZ; this is FDC, Fire Direction Control. In that hooch they monitor the radios and direct the pieces in firing.

All the work ceases around Artillery and the men man the guns, crank them around 180 degrees, and put out a salvo of six rounds each. I can see the rounds land a good distance off, partway up a neighboring mountain. The action is threefold; the guns are loaded with shells the size of rural mailboxes, the breech is locked shut, and on command all five guns fire at the same time. The outgoing rounds make a deep whistle for a split second. The artillerymen have loaded the guns and are checking the sights again before the explosions on the distant hill occur. Where the rounds land there is a burst of smoke that is first small, then bigger. During a few of the hits I can see some flame before the big puff of smoke. Eventually the sound the high-explosive rounds make comes back to the LZ, and by the time it gets there it is a lot smaller than seems logical.

Somebody has hit some shit, the war is that close.

At the bottom of the mountain is the An Loa River. From the LZ it looks smooth, what little bit I can see, but the whole river valley runs steep to the south, so the An Loa is probably swift. I wonder how far I can see down the valley. There are specks that are helicopters every direction I look, and higher are the lazy white streams left by planes. There is almost no wind, and during the quiet part of Artillery's action I can hear the sound of axes beyond the perimeter of the LZ. A Chinook comes in with a slingful of concertina wire and misses its mark so the load falls in a particularly steep and thickly covered section. Everybody who sees the sling fall moans; it will mean rough, rough work to get to it and carry its load back up the hill.

A smaller river runs down the mountain not far from us, and a couple times while we are filling bags it is quiet enough to hear the water falling over what must be Niagara. Work details are constantly hauling in timbers from the jungle and sandbagging roofs. Nobody seems especially tense but nobody is slack either; there are rifles leaning casually against every hooch, and they're loaded.

"Let's take a break," Peacock says. "I want to see Prophet."

He disappears into his lean-to a minute, then is gone down a narrow trail. I go back to the hooch to get my canteen. There's nobody inside. It is dark and cool. It has the feeling of a boyhood hut about it. Each of the four bunks is individually arranged or disarranged. The only bunk I know belongs to anybody for sure is Pops's. It is the bottom one nearest the doorway and is full of junk. Most of his rucksack is scattered on the bed. It looks like a kind of home and feels safe. Up on top, I feel like Charlie might be watching me and with the worst kind of luck I could get it, but down here there is a feeling of sanctity. It would have to be a direct mortar hit to cave the roof in. Ass was just totally unlucky.

As soon as the next hooch is done there will be a bed for everybody in the squad, but in the meantime we rotate. The bunk they put me in last night is the smallest and on the damp side of the mountain. A little peephole between sandbags on the wall above the bunk lets a very little light into that corner. I am clumsy, walking in the narrow trench between the bottom bunks, and I almost fall against the wall but I catch myself on the roof beam. There is a grenade launcher, broken open, hanging on a twig from the roof beam.

All morning long there has been a slow line of guys filling canteens and empty ammo cans at the water trailer, which was the last thing to be brought in last night. Four guys are standing together at the back of the line. They have just finished carrying a log in, because they're running with sweat and there's still bark on their shoulders. When I come up they quit talking, and I see they're smoking a bowl. The guy offers it but I don't want any.

"You're pretty new, ain't you?"

"Got in last night."

"Just in time for the party," another guy says. He is so cross-eyed I'm not positive he is looking at me.

"Yeah. One of the guys who came in with me got it."

"Heard it was an Effengee. What a bitch, first night."

This time I take the bowl when it comes around.

The shortest guy is wearing a tattooed hat at least one size too big for him. The fabric is covered with different sets of initials. I see Grandaddy spitting words through his small mouth without any teeth, the old gray work hat tipped back like half a drawbridge, a rake-handle cane drumming the edge of the manure spreader, telling me, "Live your life like a beech tree, Gabriel. Grow that way. A beech tree is one of a kind. It's the only tree that—when you carve your initials in—them initials get bigger instead of getting smaller." The short guy's hat, covered by all those initials, is one of a kind.

"Ain't no way tellin' how long a dude's been here after a month."

"Soon as a guy sees his first share of shit, he's no Effengee."

"I don't know about that," I begin. "I—"

"Wait until the next batch of real Effengees come. They won't know you from me, who's been here longer'n whoever else, same as you don't know now. Me, I'm a double-digit midget, ninety-seven days."

They don't know how scared I am.

The water is purple, treated with iodine against diseases. Tasting it is like sucking a steel comb, the metal taste gets into the back of your mouth.

■■■■■■■■■■

WHEN I GET BACK, PEACOCK IS THERE AND READY. WHILE we're digging, he tells me he has a little over four months left. I can tell he is high: he works a little slower and pauses more often. He has on an empty sandbag for a hat and nothing else except for a pair of underwear that was once white. His skin color is a deep brown, and all his zits are on the back of his neck. He seems to have less jungle rot than anybody else.

"Four more months and change, and I'll be back in The World with a brand-new guitar. I've heard they used to ship you back to the Rear when you had less than three months left. No more. The last guy who rotated out of Two Squad was out here in the Bush for three hundred and fifty days. His name was Spillson, from California. He was fuckin' losing it the last couple weeks. We were on an LZ by ourselves, just our company and three artillery pieces, and we got incoming almost every day the last two weeks he was here. He spent all day burrowing out his hooch, after the roof was on. All day long, he'd dig deeper and deeper and carry the dirt out in part of an old Air Force parachute he had. Like a goddamn mole, you know? He had to wear sunglasses whenever he came up out of the ground because the light hurt his eyes."

"Cautious."

"Fuckin'-A, cautious." He takes his glasses off to wipe the sweat away. "Smart, goddamm it, smart. I've got news for you, Gabe. I plan on digging on this hole for as long as we're at this LZ too. Even if I have to dig the whole

37

sonofabitch by my ownself, I'm gonna be down where the metal don't fall. The first part of my tour was during the wet season, and we hardly ever saw any shit. I think our squad only lost two guys, one to malaria, my first six months. One guy got killed by a short artillery round one night we were on an ambush. If it hadn't gotten him it might have gotten me. From then on, for a solid month we were hitting shit almost every day. I knew we wasted eight gooks in one fight because I counted them afterward. Prophet got hit in that firefight."

"Was that the worst shit you've been in?"

"Yeah, probably. I went crazy. After we had been pinned down for two days and two nights I was on fire inside. I wanted to get outa that jungle so goddamn bad I tried to catch some shrap in my arm. I heard a mortar tube pop and I got down behind a log and held my arm up in the air, just goddamn begging to take a piece big enough to get me medevacked. It hit close enough that I might have caught some, maybe twenty-five feet away, and was a goddamn dud."

"What's it like to be pinned down?"

"Hope you never find out, brother. Hope, pray. It's everything bad combined. Like being in jail and somebody turns a scalding shower into your cell. There were more of them than there were us and we were in a dinky little ravine. Couldn't get up the hill, couldn't get down. We had constant firepower: artillery walked rounds in every time we thought we knew where Charlie was; we had Cobra gunships up above us all day long, and nobody slept for all that time. Prophet was the hero. That fucker deserves every star the Army has. He brought misery to Charlie with a grenade launcher. I know he got a direct hit, we could hear the screams."

"How'd you finally get out?"

"All that firepower kept Charlie's head down enough that they airlifted another squad in near us. So, they advanced, and we made a little move, and the gooks had to *didi-mau*—"

"What's that mean?"

"Means 'Get the fuck going, *now*!' and that's what they did. That was when we got eight of them. We were so fucking low on ammo that the next day would have had to be the end, but they made a run for it and we poured everything we had at them."

He takes his glasses off again and his eyes are bloodshot. The look he has is one of complete distance. I know he is telling me the absolute truth.

"That sort of thing would change a guy."

"For fuckin' ever, man. Forever. I'm not the only shorttimer who has them shakes. You can only do so many things to keep your shit straight out here, and that's why this hooch is gonna be an Alamo. Not only deep, but this hole is gonna have double timbers on it. The hooch that got the direct hit last night had a weak roof. We built it in a hurry. But the Army's got plenty of empty sandbags and there's plenty of dirt on this mountain, and we haven't got anything else to do, so deep I go. Fuckin' deep and safe, that's my attitude.

"Prophet and Bull Durham are out in the woods now, cutting down a tree bigger than a telephone pole. It will take six of us to bring it in."

I feel friendly enough to try a confession.

"Peacock, I'm so goddamn scared you wouldn't believe it."

"Bullshit. How can you think I wouldn't believe it? And what makes you think I ain't just as scared?"

"You've been here for eight months. . . ."

"Goddamn, man, this is a war! You've already seen one guy get killed. It happens, plain fuckin' happens. Anybody who ain't scared belongs here forever. And there are some —but you'll know those kind right away. Gung-ho fuckers, think they can't get it, or want a Heart worse than

39

anything. Nobody in our squad is like that, but there's some in the company. Three Squad, they're crazy. Us guys are all the same, we trust each other and our policy is to keep everybody alive by staying out of all the shit we can." He wipes his glasses off again, and says, "And that's nuthin' to be ashamed of."

A shovelful of dirt falls into his lap and his hat falls off.

"Sorry."

"Fuck it, friend, fuck it."

"Nice lid you got there."

"My pride and joy, man. I listed all the LZs I've been on since I got here, among other numerous paraphernalia-isms. That, and this"—he swings his rabbit foot—"kept me alive for two hundred forty-some days. I trust 'em completely."

"Is everybody superstitious?"

He looks at me for such a long time I begin to feel uncomfortable.

"Listen," he says, sitting down, "there's no such thing as superstitious. There's only lucky and unlucky. Your chances of getting hit are very, very good, you know that? It took me a while to realize, do you understand, but the infantry is just like the lifers say it is: 'The infantry is the queen of battle, always getting the cock shoved to her,' and if you're a leg, a grunt, a peg"—his voice rises now like he is warmed to the subject and on a proper soapbox—"a goddamn Eleven Bravo, you will hit the shit before anybody else does so you are either lucky, dead, or in-between. In-between may be the same as lucky or the same as dead. And when you realize it is all luck or unluck you cease thinking and begin hoping, trusting rabbits' feet, praying—different strokes. . . ." And he trails off. He gives the rabbit's foot a push and straightens up his glasses. The foot swings across the peacock tattoo while he read-justs his hat against the sun, which goes behind a cloud just then.

The land below us yawns away like a faded patchwork quilt.

What The Nam is and what I had expected are such totally different things, I'll never be able to explain it. It's the guys here. I don't know about the fighting—the incoming last night was all so fast and hard—but the guys, how they act surprises me. The tour of duty is usually a year. Not everybody does an exact year. Some guys go to Germany first, or get held up in transit. Maybe because Ass is dead and I don't trust my thinking any further than that, I feel like there is something missing, like too much has gone on in a single day. I know this about myself, and it helps me fit in: I am no hero. I want to go home, complete. I feel cowardly, but there isn't any shame with it. I am not fighting any other war—not my father's and not his father's—I'm in Vietnam and it is 1969. The object is staying alive.

■■■■■■■■■■■

THE COMPANY FIRST SERGEANT IS A GUY OF ABOUT FORTY, and I feel like his face always wants to smile more than his mind does. He is tall and in good shape for his age. His clothes are clean and on him the jungle fatigues look like a uniform; anything he would wear would look like a uniform. He is a lifer. His face is egg-shaped and his hair couldn't be cut any shorter. He isn't unkind-looking, but there is uneasiness in his manner. He comes over to where Peacock and I are sitting on sandbags with Callmeblack, who has just been assigned to Two Squad. There is something out of place about the fact that he introduces us all by our real names. Justin Riggins meets Adolph Morrison and me.

Adolph Morrison tells Justin Riggins, "I'm Peacock."

"Callmeblack."

"You're black."

"Always have been."

41

It is our turn to be ahead of the game, me and Callmeblack. Peacock is confused for a minute, and for a minute F.N.G. syndrome falls away. Peacock looks bewildered. He takes his glasses off and rubs the sweat out of his eyes, to buy thinking time. Just when he looks so confused and I feel so sure of things, he opens his eyes and has a serious expression on his face.

"You're a nigger," he says.

Callmeblack is stunned.

Peacock has it figured out. "You're a nigger, Callmeblack, and I'm a nigger. Ever seen a nigger peacock before?"

"What the hell are you talking about?" Callmeblack asks slowly. He looks at me and goes on, like my expression doesn't matter, "Nobody ever *told* me I was a nigger before."

The First Shirt looks uncomfortable, but at the same time he looks like there is nothing out of control either. That's the way I feel too.

"Never been to Nam before either, have you?" Now his whole face, still without his glasses, is smiling. Suddenly, he hugs Callme with his left arm and the two of them go through some soul shakes with their dirty right arms, and Peacock knows more daps than Callme. We're still laughing—I'm not totally sure why—when Callme begins dancing a jig and the first sergeant leaves, laughing too.

"You two Effengees might be just what this squad needs," Peacock says. "Fresh blood. Us old guys are getting chickenshit. Can you kill?"

That's a shocker. I don't have to know him any better than I do to know he is ordinarily serious, but I don't know what he means by that.

"No," Callme says, "I can't kill. I'm a truck driver. Send me home."

"I tried that. Doesn't work. The only way you're going to get home is be a hiding nigger for a year. Call on the

42

knowledge of your slave ancestors and help us hide, man."

Pops yells that there will be a squad meeting in ten minutes and Peacock leaves. Callmeblack takes over the shovel and I hold the sandbags.

"You been thinkin' 'bout Ass?" he asks.

"A little, yeah. I liked him and it still doesn't seem possible he's dead."

"Sergeant Hightower said that was the first direct hit they've taken in two months, and Ass is the first KIA in two months."

"You know what I'm happy about though? And this is weird. I'm glad he wasn't mangled and bloody. He was just crushed to death. I'm glad they don't have to send him home in pieces."

"Yeah."

"I liked him from the start, didn't you?"

"He was like a kid, you had to like him."

"It seems logical that it had to happen, that somebody had to get killed, but so fucking *soon*?"

We're quiet. He is working at a slow but steady pace, and I am tying off the sandbags and piling them. The hole isn't very deep yet—we aren't even through the roots—but the soil has changed color, and gotten harder. Callmeblack's enormous truck-unloading back muscles ripple as he jabs the undersized shovel at the bank of pebbles and clay. His Boonie hat seems more broken in than mine and I wish I had a picture of him tirelessly jabbing at the earth, with our rifles leaning in the background. *This is real*. I can't pinpoint my feelings. I can probably spell better than Callmeblack but I couldn't write home. The dust from digging has gotten behind my teeth, my legs are cramped from sitting, and my back is sore from throwing the bags. The only smell around is the scent of new-cut weeds. It makes me daydream until they holler at us from the squad hooch. Like an act of kindness, Callme cleans the big hunks of dirt off the shovel and lays it out of the hole.

■■■■■■■■■■

THE INSIDE OF THE HOOCH IS DARK AND COOL BECAUSE THE poncho liner over the doorway is down. Big Bull Durham is already there and has a big bowl going. When we come in he passes the pot to Callme and starts a Janis Joplin cassette going, without saying anything. His tape player is beat to pieces; its plastic case is cracked and covered with tape; hunks of it are missing. It runs off old commo batteries and these, too, are taped to the player. The setup looks like a kind of hobo kit, which fits Bull's character. He's smoking a cigar. Somebody walks over the top of the hooch and he yells, "Would you do that at home?"

Everybody else is just sitting on the bunks, but Bull has that look about him like he knows we're all watching him. He pantomimes a fat guy sitting down. The song is "Cry Baby," and he goes so far as to get at least one real tear.

Big rounds explode somewhere near enough that we can feel the concussion. It's weird to be inside the hooch and feel the big rounds; a little claustrophobic yet safe. Bull has quit his pantomime and is lying on his back with his feet tapping to the slow beat of the music.

"Calling in the big one on Charlie's ass."

"Wonder how much it costs to drop one of them babies on top of some rockpile that Sir Charles is already under."

"I read somewhere, or heard on TV once, that a one-oh-five round costs five hundred dollars."

Two more rounds hit and somebody says, "There's another grand up in smoke."

"If your conscience bothers you, tell it to the chaplain."

Pops isn't in the hooch yet. Bull, Callmeblack, Chickenfeed, me, and Peacock are there. Bull packs another bowl, and it goes all the way around in silence. Chickenfeed blows his smoke out in rings and Peacock stands up to follow the floating smoke, sucking at it. Then he takes his hat off and makes a game out of putting the hat over the smoke ring. Once, when he removes the hat, a ring is still intact. There is very little extra room and now the hooch smells like BO. I am sweating and the bugs have found me. Just for the hell of it I let a mosquito suck on my wrist. After thirty seconds or so Callme urges me to kill it, but I let it go another few seconds and nail it just as it pulls out its stinger. It leaves a spot of blood as big as a nickel.

Peacock is reading his Bible now. The cassette turns slower and slower toward the end of the tape and finally winds dead. There is so much sand and grit in the mechanism that it sputters in half turns for a minute before it finally spits the tape out. Bull has the hobo kit on his knees, and he bends up to flip the tape over and cuts a fart.

"Would you do that at home?"

"Only in the privacy of my bath."

"See, you're a goddamn animal here."

"Farts move in waves, and them waves are very beneficial to my tape recorder. It's a little thing I discovered on guard one night."

The artillery rounds keep hitting. They don't sound that close, but there is a definite concussion. They might be bigger than 105s. Maybe 175s or Navy 8-inch guns.

A sudden wind sweeps the poncho liner and brings a burst of dust through the door.

"Rain tonight, fellows."

"Muthafucker, muthafucker, I am too too short to be dealin' with the rains, the rains," Peacock says. Then, to me and Callmeblack, "You've never been miserable. Never in The World and not even the other night when the shit hit have you been miserable. Scared, maybe. Pissed, maybe. These are showers; when the monsoons are here, then you'll be miserable."

"Pea," Bull says, "I'm gonna piss on a sweatband and give it to you. It's the squad's Mister Cheerful award."

"Our mail is a good month behind us."

"Now I'm gonna get a dink to piss on it."

"They'll move us more for the first month of the 'soons."

"I'm gonna wipe my ass and a Chieu Hoi's ass with it, man."

"My *Playboy* subscription runs out next month."

Bull is up on one leg and grabs Pea in a headlock. Pea takes a couple half-ass swings at Bull's head, but Bull lets them glance off his sweaty back with a grin on his face that is infectious.

Just then Pops comes in whittling a bar of soap. We make room for him to sit down. He says hello to everybody individually and lights a cigarette. As he whittles, small flakes of soap cling to his pants and get scattered along the floor planks. There are even flakes in his eyebrows.

Only Prophet is missing. Bull is still talking. He's always talking. Now it's about playing baseball, and in a few minutes he is standing in the aisle so the downdraft from the doorway brings me his smell, which isn't any different from anybody else's—putrid—like a set of gym clothes left a month in a gym bag. Wearing only a ragged pair of skivvies and his hat, he is in a Vic Power hunch and is taking small swings at an imaginary pitch with his rifle. *This is how accidents happen. Maybe there's a round in his chamber. He could stumble.* I think of Lonesome, about how he is half a hand short because of carelessness, and I think of my shotgun going off ten years ago, almost getting my grandfather. But when I stop worrying, Bull's act is funny.

"I hit the fastest pitch Sam Levine ever threw," he says, "and he woulda been the fastest rookie in the Bigs, but one night he called some tomato-picker a spic and the spic laid his head open, so nowadays he just rusts away with his granny, who always wears cowboy boots and takes snuff through her ass . . . but I hit his best pitch."

The hooch is crowded and stuffy. Everybody is a smoker, and there is a regular cloud of smoke hanging against the ceiling. It is late enough that the sun is starting to fall fast and I feel like I want to get outside to use it up, but we're still waiting for another guy. Chickenfeed is the only one who looks uncomfortable. The back side of the hooch is hollowed out for a place to store rucksacks and he is curled up on that shelf with his face to the aisle, but, from where I am sitting on the top bunk, all I can see is the toes of his boots with peace signs carved into the leather.

Pops is afraid one of the old guys is going to get transferred out of the squad. He didn't expect to get two F.N.G.s. None of those guys wants to go, and I hope I'm not one that gets transferred either because I like these guys.

■■■■■■■■■■■

A BIG GUY SHOULDERS INTO THE HOOCH AND STANDS IN the doorway. He blocks most of the light from outside but there is still enough to show his face. It is the most intense face I've ever seen—long and thin with pointed cheekbones and a huge mouth. His hair is totally black and long enough to stand up out of a cowlick on one side.

He smells incredibly bad. He is leaning on the main roof beam, and the odor from under his arms is past ripe, pungent. His eyes are deep-set and they have the same riveting quality that Ass's had, but there isn't anything kind-looking or innocent about them. He makes me feel like he can see a layer deeper than anybody else when he looks at me. He stares, and when Pops introduces me he only nods.

"Sit down, Prophet," Pops says. "We were just talking about how full the squad is. If they try to transfer anybody, nobody wants to go."

"Hell, no. Two is the best fucking squad around. We haven't lost anybody in four months. If they try to split us up we'll tell 'em to take one of these new guys or go fuck themselves."

He looks at me and I expect a very hard look but instead it is open, honest. He looks at Callmeblack too and Callme seems to feel the same thing—his face is as open as Prophet's. I hope mine is, although I don't want my apprehension about being transferred to show.

"Well, remember what it was like when we were new, man. Anyway, here's the guard roster. At the meeting this morning they said we might go out tomorrow for a two-day hump."

"That figures. We get our hooches dug and they're pulling us for detail to sandbag for Artillery, so we'll go out and when we get back we'll tear all this down and move. A hundred and twenty days, that's all I got to say."

"You got it, brother."

"Short."

"Fuck you guys."

"Anybody got any deodorant?" Prophet is stripping out of his utilities and takes a crusty towel out of his ruck.

"You goddamn need it."

"Keeps the mosquitoes away."

He takes his rifle and loads it with two clips taped to each other. He is gone.

"That fucker is crazy, going down to the Blue Line alone."

"He ain't afraid."

"How can anybody not be afraid?"

"He's an animal."

"Sure as hell has bad breath too."

It gets some laughs.

"Permanent shell shock. He's been hit three times."

Something, some other crutch snaps: I have been thinking getting wounded would send me home. I've had sneak-in daydreams about taking a small wound and getting sent back. I guess I never believed them; anyway, I know the real score now. I can't count on luck, just believe in it.

"Hit three times?" Callmeblack asks loudly, his eyes as big and clear as hailstones.

"He's a living lightning rod. Nobody near him has ever been hit. The first time he took a round in his gut it came through another guy's helmet and never hurt that guy."

"You're shitting me, he still goes with you?"

"We go with him, man."

"He's the number-one man out there. He pouts when he doesn't get to walk point."

"Is he gung-ho?"

"Not at all. He's plain good at it, and I guess he feels best when he's up front, looking."

"Prophet is the guts of this squad. Nobody who's ever been in Two Squad with him would make a trade. He's the walking rabbit's foot. Everybody out here in the Bush seems a lot alike but Prophet; he's special."

Pops goes to another meeting and Peacock leaves too, to scrounge C-rations for the squad. Chickenfeed is still asleep. Callme is leaning against the wall with his eyes closed. I want to ask Bull Durham how Prophet got his name but I don't feel like breaking the silence.

There is radio music in the distance. Gray slices of light cut through the smoke. Pops's rifle is loaded and hung on one roof beam. I begin composing a mental letter to no one in particular.

Vietnam? Like hunting so far. Except we get hunted too. We hide under huts of sandbags and behind great big guns. . . . I wish I was home there, get me a new shotgun for duck. These M-16s put out eighteen rounds in two seconds. Big rounds that tumble like a hatchet after they hit something. A clip could shred a bear. A shotgun whams, a rifle whings, shrapnel sings. A friend got killed last night.

That still seems impossible to say. The truth of Nam isn't believable yet.

A rabbit is the biggest thing I've ever killed and a fox is the smartest. Until last night I'd never seen anybody who had been killed, just people who were dead. Now I am with a bunch of ordinary guys who've seen men killed, and maybe killed themselves. It's no wonder I feel so weird, so scared. I'm no hunter now, I'm part of a war.

That white morning: me and Grandaddy: "Flush, you goddamn hopheaded bunny bastards. Come on up outa them warm holes. Tramp them woodpiles, Gabie, I got a feel there may be a convention in that woodpile. Flush 'em, make one hop, so that beagle don't feel so bad comin' out on a morning such as this . . ." then up, going a yard a hop for the creek, going away from me and the old man with his rabbit hat and old double-barrel, a cottontail trailing through the woods: wham! and a pretty big rabbit nailed in the beech grove, flopping. The dog sniffs him once.

I am tired. It is as stuffy inside as a plastic sack. The sun is round but not happy-looking. Eyebrow clouds in crowds plaid the west. The east is clear and the color of stainless steel on the horizon. It seems awfully quiet. There is a volleyball game on the other side of the LZ and it looks like it is being played in slow motion.

I flash on the whore, the old woman with squirrel teeth, and the dinks I saw sitting around the gates and convoy points. I have an image of Charlie that hasn't been changed yet: little yellow guy, all wicked face, smile of brown teeth like machine-gun ammo.

"Sauers. Hey, Sauers. Wake up. We're on."

The middle of tonight is darker than the middle of last night, I swear. I'm awake fast. Chickenfeed is shining a flashlight in my face. When I light a cigarette he turns it out and starts rummaging through his ruck.

"Bring an extra bandolier of ammo," he says.

Then I watch him go out and I notice he puts his jacket hood up and I wonder why, until I hear a sound like crow's feet on a tin roof. Rain. I've never liked rain.

He comes back inside while I'm smoking and shivering and lacing my boots. He sits down and lights a cigarette. He is small and very black. He's the only one I haven't seen with a Boonie hat on, evidently because of his hair, his Afro. He takes the best care of himself of anybody here; his clothes seem a little cleaner and his long pink fingernails are so well kept they look artificial. They glow as he sits on the edge of the bunk across from me, cleaning them. Bull is in his bunk, asleep on his back. The hooch is lit by a Christmas tree bulb hooked up to a PRC-25 battery. The battery is as big as an ear of corn and the bulb hangs from it by wires, swinging just enough to cause the shadows to move. I'm still sleepy, and I wonder if I can stay awake for the duration of guard.

Now the rain landing on the sandbagged roof sounds like shrubbery blowing against a window, and I can hear water drip steadily onto something metal near the door. There are explosions somewhere and their thuds sound wrapped in the rain too, not quite loud enough to believe in. But outside is a different story. It isn't raining hard but there's a gusty wind and it almost immediately soaks me around the collar, like an initiation. It isn't cold.

There are a few lights showing around the hill, but like the last ashes of a fire they don't illuminate anything and there's no way to read the hillside in the rain. I couldn't have found the trail that leads to the guard position; I can only follow Chickenfeed's back. It is logical that I think of Lonesome, following him to the whorehouse in the dark my first night. I'm thinking of him when I run hard into Chickenfeed. He grunts.

We're at a radio conex that is bright inside. The light is run by generators. One whole wall is radios. The radioman is monitoring something through headphones and scratching rot around his armpits with a letter opener.

"What's happenin', bro?" Chickenfeed asks.

"Hong Kong radio is bouncing in," the radioman answers. The headphones are around his neck now. He tells us the frequencies we need. When we're leaving he says, "Ain't these rains hell on grunts?"

"Sweats me not," Chickenfeed says, "I'm so short I be steppin' on my mustache."

●●●●●●●●●●●

WHEN WE LEAVE THE CONEX WE HEAD DIRECTLY DOWN the slippery hill. The guard position is far beyond the perimeter. It is an LP: listening post. We relieve the two guys there and I'm suddenly shaky, nervous. The LP isn't made to be comfortable. Two ammo crates filled with dirt are stacked and for a roof there is a small piece of plastic held up by four sticks. The plastic doesn't stop much of the rain, but it's a soft rain right now. Chickenfeed and I are both sitting on an ammo crate, and I can't see a goddamn thing. For my nervousness I want to talk, or I want him to talk.

"Kind of peaceful out here." My voice seems to be full of the fake; it quivers.

"Peaceful?" He chuckles deep in his throat. "On really warm and star-spangled nights it's unbelievable. So damn quiet. I mean, hell, man, no where in The World be as quiet as it get here. One night it was quiet like that and I am pulling the middle shift with a cat from Philly when all of a sudden we hear this goddamn racket and called Artillery in. Sound like a regiment of NVA was moving up the ravine. But no return fire, couldn't hear no cries, nothing. Next day we found some dead orangutans. Can you dig that?"

That makes me try to imagine what the jungle must be like. I still haven't been *in* it. I've got some ideas about it, but most of my ideas have been modified by degrees. I don't even know what to listen for, what kind of sound to stretch my hearing for. Even though I know Charlie isn't going to show himself to me I am straining, looking hard at the blackest black I've known, but I don't know what for.

The guard pit is about as big as a batter's box. I momentarily think of standing on deck and watching a pitcher throw, looking for a good spot to pull a fastball if I get one. My boots are soaked through and I keep my feet bouncing and the bouncing sends out little splashing sounds. So I quit that. I try to keep my attention on looking out at the blackness. I can hear frogs or something chirping. Small night birds, maybe.

Once, I think I hear some talking. Just a few sounds. It sends chills all through me and makes me grit my teeth. I'll be damned if I know whether I heard it or not. I'll trust Chickenfeed. I'm scared but I think my nerves might be playing tricks on me. I feel dizzy and there are spots, black spots in the black night—impossible. Shapes, too, like I am watching something as black as a box of black pups in a coal room.

"Chickenfeed, what the hell do we listen for?" I try to whisper.

The rain is all the sound there is and it's gentle. He laughs a little again.

"Listen for a motorcycle."

"What?"

"One time some guys was pulling a dawn shift and they hears a motorcycle, so called it in to headquarters. HQ came out and got them, figured they was loaded. But next day there was tracks, mosquito-bike tracks, goin' down the trail. Can you 'magine ridin' a bike through this goddamn jungle at night with all kin's o' cannons on the hill above you? Charlie been fightin' this war so long, man, so long. He know GIs ain't no match for him. He know most of us don' give a shit about the war. We ain' here for the duration, we just here a year or less, and we got nothin' to do but hide from him and watch the sweat roll down our chests. Even if we hear a motorcycle what we gonna do? How'd you know where to call the guns in? Me, I might take one shot, but chances are I'd let him slide on home."

"Yeah. How long you been here?" I realize the object of our listening duties is to be quiet, but talking feels so good.

"Two hundred fifty days. Either too long or not long enough."

"How so?"

"Fear, man. The utmost fear. I know how much 'fraid you are, 'cause I been there. When I first came in-country I expect to get hit all the time. I expect to be plain unlucky every single day for, say, a month. Then I got use to it. I quit thinkin' about it twenty-four hours a day. I begin to believe it was possible to make it. I been in incoming a dozen times probably, in three firefights, been on a LZ that got a direct attack, and was on the patrol that got ambushed when Prophet got hit the second time. Ever' one of those times was a surprise. It all happen so fast, I react automatically. I fucking hid if I could, I fucking shot back when I could, I fucking began to hate Charlie. I've survived. But, jus' lately, the fear is comin' back. Bein' out here, on LP, don't bother me anymore. We never hear anything, and this is so routine it like a job, but sometimes in the middle of the day I get the shakes. I be thinking about something else, back home usually, and all of a sudden I'm out of my mind. I get feelin's that we're gonna get hit and it gonna get me this time. I go into a state of shock. Now that I'm close to bein' under a hundred days I count every single fucking day. Between now and when I rotate, I'm into prayin'. I pray I won't see any more shit. I make bargains with God. I figure I paid my dues, that a cat can only take so much and I took it. This fear now, this's different than the original fear, 'cause I seen it happen. I wish I was crazy as Prophet."

I don't know Prophet well enough to say anything back to Chickenfeed, but the first time I saw Prophet I saw something in his eyes I'd never seen before. Like he looks at you to see your future. He's intimidating without meaning to be. Chickenfeed says he's crazy.

It amazes me that it can rain so steadily yet softly.

Half an hour later I feel very much awake and not so nervous. It is still raining the same way.

"You drafted, Chickenfeed?" I feel stupid asking him.

"Fuckin'-A. I figured they'd never get me but they did. I had me a good job, pullin' steel out of furnaces. Money. Man, money. I wonder if any o' that steel I pulled is sittin' over here with holes in it. That's one thing I can't get over, dig it? I seen so much goddamn steel with holes in it since I got here, I can't believe it. Choppers blown to shit. APCs shot up, bulldozers blown into pieces, conexes and corrugated base-camp buildings patched with plywood. It's amazin', man, fuckin'-A amazin' what kin' of power plastic explosive packs. The dinks do more damage with explosive than they do with anything else. Satchel charges. Scares the shit out of me to know they can walk onto this LZ, a suicide squad, and drop a satchel charge into my hooch. Anyway, I was an innocent American, I didn't think they'd draft me. Married, a kid now that I've never seen. . . ."

"You should've had the kid sooner."

"We try, man. When they started draftin' married guys without kids, I start on a kid. I used to—get this, compared to what I've got right now—I used to come home on my lunch hour and get laid." He laughs that whispering laugh.

It stops raining. He hawkers and a glob of snot lands on my boot that I've propped out of the water. It is so dark I can only see as far as the end of my boot, and what's there but a greenie.

Like an afterthought, he goes on in the same whispered

voice without the rain as background. "Quite a feelin', a kid. So I'm no kind of fuckin' hero. I get as deep under anything I can fin' when the shit hits."

"No such thing as a coward here." I feel confident saying that.

■■■■■■■■■■

THE BEAUTY OF THE COUNTRY HERE MAKES IT SEEM LIKE A funny place to have a war. I can see a very long ways this morning: mountains, mountains, mountains. Smooth like snowdrifts, wet green like seaweed. There are clouds in the east and the sun is the color of a fresh egg yolk. The yolk runs over the clouds in tree-limb patterns. Taking a deep breath is a rush, listening to the near-silence with my eyes closed calms me. I'm glad I am sitting alone on top of an empty water blivet.

The Nam. Here it is. The Nam and The World; nothing else exists for us. Nothing in The Nam is like anything in The World, not even the guys. Especially not the guys. I've been in the Army long enough that in a way I'm used to living without girls and without family, but I'm not used to being a part of it.

Now the sky is all one color in the east, lemon custard. The clouds are getting wispy, random like swallow shit on a frozen pig trough. I've got a cup of C-ration coffee and I'm letting myself be homesick, thinking of The World, where I'd likely be getting ready to work, to paint a house. Some of the houses I've painted floated through my memory. I see neighborhoods of big houses and clean bungalows. Nam ain't that. LZ Niagara is sandbagged huts, no painting.

I think about writing a letter home but even the thought doesn't get off the ground. Home is both too far away and not far enough. I can only write myself.

I don't want to get killed or wounded into ugliness or crippledom. I don't want to see anybody else get killed. I

56

wonder what Charlie thinks on mornings like this. I wonder if somewhere within a few kilometers there is another, smaller compound, hidden from our helicopters, where there is a guy sitting with a cup of something to drink. I wonder what he is thinking about. I'm sure he has never painted two-story houses and I'm pretty sure he isn't thinking about one year at a time.

BUSHWACKY

THE DAYS ARE CRAMMED FULL OF WORK. THIS TIME OF year, it rains at night, never very hard, and is hot during the day. The only cool places are inside the hooches, where moisture condenses on the underside of the sandbags. Outside, the vegetation is gradually disappearing and the red ground gets so hot we can't go barefooted, so one day my feet begin to come apart inside my boots and their smell is indescribable. By general consensus I qualify for the squad's ration of foot powder, and Funkfoot looks like it might become my nickname. The second day is painful because my feet crack and the open sores rub against my boots. I hold up my share of the work, though, and soak my feet in the morning's shaving water. About every other morning we shave out of water in our helmets and I recycle this—after it already has been recycled from man to man —by putting it into two rectangular ammo cans. At dark I take my boots off and sit for an hour on the edge of the hooch roof with my feet in the water.

During the day about half the squad is on detail, unloading helicopters on the pad or filling sandbags to protect the communication conexes or helping build parapets for Artillery. The other half works on digging another hooch. We constantly kept a pair of guys digging and filling sandbags, and now the hole is about five feet deep in the middle and there are sandbags piled five feet high waiting to go into the walls and roof. Tomorrow we will go into the Bush for overhead.

I am so tired I usually fall asleep right after dark. Tonight I am outdoors underneath a poncho and beside a trench. I can't get to sleep. I hear everything. I listen for mortar rounds and I welcome the noise of outgoing artillery rounds shooting Night Fire patterns, because at the very least I know somebody else is awake too. I feel entirely vulnerable underneath the poncho. My only protection if we were hit is the trench. I could roll into it and point my rifle downhill, which is my territory if it happens. In the event of incoming mortars I'd be lucky it all missed me if the rounds landed very near. But as frightened as I am at night, I dread going into the Bush for the first time. If I had to, I could run into the hooch during incoming here; no place to run out there.

During the first part of the night, the sky is clear and right above me there are enough stars to fill a washtub. Very, very high I can sometimes see the lights of a helicopter or a plane, and now and again the immediate sky is filled with the instantaneous and short-lived eerie light of hand-held flares that go up from the perimeter. Every time one goes up I listen as hard as possible and make sure I know where my rifle is. My feet hurt and smell. There is no reason to try and quell the quick breaths that come so often—I'd cry if I thought it would do any good. It is at night I feel so alone and unprotected; during the day it isn't as bad.

Tonight there is a sound that I can't trace. First it seems to come from directly on top of the hill, then it sounds closer, then farther away. It is a hollow pinging that makes me think of my mother taking the wash off the line and dropping the clothespins in a bucket.

It isn't warm. I have on my jacket although it isn't zipped up. When the clouds come in like seaweed and blot away my cluster of stars, a wind comes with it. In ten more minutes the rain comes, like feathers somehow, and I need to put my hood up to keep the water from dropping off my poncho and running down my neck. I don't expect to get to sleep and I wish I had drawn a guard duty so I could soak my feet. The last thing I remember thinking is whether or not it would take the sting out of my feet if I soaked them in my slit trench, into which I can hear the water draining.

I dream of a river bottom near the Ohio. I haven't seen anybody for days and I'm engrossed in tracking a big rabbit but I can't see the ground very well. I stoop down to look at a rabbit squat pressed into briars that are young and green. The ground is split right there and I see a cavern that holds five dinks sitting around a broken-down combine. Prophet is looking in through a slit on the other side, and he drops a frag down the feed chute of the machine. Then music starts. Bull Durham is folding back my poncho. It is morning and I am awake in wet clothes.

"We're going out in half an hour," he says, "if you wanna eat something warm."

Out. So today will be one of the days I've been afraid of. The Bush is no-man's-land. Charlie is waking up somewhere out there too. For months I've thought of this and wondered if it would ever really happen. Very few patrols see anything, but *what if it's in the cards?* Not many guys see incoming on their first night either, but I did. The last time I thought about luck I felt lucky to be in Two Squad, but right now that feeling isn't doing me much good.

In my own way, I say a prayer. I just say, *Oh, God, watch me.*

Something is burning. Peacock is sitting on a rock in front of his lean-to, holding a C-ration can by its lid. A small, white-hot fire from C-4 is heating the can. C-4 is an explosive that comes in wrapped cakes twice as big as a giant Hershey bar. Food doesn't sound at all good to me. I turn my steel helmet upside down and sit on it, chain-smoking.

Even though it isn't much after sunrise there is steam rising from the ground. In the valley is a cloud the color of newspaper. Higher, smaller clouds drift over our mountain. There isn't any wind and hardly any noise. One radio is on and it's off the station. The guy it belongs to has red hair and is asleep with his head downhill and one boot in his slit trench.

Bull Durham is shaving. He has water in his helmet and is lathered up. The lather on his face makes him look totally out of place, standing twenty feet around the hill from me with the clouds moving behind him. It makes me think of a religious painting. My basic training comes back to me all of a sudden, and it seems so bookish, pretend. I almost expect Peacock or Bull or somebody else to laugh as I take my rifle apart to be sure it is clean. I take down my poncho and fold it into my rucksack and I make sure my bandoliers of ammo are where they belong, so by the time Pops and Prophet come out of the hooch carrying their gear I'm as ready as I can be.

"Mornin'."

"Yeah."

"How long are we going out for?"

"Three days."

"Anything I need to know?"

Prophet stops on his way by and looks like he is thinking about my question. He says, "Know which pocket your toilet paper is in," and is gone before I can see if he is smiling or not. I check to see if my toilet paper is where I think it is. It's not.

One time, fifteen years ago: Following the old man through the path in the briars. My gun is too big and gets snagged by bushes over and over again. Thanksgiving morning. Somehow my double-barrel hand-me-down doubles a maple sapling that would've been the old man except

61

that I fall backwards when I fall. My hands are stiff from the cold, my nose is running, my boots leak after all. I never want to hunt again.

My knees are shaky and my hands quake as I shoulder my ruck and walk to the perimeter, where there is already a work party stretching concertina wire. Prophet and Pops are throwing a Frisbee with two guys from the work party while they're waiting on the rest of us. They don't look the least bit concerned and I wonder what my face looks like but nobody looks at me. Chickenfeed is coming down the hill behind me, dragging his ruck with one hand. The Frisbee sails into the pile of concertina and the guy chasing it can't stop himself in time so he gets a quick cut on his leg from one of the barbs.

"Cheap way to get a purple one."

"Just my goddamn luck this wire isn't rusty so I don't go back to the Rear for a shot."

"A good infielder could've had that anyway."

"Fuck you."

"Let's go, it's getting hot fast."

"OK. Gabe, Callmeblack, listen up. One of you is gonna be walking second. Prophet will be walking point, the radio is third. The other one of youse two will walk behind the radio. Gabe, you take second and you watch on your right. Pea will have the radio and he'll watch left. Callme, you watch to your right. We're headed straight down the hill at first and the trail is pretty open. Keep your fucking eyes fucking open, no daydreaming. Be damn sure you know where the guy in front of you is. Don't think about the guy behind you, it's up to him to watch you. We'll probably hump from here to the Blue Line before we take a break. It's downhill all the way. Be as quiet as you can, don't talk. If you see anything, hold your hand up and get down low. I'll tell you right now we ain't likely to see anything before the Blue Line. Once we get close to the water we'll put on flak jackets and you can put on your helmet if you wanna, it's up to you. Charlie isn't gonna ambush us before we get there, we're too close. The only way we're gonna see him is by surprise, and more than likely it'll be Prophet who sees anything first. Gabe— Funkfoot—stop shaking." Pops smiles and walks a couple steps to put his arm around my shoulders.

"I'd like to."

"Brother," Chickenfeed says, "if there was anythin' to worry about I'd be shakin' too, but this is a pud hump, so relax." He begins to load his rifle and pretends his hands are shaking too much to bring the clip and gun together. It is that beautiful white grin of his that calms me enough to take a deep breath and load my weapon.

The guy who cut himself has a green handkerchief tied around his leg and has a Frisbee on his head like a beret. Prophet rams a clip into his rifle and says, "Let's play William Tell for a case of C's," and the guy scrambles in mock fright. We saddle up and head into the thick stuff. I can hear Prophet chamber a round. Only the point man carries a round in the chamber.

I keep my eyes right, all the time making damn sure I have my thumb on the safety and very aware of how to get a round into the chamber fast. The first part of the trail reminds me of grown-over pasture track. It is rugged, and there are rocks and lengths of vine lying across it because of work parties dragging logs for hooch roofs. By the time we are fifty meters out I can't see back to the clearing of the LZ, and in another five minutes the jungle is closing down on the trail. Even though Prophet is only about six meters ahead of me I constantly lose sight of him when he rounds a curve or drops over a rock. My heart drums panic for these moments. We are going down the mountain at an angle, toward the small river that runs down to the wide An Loa at the bottom. My rifle keeps getting tangled until I learn to point it down. Like a hardon in Sunday school, one too many things to keep track of. My sore feet rub against the rough insides of my boots, and that discomfort feels real because everything else still seems impossible.

After about fifteen minutes I want to stop and rest. It is hot and the sweat is constant. My eyes fill with sweat to the point where I can't see anything clearly. Prophet is setting a fast pace. He is in shape. At first I try to watch him but soon it is all I can do to keep going. My feet feel hot and the sweat is coming off me like rain. The shoulder straps of my ruck are two inches wide but in fifteen minutes I would swear they are only as thick as rope, they cut into me so bad. The trail is rock and dirt for the first few minutes but then it gets narrow and is covered with weeds that have been beaten down a little.

I keep looking right but all the time I want to sneak a look to the other side too. All the vegetation bleeds together through the sweat in my eyes, and about the only distinctions I can make are between different shades of green and yellow and different shapes of leaves and vines. Every so often my side of the trail thins out for no reason that I can tell, and I can see into the jungle a little farther. Each time I see one of these clearings I expect to see something, somebody, I don't want to see.

Just when I come to a big rock there is a small whistle. Nobody said anything about signals but I've got a clear view of Prophet, and when he hears it he backs up to another rock and leans his ruck on it. I stop too. Prophet is wearing a green headband and he wrings it out with one hand. I happen to be looking at his rifle, and I notice he flips the safety switch. I can hear the murmur of Pops and Peacock talking behind me, although I can't see anything but the radio antenna.

"How you holding up?" Pops asks me. His butterscotch face is slick with sweat and I notice a mole on his chin I'd never seen before.

I am still huffing, out of wind. He doesn't wait for my answer, although he looks right at me and squeezes my shoulder. He says, "Wait until we start *up*hill," and winks. He unshoulders his ruck on the other side of my ruck and slides down toward Prophet. I lean back expecting the rock to be cool but it isn't. Nothing is.

Peacock startles me when he moves up to where I can see him. He is still wearing his ruck and the radio and I'm surprised that he doesn't seem to be breathing hard, but he is wringing wet too. He gives me the peace sign and closes his eyes.

The only thing I can hear is birds, and they aren't very close to us. Most of the sounds they make are thin and pleasant, in a rhythm that makes me think of tree frogs. There's also a mid-range call that sounds like a screech. I wonder what kind of bird it is and what the sound means, whether he is warning other birds—or maybe Charlie—about us, or whether he is simply talking. There doesn't seem to be any alarm in the sound; the alarm is within me. My breath comes back and I think of lighting a cigarette but I know that would be stupid. Peacock hasn't moved. I'd be afraid to close my eyes. Pops and Prophet are sitting back to back and talking.

We start again. My feet feel like cinders. Instead of going on straight down the hill, we move laterally this time, along a trail about the same size as the last one. It seems a little different to be looking uphill, even though the foliage is too thick to see the ground. I think it is being able to see the underside of the leaves that tells me my side is uphill. The sunlight shining through the canopy makes it look much like cloth.

My tongue begins to feel like cardboard. Walking along this trail is easier than the last but it seems to be getting muggier too as we gradually descend. In another twenty minutes my ruck is cutting so bad the pain moves up to my neck and into the back of my head. I have to stop momentarily to shift the weight higher onto my shoulders. Peacock comes up behind me with the radio. That fucking radio is another thirty pounds. I don't have to stop long enough for him to catch up with me but I have to hurry to catch sight of Prophet. I feel bad when I see that he's far ahead of me and I feel like I should do something about it, like whistle. Just about then Prophet must notice I'm dropping behind because he stops. When I catch up to where I should be I can hear the river falling over rocks. I have enough sense to know this is a critical point. Prophet catches my eye and the look he gives me is part exhaustion and part perplexity.

When we come to the river it is falling over two big boulders. There are vines over the water so old and thick they look like the black ironwork of a bridge. One by one, we hop across the boulders and take turns filling our canteens. This side of the river is rockier and there are little patches of kinky branches.

"We'll lay around here a little while," Pops says. "Set up in pairs. You come with me."

He and I go up the hill a little to one of the kinky patches. Another pair goes down the hill, and Prophet and Bull Durham are stripping to get into the water. My blood pressure must roar, I feel flushed. Peacock fixes the radio against a big rotten stump. Pops sits down in the thicket and I sit down looking the opposite way. I see the trail we were following where it disappears into the bush. This kinky stuff is a lot less green than everything else; partly yellow and partly brown, it grows sideways instead of up. Pops lies back and pulls his hat down to shade his eyes. The weird thing is being the same size as all the plants around me. I feel like a rabbit must feel. I keep my eyes riveted on the trail's end for the most part, but pretty soon I begin to scan all around. I don't know why I expect Charlie to come walking down the trail; if there are any dinks around here they're probably watching us look for them.

Pops stirs. "Keep your eyes on that trail over there," he says. I feel a glint of pride because I have been eyeing it.

"I'll watch these two." Now he points out two I didn't see and that pride eats itself, and I feel depressed. The World, Nam, the Bush; it's a downward flight into basic survival, and now, with OVER THREE HUNDRED FUCKING DAYS LEFT, my dream is to make it home, fuckin' home, *make it home*.

♦♦♦♦♦♦♦♦♦♦♦

I SEE POPS NOD OFF FROM TIME TO TIME; HE HAS DONE ALL this a hundred times. The only thing that changes for me is the spots in front of my eyes. I play little games with the spots, make them blend into the jungle, watch them dance on the water, blink them away. I'm curious about why they are there—I guess it's my nervousness. The other pair of guys get out of the stream now, but I don't feel like getting in.

When he looks at me and winks I ask Pops if we ever see any dinks at times like this. "Well, hell, if they hear us they'll lob mortars in at the guys in the water. But mortars aren't all that accurate. Of course, if there are very many of them there's a chance they'll take us on, but if there's very many we don't have a chance. About the only good we're doing right now is if there's a couple trying to sneak up on us to throw a frag."

"Does it ever happen?"

"Over near Pleiku there are more VC. Over here we're after the Trail, and it's mostly NVA. They travel in regiments and you never hear about them or see them until they're ready for you."

In The World it is inconceivable to imagine that there could be a regiment of NVA so close and we wouldn't know it, but sitting in a kinky little patch of jungle, still scared shitless, the possibility is as clear as the clouds that I see through the canopy.

"What good do these short squad patrols do?"

"We find signs."

67

"Like what?"

"Usually a fresh trail." He takes a minute to pick his nose, and then another minute lighting a smoke and carefully scratching his rot. "Most of the dinks around here are coming from the DMZ, on their way to the delta. Or they're headed for Cambodia to recoup. This whole area is a switching yard, big trails meet all around here."

"How big?"

"They drive trucks down the Ho Chi."

"Where's that?"

"It moves all the time. Way the fuck into Cambodia now, I think, because we see a lot of bombers going over, then we hear the drops, and it's a while before they come back over."

I assume they're bombing the Trail. I ask Pops about it.

"Who knows, man? The big guys run the show, and the ones that run it the most are the ones up there in helicopters or planes, or way back in the Rear with the gear, working eight hours a day and living the rest of the time with a cute little whore somewhere. I could never figure out why we do what we do. We just make these fucking humps, move when some lifer thinks we oughta, and count our days; that's all I know, man, that's all I care about." He opens his mouth to say something else but doesn't.

"How often do we move?"

"Depends, goes in spurts."

I take a drink of the stream water. It's good, very good. My throat has dried out and the water is much colder than I thought it would be.

"When we move, that's the tensest times," he says. "If the lifers happen to be right on their guesses, then we move into what is supposed to be Charlie's area. But, hell, I like it, passes time faster. Have to admit, though, the shorter I get the less I like to think of hitting any shit. Funny, we'll go a month without seeing anything, then we might hit some shit and it can go on for a week straight. Incoming, mostly, and believe it or not, you get used to that. I don't mean to be telling any war stories, but when we were over nearer Cambo, back in March I think, we took incoming for nine straight days. We could hear the rounds leaving the tubes and knew we had about twenty seconds before they would hit. You'd be surprised what you can do in twenty seconds. Shit, man, I can remember finishing a hand of cards between the time we heard the pop and the time we headed for a hole. It's funny little things like that that keep you sane, dig it?"

"Seems like the scariest thing is this, these patrols. I worry about getting ambushed, don't you?"

"Not so much. Prophet is probably the best point man in the Central Highlands, and I'm not exaggerating. He gets feelings that nobody else gets, and they're accurate. I'm glad I'll rotate before he does. I'd swear he has saved my life at least twice, or at least saved us from hitting shit. He stopped us once for no reason, and five minutes later an NVA squad came past us."

"What'd you do?"

"Kept as quiet as I've ever been in my life, shit my pants, almost fainted. Bravery sucks, man. This army you're in, man, isn't a fighting army in this war; this ain't ours."

I sense that he tells me this with some kind of regret, and I feel like I ought to say something. I am relaxed now. Talking to Pops, or listening to him, makes me feel better. A great feeling of warmth comes over me when he reaches to squeeze my shoulder. Bull Durham is coming up the trail naked. Pops looks away from me, I think, rather than away from Bull. He seems embarrassed, I guess because he told the absolute truth, and again I wish I knew what to say. I smile, that's all. I wish he knew what I was feeling. I am not gung-ho; I don't want to fight, and one guy killed was one too many. But I figure he's heard, maybe said himself, everything I could think of. And Bull isn't walking up the trail anymore, he's dancing.

"Hey, look. Out here in the middle of nowhere, a real swinger."

I'm surprised how deft the big Bull is. Light on his feet. I begin chuckling to myself at the sight of him doing pirouettes up a jungle trail, completely nude except for his beads and hat.

The sun passes straight above us and comes now from the valley side. Eventually we all get careless. It starts when Bull throws Peacock in the water, then Chickenfeed shoves Bull in. Although we never let our guard down completely we begin to have some fun. Prophet discovers a pool downstream that is not covered by canopy, so the sun shines on it. Sometimes there are four guys in and the others are far from ready for combat. However, we all chamber a round and leave our rifles close by. The pool offers a little protection of its own because it is surrounded on every side but downstream by boulders. As if it is fatal, I panic momentarily when I catch myself appreciating the beauty of it all and plain having some fun. The water is warmer here. Everything seems so peaceful. The reality of live ammunition and the possibility of an enemy seems dreamy. I get inside myself so I feel hidden. Not like I belong here, but like I can hide.

We decide to move on before it gets dark, because we don't want to be too near the Blue Line. Any decent-sized river on a map is marked in blue, and when Artillery sets up its Night Fire Program, a likely target is Blue Lines. Night Fire pinpoints a series of defensive targets that the big guns shoot at all night long at random. Charlie knows where the LZs are, so Night Fire targets are usually close to the LZ in areas where there are trails, to defend against a lot of dinks coming at night. The spot we are in seems a logical spot for Artillery to shoot.

AFTER A SHORT DISCUSSION, WE DECIDE THERE SHOULD BE another gully across the big river that would be a good place to set up for the night. We scale the distance at two kilometers as the parrot flies, mostly downhill. We get into line again and move out. As soon as I shoulder my ruck and start to sweat I feel afraid again. Maybe there is another description besides afraid. Apprehension, maybe. I felt better while we were stopped. Humping down this trail makes me feel vulnerable. Even though our weapons are probably better than Charlie's, and even though we've got the support of big guns and helicopters, Charlie has been in this jungle forever. I am beginning to believe in Peacock's luck and unluck. If the dinks hit us, there wouldn't be much to do except hope you're lucky, and that everybody else is lucky too.

The trail we use runs right along the stream. It is a fairly wide trail and hard-packed. I keep remembering things from years before. Grandaddy hunted his food for fifty years and is as likely to be hunting squirrel today as not. I went hunting with him. I was Grandaddy's favorite. He kidnapped me more than a few times. In the winters after I left for school he would meet me at the bus stop with our guns. Some of those days stolen away from the boredom of school are my fondest memories. I am a good shot. My father went hunting with me once right before I got drafted. We didn't talk much and I was a little humiliated that he is still a better hunter than I am. In the heat of this goddamn jungle, through the sweat underneath my eyelids, it isn't hard to imagine him walking like Bull Durham is, carefully and expertly.

The Bush is its own kind of world; there isn't anything remotely like it in The World. Down here by the river it is extra thick. The trail is both steep and slanted toward the stream. I am always on the lookout for snakes. Stateside, the veterans of Nam told us snake stories, of pythons in trees and bamboo vipers in sandbags. Prophet is setting a slower pace this time. My feet are the sorest they've ever been, and walking on the double angle of the trail causes them to rub against my boots. When I catch sight of Prophet he is standing beside a big boulder where another trail comes in. He makes a sign with his fingers that means the stream and river come together here. He waits for me to catch up to him. The An Loa River is about twenty meters in front of us. I see it by looking down the valley of the small river. It's not moving very swiftly, but it is wider than I thought it would be. I wonder how deep it is.

"Wait until Peacock and Bull catch up but be ready to go across," he says.

Jesus. I'm going to be the first one to cross? This is it; I expect to get shot at. It is impossible to see into the bush on the other side. There's a slight wind blowing the top of the water. The river is probably a hundred meters wide here, and it is extremely shallow as far out as I can see. I wonder if there's a channel down the middle. The rest of the squad catches up and very quietly settles into points of security, two looking behind us and four looking across the river, where I'm going. I stall for a minute, watching Prophet and glancing at Pops a time or two. Nothing is ever said. I wonder why they are sending me first but I don't question it.

I'd be an easy target out there in the middle, a duck. I'm not sure how much out of the water I'll stick up in the middle. I put on my steel pot, mostly as a precaution against bullets, but also so I can stick my cigarettes in the band that holds the camouflage cover on the helmet. Prophet just looks at me while I get my shit together. I remember to put my toilet paper with my smokes. When I hit the water I chamber a round and glance at him once more, not expecting anything. He gives me the peace sign. I'm in too much of a hurry at first and I almost fall face forward. I try to make it look like it was part of getting into my crouch. The water is pretty warm and makes my feet feel a lot better. For the first twenty-five meters it doesn't get above my knees even though I'm crouched fairly low. Then it gets deeper slowly. The bottom here is mostly rocks about the size of a cookie jar and it isn't easy to walk. I keep my eyes trained on the bank across from me. I rationalize that Charlie wouldn't open fire while it's only me in the water; he'd wait until there are three or four of us crossing. I look back and Callme is getting ready to come next. He has his pants legs rolled up to his thighs for some reason and looks tall and black against the green foliage.

Suddenly there's a drop-off and once more I stumble. I keep my rifle up high. I'm dog-paddling now and couldn't fire a round if I had to. I begin to swim faster and think about how Charlie would bring pee if he chose to. *Rockets? Small arms? Machine guns?* My boots are heavy, my mouth is dry as dead leaves, my heart is beating hard, and my helmet is getting crooked on my head but there's nothing I can do about it. When my feet hit the bottom of the other side of the channel I let myself piss. Now I remember I forgot to put my stationery in the helmet. I am panting when I reach the other side. I feel worn out.

Something is wrong with Callmeblack. He is only fifteen meters away from the other shore and standing straight up, looking all around him very rapidly. I listen for anything strange, but all I can hear is the water running over a small rapids near me. Now I can see Prophet on the other side, standing at the edge and holding his rifle by the handle, waving it at Callmeblack. He isn't yelling but his actions are obviously frustrated. Then Bull Durham is in the water. Suddenly aware that I should be scouting my side of the river, I move up the bank a few feet and my heart quits when I see the trail. It's like a bicycle path and it looks fresh. During the moment of panic the spots come in front of my eyes and I literally gasp for breath. I don't think about it, I hit the dirt with my rifle ready. Nothing is moving anywhere and there aren't any sounds except the wind and the water. The trail is only about five meters away from the river and I'd have to be real stupid not to know it is fresh. There is a lot of vegetation broken off and it's still green. I can smell it—a kind of celery smell.

Bull is about halfway to Callme already and just then Callme gets over his fright and crouches and moves again. Bull goes down on one knee to allow Callme to get farther ahead before he starts again. Callme is coming fast now and when he hits the channel he lunges forward and dog-paddles like a spastic. I'm surprised that he lets his head go under for a moment, I guess he just does it to cool off. I meet him at the edge and take hold of his rifle to help him up. His face is wrinkled funny; I've never seen this look on his face. I wonder what it is, and whether I had it on my face too. I put a finger to my lips and point at the trail. His eyes get big like I knew they would; then we point at the spots we'll each go, and with one more look at the river I lie down about the same place I was. He goes downstream but not very far. We look opposite directions. Bull is most of the way across and Chickenfeed is in the water to his knees. Now it occurs to me how vulnerable the last guy will be, alone over there.

"Oh, fuck" is all Bull says when he sees the trail. He scrambles across it and goes upstream. He wears a big ring on his right hand and I've seen him nervously click the ring against his rifle; I can hear him doing it now.

Both Pops and Prophet are in the water before Chickenfeed gets out. Pops is last. When he gets across we gather around two old stumps on the high side of the trail.

"Fucker's fresh, ain't it?"

"Very. They ain't far away."

"Anybody wanna volunteer to scout it a little?"

"No."

"Fuck no."

"I'll go down it a little ways," Prophet says.

"Take Bull's grenade launcher with you."

"Nah, I ain't going far."

"Want anybody to go with you?"

"Nah. If they're anywhere's close they would've blown our shit away when we were crossing."

"True."

Pops is looking at the map and picking at the mole on his chin. Peacock goes uphill a little to another tree, and the rest of us stay still. In no more than five minutes Prophet is back. He moves so quietly I don't even hear him before I see him.

"They set up about thirty meters downstream," he says.

"How many?"

"I think probably only a squad."

"Let's take a look."

The camp is fifteen meters up the bank from the trail. I wouldn't have seen the small trail that leads up to it. There is really nothing to the camp except five small trenches. Bull finds an empty C-ration can and Peacock finds some cooked rice. It is the weirdest feeling ever, to be standing here, knowing a squad of enemy soldiers stood here within the past few days. The camp disturbed almost nothing of the jungle. There are two sets of three sticks that must have been used for making a shelter, a few places where the grass has been beaten down, but, except for the trenches, this jungle will erase all the traces they left behind within a week. A big difference between them and us. I wonder where they are now.

"Figure they were only here one night?"

"Yeah."

"Looks like they had a mortar with 'em."

"Couple days old."

I still have my steel pot on, and all of a sudden it is heavy. So is my ruck, and my feet hurt. I'm tired. I'd guess there is probably three hours of light left. There is a spot of the river visible from here and it's just where the rapids are. The water going over the rocks reminds me of spunglass insulation, small windows of light. Nobody has said anything for five minutes or so. Bull taps his rifle with his ring a few times and we all turn his way at once. He stops, a shit-eating grin on his face.

"Let's get the fuck going."

"We gonna call this in?"

"Not unless we can tell they're going the same way we are."

It almost feels good to be walking again. Pops trades positions with me and Callmeblack moves up behind them and carries the radio. Merely helping him shoulder it makes me glad I'm not the one who has to carry it. We follow the trail for the first twenty minutes, and even though I worry about hitting some shit, I'm so tired I'm glad it is easy walking. Before I even realize it we are off the new trail and heading directly up the mountain on a trail that is mostly boulders. I do my damnedest to think about something else.

■■■■■■■■■■■

SOMETIMES SOMEBODY WILL REFER TO THE ENEMY AS dinks or gooks, but mostly it's Charlie. The only Vietnamese I've seen up close were ARVN soldiers who rode with us in a convoy at Cam Ranh, skitterish little men in whose eyes I could see almost nothing but fear—actually, they never look into your eyes. They didn't trust us and none of us trusted them; they are allies, but it's their war. There are three Chieu Hois on the LZ. *Chieu hoi* means "open arms" in Vietnamese, and Chieu Hois are former VC or NVA who the U.S. Army uses as scouts. Nobody trusts them either, and they stay alone in a hooch on the perimeter. I've never seen them, and the only reason I know about them is that somebody told me.

Charlie is still the pictures and drawings we were shown in Basic Training and memories from TV newscasts for the past few years. Even though I've been in his house now, he's still not real, just Charlie. I'm afraid of him. Nobody could convince me I'm as good a soldier. I never want to see him, especially not alive.

I keep a steady watch on my side of the trail. Pretty birds the size of crows take off from the trees, and aside from their calls the only other noise is the sound of somebody's equipment rattling. Mine rattles each time I rearrange the weight of my ruck. The trail has gotten steeper all the time and now I have to use my free hand to help pull myself up. This moves the weight of my ruck higher up on my shoulders, but at the same time it plays hell with my feet. Instead of just being sore now, there is steady pain from my ankles being strained. My lungs hurt too, and the short stops we make don't last long enough for me to catch my breath. We have to hurry; the light is going fast now.

Just about the time I can't go any farther we stop. The spot doesn't look any different from what we've been coming through and we can't see more than ten meters in any direction, which is what makes it a good place. We set up in a small circle, everybody facing out. Callme and I dig the trenches; it's easy digging.

I'm surprised how good my C-rations taste, cold, and I drink too much water. It is dark as hell, and the only thing I hear for a few moments is individual can openers working, then the sounds of eating. Callmeblack starts giggling.

"What's so funny?"

Now more than just a giggle, he's laughing. "I just learned to swim today."

"What?"

"I've never swam before in my life."

"Watermelons float."

"So do niggers when we has to," Chickenfeed says.

"So you've got a good war story to tell your kids, how

77

you learned to swim in full combat gear right under Charlie's nose."

"Where do you suppose Charlie is now?"

"A long ways from here, I hope."

We call in our position so Artillery can shoot for us if we need it, then get a guard roster together and pass a couple bowls of dope around. My eyes adjust and the moon gets high enough to shed a little light through the canopy. I can just make out a couple of outlines——Chickenfeed and Peacock, who're next to me—and I can see the orange glow of the bowl go around the circle. Everybody hears a noise, a stick breaking maybe, and the next noise is when we all take hold of our rifles. My heart is a piston. As if he could see well enough to be positive, Prophet says it's an animal. Still, even though his confidence helps me out, all I can hear for a few minutes is my heart and my breathing. My feet stink through my boots. This is my first night in the Bush.

I will pull the second guard shift so I try to get some sleep beforehand but I barely drift off. I have a weird dream in which three Charlies are waiting for a train in The Depot Restaurant. The Depot is on Railroad Street but it's made out of bamboo. The Charlies all look alike and have a uniform tattooed onto their bodies.

Chickenfeed wakes me up. Callmeblack and I pull our guard, listening to the guns on the LZ fire, then the rounds hit in clusters. We talk a little bit about being scared and agree there isn't much to say or do about it. Right at the end of our shift a wind comes up that makes the huge vines move. The sound is one of a kind: too massive to be a creaking, but something on that order. Callme goes to get our relief and it's only me out there. If I heard anything I'd probably sit quiet as hell and wait for help, but all I hear is the bare sounds of him talking to somebody six meters away. It makes me think of people whispering in a theater.

I'm not sure I sleep where I mean to. I wonder if flash-lights are ever allowed in the Bush.

When we call in in the morning, Headquarters tells us where to go. It isn't far but it's straight up again. We are supposed to set up tonight at the junction of two trails. An ambush.

After we saddle up and go for twenty minutes the sweat begins to chafe my asshole and I have to use my towel to pad my shoulder straps the first time we stop. Basic Train-ing wasn't shit compared to this, and I am preoccupied wondering if I would freeze if we hit any shit. In an hour it suddenly clouds and rains and just as suddenly stops. The rain makes climbing more miserable because now there is mud on the trail. Once I slip and fall on my crazy bone. I get that feeling that makes me want to cry out and laugh at the same time. After a long break it is my turn to carry the radio.

Jesus Fucking Christ, I can't. It is the size of a sack of potatoes and weighs more than three gallons of paint. Its straps fit differently than my ruck so now I've got four lines of soreness by the time we crest the hill and stop again. Up here we can see a long distance, and the green-yellow mountains look like pile upon pile of cauliflower heads. There are little clouds everywhere; above us, below us, even with us. Like being in a wet box of tissues. I want to take my boots off.

"Caterpillar Four," the radio says. I wait for somebody else to answer.

"Get back to him, dumb-ass," Prophet says impatiently.

"Uh. . . ." I can't remember shit. "Uh, Caterpillar Four. Go."

"What's your Lima?"

"Wait one." I'm relieved that we have to figure our co-ordinates. I feel like a fool. Pops codes the numbers and I relay them to the base.

"Roger that. A bird sees you, didn't want to call in The World on your asses. Break."

"Out."

"Out." Talking into the hand mike reminds me of being broken down on a highway at night somewhere and using a phone—so removed. I look for the helicopter but can't see it. I feel like I should know which range of mountains the LZ is on, and if I'm right it is covered by a puffball cloud as bright as porcelain.

Charlie would go for the radio and I wish the antenna was at least painted green. Every so often I can feel it snag on the branches over the trail even though I am walking bent over. Going down isn't as rough as coming up was but the mud is a pain in the ass. My boots look like divers' fins but at least some of the spanking newness of the canvas is changing. I wish Ass could see them. I don't think it's a lump that comes to my throat when I think of him, but I think of him. And I wonder where his body is now.

The trail that intersects ours is the same size as the one we're on. We approach the intersection one at a time, and the first three guys each go a different way for a few meters. Peacock finds something on the new trail and calls Pops over. They decide it is a tire track, maybe from a wheelbarrow.

"Let's get some claymores up and get the hell into the woods."

We pull nonstop security and arrange the claymores; then we go uphill a little to a spot behind two trees and dig our trenches. I have to take a shit and it's pudding; it uses all my toilet paper, and immediately draws flies and a bug that looks like a button.

"I wanna go home."

"Tell the chaplain."

It rains again, hard and fast. My cigarettes get mostly wet and I get pissed off because I can't get one to stay lit. I oil myself up with mosquito repellent and lie back in the grass to at least rest my eyes. The sun is no longer bright but the visions behind my eyelids are all colors. Nothing definite, mostly shapes and dancing rainbows. I am hungry and don't even bother to look at which can I draw out of my ruck. My plastic spoon is in the bottom pocket of my utilities and its handle isn't much longer than the rest of it by now. After I'm done eating I want another cigarette and again go through the absurd task of lighting a wet one. It seems strange, but I feel chilly so I put on my flak jacket, which isn't really warm but at least it is somewhat soft when I lie back again.

I'm exhausted and sleep comes easily. I don't have any idea what time it is when they wake me up, but what surprises me is that I've been sleeping while it is raining. I had put my shelter up, but when I wake up I'm out from under it and soaking fucking wet. It is me and Prophet on guard. I feel like about half my mind is all that wakes up for the first five minutes. I am lacing my boots, not really caring that it is so dark I can't see to do it. I would like to smoke a cigarette, but there is no smoking on guard in the Bush.

There isn't much of anything on guard in the Bush. Just listening. It's insanely dark. After half an hour of wishing I had a cigarette and sitting as still as I possibly can, my eyes acclimate just enough to pick up glows here and there, some kind of phosphorescent insects. The only thing I can think of comparing them with are lightning bugs, but these bugs are a few different colors and they don't fly around much. They might be worms on the leaves, I don't know.

"You still awake?" He whispers so softly it doesn't even startle me.

"Yeah."

"You know which way is downhill, don't you?"

"Yeah. You're slightly downhill and the claymores are on our right."

"Good job. We ain't gonna see anything tonight, but keep your detonator handy."

Jesus. I forgot. Pulling goddamn ambush guard, claymores in front of us, and I fuckin'-A forget all about the detonators.

Another thing I forgot about is the watch, and about the time I figure it has been two hours I'm beginning to wonder about Prophet because I haven't heard him stirring around for a while now.

"You awake?"

"Yeah."

"How much longer?"

"You got the watch?"

"Thought you did."

"Fuck it. Go to sleep if you want to. I'll either stay awake or get somebody else up in a while."

The rain has started and stopped over and over again. It is started now, and it seems incredible that the soft sound of drops spilling from leaf to leaf overcomes the distant thunder of artillery, enough to drop me off almost immediately. The last thing I hear is Prophet yawning. Like my babysitter.

●●●●●●●●●●●

"CATERPILLAR FOUR." IT'S LIGHT OUT, NOBODY IS AWAKE.

"Go."

"Sierra Lima?"

"No, wait one. . . . Pops, wake up. CP wants you."

"Bad news."

He has a hardon when he gets up but it doesn't bother him. He goes to the radio and turns the volume down while he's listening. I go outside the perimeter to take a piss, and when I come back he is leaning against a tree with a nasty look on his face.

"How's your feet?"

"Sore, why?"

"We're going another five kliks."

"Kiss my petunia," Peacock says, putting on his glasses. "Maybe we shoulda turned that fresh trail in, they'd send us back down there."

"Maybe, maybe not. Four Squad hit some shit last night. Two WIAs, one dink. They're south of us about ten kliks and CP wants us to head that way. Evidently just a NVA patrol. So, let's eat and ride."

When we left I packed what I thought was enough food for three or four days but I haven't eaten much. This morning it is peaches and pound cake, the best possible meal.

It is hot when we start moving again. I am still humping the radio and my feet are tender. I try walking on the sides of my feet then on the heels, but nothing works. After a while a numbness comes, or I start thinking about the rest of my aches instead. We are going away from the river. I am following Peacock this time and once when I can see him he points with his rifle. He doesn't slow down or stop, but when he points a panic hits me hard in the chest and my breath disappears. At first I don't know what he sees, and then I see a large crater, evidently where artillery rounds once landed. The crater is fairly fresh but already the vegetation is growing over it. It's just off the trail and I wonder if it is that close to accurate or simply chance. Everything within twenty-five meters has been scorched and torn by shrap metal. As we keep on walking we pass more of the same and I wonder if there was a firefight here once, whether this is evidence of a barrage called in or whether it is random Night Fire targets. Once, when I happen to stumble and look down, I see a piece of shrap the size of a cigarette lighter lying in the trail.

The rain comes and it's hard; it feels good until it lasts too long. It makes it hard to see, hard to keep my eyes open even, and isn't as cool as it seems like it should be. My back is killing me now, and I know we won't stop for a break as long as it is raining. When it stops we do too. I am unbelievably sore.

The terrain turns brutal all at once. Now we are walking almost exclusively over torturing rocks. The rocks are red and there isn't as much vegetation as there has been. Our progress gets slower and slower because we have to find footholds and sometimes pull ourselves up by small trees that grow almost sideways.

There are three quick shots and my heart falls all the way to my sore feet. Once shot hits the top of the radio and breaks off a chunk of the plastic. I go down with my rifle pointed in the direction I think the rounds came from. I am waiting for more. We are in a crevice with three sides protected by the steep rock cliffs. The fourth side is somewhat open. I can't get my breath.

"Peacock, the radio!" I shout at him because he is the only one I can see.

"Hang tight. Stay the fuck down. Are you hit?"

"No."

Chickenfeed comes running up to where I am from behind me and dives headfirst into the crevice.

"It came from in front of us," he says. "See if the radio works."

"Alpha Six, Alpha Six, Caterpillar Four, over."

It seems like too long but finally Alpha comes back. "Caterpillar, go."

I don't know what to say but I am glad to hear the radio. I still expect to hear more rounds. Pops comes running back and dives into the fissure with us, then Prophet and Callme come too, one from each direction.

"Where's Bull?"

"He was behind me," Callme says. His voice trembles and he is breathing hard too. "I hit the dirt, then got up and ran here. I thought he was right behind me."

"Bull!"

"Behind you. I'm hit!"

Prophet quickly puts on his flak jacket and begins to crawl back down the trail. Five or six rounds rip near him but he keeps crawling.

Pops and Peacock open up, shooting over Prophet's head. As if I am seeing everything from somewhere else, I can see a lot of their rounds peppering the rocks on the other side of the trail.

"Get on the horn, tell 'em we hit a sniper and are pinned down. Keep throwing shit out that way. Tell 'em we can't tell where it's coming from and that we want some artillery. Have 'em shoot a smoke round about five kliks south of our last night's position. Hurry. I'm going to see if I can help those guys." Pops slaps his steel pot onto his head and starts crawling too. Peacock and Callme cover him with rifle fire and Chickenfeed starts putting out rounds from his grenade launcher. Some of his rounds seem to land dangerously close to where I think Bull is. They make a red-yellow fire when they hit that burst behind the rocks and shower shrapnel back toward us.

"Alpha, we're pinned down. Suspected sniper. Need Arty smoke round approximately five kliks south of last night's papa. Will adjust."

"Caterpillar, roger. Will advise."

"Come on, Charlie, you bastard," Peacock says. "Lay a couple more rounds in the dirt and we'll have your ass on a stick. The only angle he can have is that direction, so be goddamn ready if Pops and Prophet start bringing the Bull back. Get your fuckin' ammo out of the bandoliers. Keep some kind of fire out there all the time and stay away from those guys."

He jumps up and runs over the first big rock. When he does the sniper fires a few rounds at him. He yells back that he is all right and that the rounds are coming from two o'clock. There is a smell of powder as Callme and he pump out single rounds in the general direction of two o'clock. Chickenfeed jumps over the rock on the other side of us and begins lobbing grenade rounds again.

"Round out," the radio says.

"Round out."

Ten seconds later a smoke round comes in at about eleven o'clock, not far from where a peak of rocks that looks like a Christmas tree stands up above everything else. It occurs to me like diarrhea that I am in control of the radio and hence in control of guiding the artillery. I am momentarily lost in thought but snap out of it when there is another burst of AK fire and I see Pops first, then Prophet, dragging Bull down the trail toward us. The AK rounds go high and Pops spins and fires in the direction they came from. My wits come back.

"Alpha Six, right two hundred, add fifty, smoke again."

"Roger." Then, "Round out."

"Peacock, watch for that round, I'm gonna help get Bull." I say it before I think, and when I think I realize I am scared shitless, but instead of thinking anymore I dive out to where they are and Pops hands me Bull's rifle. Then he and Prophet get hold of Bull under his back and together they make it back to the safety of the rocks. He is hit in the shoulder and blood has splattered all over his cheek. There is a lot of blood and I can't tell how badly he is hit. He has his eyes closed at first and I fear the very worst until he opens them and grimaces. He tries to roll over a little bit and screams. Prophet puts a leg across his stomach and holds him down. Pops strips away his shirt and the wound isn't big on the front but when he lifts him up a little I almost faint at the size of the hole in his back where the bullet came out. I look up in time to see the smoke round land, just where I hoped.

"Fire for effect," Chickenfeed yells from the other side of the rock, and he puts out three fast grenade rounds. Then Chickenfeed circles around to Peacock's position and I see him squirming up to the top of the rocks. Chicken lies close to the top. Pea's helmet comes off. When he goes for it there is another burst of AK fire. He dances, and I know right away that he is hit in the leg.

"Fire for effect!" I scream into the radio. No reason for caution now.

Bull is writhing as much as he can under the weight of Prophet's leg but he is getting tired fast.

"Hold the fuck on, Bull. Let us get the fucking thing dressed or you'll bleed to death."

Five rounds of high explosive artillery rounds land. One is dangerously close and the shrap bounces off the rocks around us. Chickenfeed has worked his way back to Peacock now and they are lying against the rocks. Chickenfeed is cutting off Peacock's boot. Peacock isn't moving and isn't screaming. Pops has a field dressing on the wound in Bull's back and he and Prophet have rolled him over so Pops can apply direct pressure on the dressing.

"How bad is Peacock?"

"Superficial, in his ankle. I've got him patched but we can't get back to you. Call in more artillery."

"Has anybody seen anything yet?"

Callmeblack is in mild shock. He is leaning against the rock wall opposite me and shaking his head sideways. I want to go over and comfort him but I can't leave the radio, even after I call for more artillery.

"Caterpillar, sit rep. Over."

"Two whiskeys. Need a Dustoff."

"Roger that. Bird on the way. Go to the other net when you have him in sight and pop smoke. Over."

Callmeblack snaps to all at once and before anybody can say anything he is up over the rocks beyond Peacock and Chickenfeed. He is on full automatic, and for an instant I am afraid he is going to charge in the direction of the sniper but instead he halts in the second position and lays rounds out one at a time.

"Atta baby, Callme. Keep his fucking head down. Get

some, dude!" Pops is almost ecstatic. I am full of admiration. Prophet goes next, and he goes one more leap beyond Callme, firing on automatic when he is exposed. He unpins a grenade and throws it as far as he can. Its concussion is incredibly loud and echoes all around. Even before the echoes die he throws another one and moves out farther yet.

"Alpha."

"Go."

"Hold the Arty, danger close."

"I think Charlie is either fried over there or has made his *didi*."

"How you doin', Bull?"

"I'm OK."

"Hold on, there's a Dustoff on the way."

Pops shakes out a pack of cigarettes and everybody takes one. I expect my hands to shake when I light it but they don't. Bull is lying at my feet and smoking with his good arm. The last thing I expect to see when he opens his eyes through the pain is a smile, but I get one, and a wink. It makes me want to cry.

"I owe Charlie one when I come back," he says, then closes his eyes again and lies there smoking. The field dressing is soaked through and Pops puts another one on top of it. Together, we roll Bull over so he is lying on it. His eyes are still closed but tears drop through his lids.

Prophet hops one more rock and throws another grenade. The ground falls away fast on the other side of the rock he is behind and the sound of the grenade is all away from us. No more AK fire.

The Dustoff comes, high up, and Chickenfeed pops a smoke. It happens to be yellow and I halfway expect Charlie to open up on the bird when it comes down toward us, but nothing happens. The bird hovers ten feet off the ground for a second or two, then comes low enough that Pops and I can heft Bull up for the door gunner to get hold of him. He screams in pain because the loading is clumsy, but there is nothing else to do. Peacock hobbles over and with very little help pulls himself up on the landing strut, then into the bird. His bootless foot is the last thing in. The rotor wash makes it hard to look up at the helicopter but I manage and I'm glad I do because when the bird is slowly ascending, Bull hangs his good arm out just enough to flip the peace sign. It makes me think of a preacher's blessing.

It is very quiet. Chickenfeed and Prophet come back. I keep staring at the marks left in the red rocks where the rounds hit. I think of cowboy movies.

"All right," Pops says, "somebody stay here with the radio and one other guy stay for security. Us other three will go out and see what we can find. I'm pretty sure there was only one guy and I'm about as sure he's either dead or long gone."

"I'll stay at the horn," Prophet says. That surprises me. It almost surprises me more to hear myself say I'll go out, so Callmeblack and Pops and I don our flak jackets and helmets and advance carefully over the red rocks, which are slippery now because the rain has started again. We move one at a time toward where we think the sniper was. Closer than I thought, Callmeblack finds shell casings, brass canisters that glitter in the rain like ice cubes. We count ten. The sniper's spot is a perfect V between two big rocks that are pockmarked from where our shrapnel chunked some of the redness away. A perfect escape route leads downhill and disappears into the jungle fifteen meters from us. None of us says anything about it, and Callmeblack and I stand in the sniper's nest while Pops goes cautiously down the escape trail

"Ah," he says.

"What?"

"The fucker is hit. C'mere."

There is a blood trail. It is heavy only at the start. After a few meters we can't find any trace of the blood.

"That sonofabitch had balls, I'll say that. Taking on a patrol, even though this vantage point is perfect. I suppose a grenade or a round from the launcher hit him with some shrap."

"So the score is two to one, evidently. He's ahead."

"Maybe. He can't get medical attention as easily as Bull and Peacock. He might die on down the trail there, but you can bet your sweet ass we'd never find him if we went looking."

"What're we going to do now?"

"Wait on orders."

Our orders are simple: wait. So we sit around for two hours. A relief the size of a two-gallon piss comes over me when HQ says they are going to extract us and we hump to a decent landing pad. This time I get the privilege of popping the smoke that guides the bird in, and when we lift off and the jungle gets farther and farther away I once again get one of those feelings I can't describe.

Back at the LZ, I borrow a black felt pen and write *Niagara* on my Boonie hat and on my helmet liner. Again, I think of Grandaddy telling me about initials carved into a beech tree. Writing on my hat and carving on a beech are acts of faith, of confidence. After my first firefight and first time in the Bush I feel something new.

JUMPING OFF

I LOSE TRACK OF HOW MANY DAYS IT RAINS ALL DAY long, how many days the helicopter can't get in with our mail, how many nights I go to sleep in wet jungle utes, how many Thousand Island shits at holes dug too wide to squat over and so shallow the water splashes back, how many card games I played in the light of the smelly sealing-wax candles, how many hundreds of sandbags I fill, how many nights I am on the verge of screaming from the pain in my feet and how many midafternoon daydreams of painting three-story houses I have.

Everybody was right. When a new shipment of guys comes to the fire base I realize how old I've gotten. They are green and white and I am red and brown. They are insanely scared and I am not. Quite. None of them comes to Echo Company.

We have moved once, to a mountain surrounded by two other ranges that we named LZ Clitoris. I put the name on my hat the second day we are there. The next day a patrol makes contact, four wounded, and in the middle of that afternoon we are told we're going to move again. A few fuck books go into the fire. Chickenfeed goes on R&R, so I've got his machine-gun ammo and claymores to carry. I have an extra poncho liner souvenired by some guy I never knew except we shit in neighboring holes in the rain the day before he left the Bush, part of a mirror from a guy who got dusted off for malaria, C-rations enough for two weeks because I only eat once a day, and, like everybody else, an ammo can to keep my matches and toilet paper dry. I've got a peculiar vine I want to carve into a pipe and a heavy-duty case of rot, a forest of raw welts that I salve every day.

We cave in the hooches, set fires, move equipment to the landing pad, squat in the rain, smoke pot beneath a poncho, listen to cassettes over and over while the helicopters come and go. The new LZ is about twenty minutes away by helicopter and I have counted seventy-five flights by now, a little after noon. There are three different kinds of birds for this move. Loaches are for the officers, who fly high to command the move. They're small, about the size of a panel truck, and they look like a transparent tree frog, bubble mostly, with a fragile high-pitched sound without cadence to their rotors; they pop onto the pad and suck in an officer. They seem like giant and expensive toys. Their specialty is mobility and the pilots handle them like motorcycles. I never see anybody lower-ranking than a captain get into one.

The real workhorses of the Army are the Slicks, helicopters that carry five or six men and all their gear. They are basically resupply birds—no doors, and they're armed with two 60mm machine guns. All morning long they come in, lined up behind each other. The operation is simple in design: you cram as much stuff as you can into one, then the pilot lifts off to test the weight, and if it is OK the bird lifts, then dives sideways off the landing pad and the next one comes in. This is all coordinated by a padman who has a radio headset on and gives instructions mostly in sign language because the noise is so massive and constant. For four straight hours the pad is like a honey hole, with a bird landing and taking off about every five minutes. There are probably three hundred men to move. Delta Company was the first company into the new area and they've been there for two days. Another wave of grunts from each company goes in next to pull security; then the move is on in full and everything depends on speed. There are work parties assigned to load the Slicks and the slings for the bigger birds, Chinooks, "Shithooks." There are other parties for destroying the LZ as we leave it. I'm on a work party that carries stuff to the pad and destroys the hooches. The hooches on the outside of the perimeter have been partly weakened by knocking out some of the sandbags in the walls, and we finish destroying the roofs with grenades.

"Run *downhill*, dumb-ass. Are you a goddamn Effengee?" Prophet is downhill from me. He looks into a hooch and comes back out again.

"Fire in the hole!" he yells, then runs lumberingly down to the next hooch. The explosion is muffled but still loud and the hooch falls only halfway in. "Goddamn, whoever built that sonofabitch must be an engineer."

We blow about a dozen hooches. In the meantime a Shithook comes in. The whirlwinds of its rotors force everybody down and all kinds of shit starts whirling around. Something big hits one of the front blades and they have to shut it down to check it. This is an emergency because Charlie might lob a mortar into the pad to get the big bird, so the detail I'm on goes into the Bush with our rifles for security.

After fifteen minutes the engines fire up again, in that peculiar, halting-then-sudden way. Twenty-five or thirty guys get into the back of the Shithook and it goes straight up like a long green balloon and hovers forty feet off the ground. It will take a sling of artillery pieces and equipment beneath it, and getting the giant sling fastened is a major operation. The commotion caused by the helicopter is enormous. When it is finally gone, the LZ is suddenly skeletal. There is one other big sling left, waiting to go on

93

its ride, and only about twenty-five guys now. Our squad goes back to destroying the camp, mostly by setting fires.

When the last Shithook comes in, a Cobra gunship comes with it. Cobras are jet-powered and so fully armed they can put a round in every square inch of a football field within seconds. It stays up higher than the rest of the helicopters and circles like a queen while the Shithook gets loaded inside, then ascends and hovers until we hook up the sling.

Me, Pops, Callme, and another guy are standing on the sling underneath the powerful 'Hook trying to fasten the sling together. All the activity and the constant force of wind from the birds has sucked the rain out of the ground, and the pad is one intense dust storm: dust in my eyes, up my nose, on my teeth. Rocks as big as golf balls get lofted with the dust; I've caught two in my shins while we are working. My arms get so fucking tired I will drop my corner in another minute, but just then I feel the stuff I'm standing on begin to lift. The load jerks, and since we're five or six feet off the ground by the time we jump, we all land in a heap. I land on top of Callme, who elbows me in the neck and yells something I can't hear because the 'Hook is gaining RPMs. The giant bird beats off and sends back pockets of *thump thump thump* through the thick air, then floats over the side of the mountain. We watch it for a few daydreamy seconds, nobody talking. There is an impression that's hard to describe when something bigger than any truck we've ever driven flies into the air over the river valley with a slingful of guns so big the courthouse pieces in The World look like harmless pistols. For me, it's simply unbelievable, something I'm not going to be able to explain when I get back. A modern war.

"So we're following a NVA regiment to the Cambodian border."

"Ain't that the shits?"

Our panorama of the countryside is beautiful. The sky is

clear except for a few wadded-paper clouds bouncing across a range in the east. The range is dark green and from this many miles looks like a raked-up pile of gooseshit. The work is done and all the helicopters are gone to the other LZ. It is utterly peaceful, quiet enough to hear lively birds jawing away the last couple hours of light. Everything left on the LZ is surreal, dusty. Part of the sky in the north is that color.

"Kills me," Prophet mumbles almost to himself, scratching his rot with a cigarette, "kills me that the lifers say we're closing in. Like we're goddamn sneaky with a million helicopters all flying to the same hill. Charlie ain't fuckin' blind. I think the lifers just pretend we're gonna kick ol' Charles's ass."

We can't see or hear any helicopters now. There are only two squads left on Clitoris. We have a radio but the new LZ is too far away to pick up and there isn't any traffic on the helicopters' channel.

Prophet emerges from the only hooch left, a scowl tightening his face like a dried bean.

"Where's our goddamn birds?"

"Let's do a bowl while we're waiting."

Callmeblack packs a big bowl and lights it. We all crowd around the hooch roof and pass the dope. I get a warm feeling of belonging. I almost feel snobbish toward the new guys, who are hanging back with their fear showing plainly. The only thing I have to feel snobbish about is the fact that my fear probably doesn't show as plainly.

"We better blow this hooch."

"Let's wait on the bird. Goddamn if I even like being left last on this LZ, let alone not having a hole to get into if we need it."

"You heard the lifers; we're *following* the dinks."

"My ass."

The pot lays me back a bit, numbs me. I wish I had a hammock.

"I got laid in a hammock once."

"What'd you fuck, a seahorse?"

Pops's shoulders are sagging. He is pacing around the hooch drawing hot and hard on his cigarette. He holds the smoke funny, between his ring and middle fingers, and when he's smoking he seems out of place—not as much like a squad leader as a bellhop somewhere.

"I wish they'd get me a bird here, just pick us up and fly my sweet ass over them mountains." Like he's the only one he is talking to, he points dramatically at the mountains with the cigarette perched funny between the two odd fingers. "I want to get there before dark or Charlie is gonna be drawing beads on that LZ with his tubes, and I won't even have a trench to get in."

"You're gettin' short-timer's shakes, Pops."

"I'm fuckin'-A nervous. Bank on that. Don't joke me, muthafucker."

"Take it easy, you asshole," Prophet says.

"Hey, fuck you."

I can't tell if there's any venom in his voice or not. The two are standing three feet apart and looking directly at each other. Everything else is forgotten when Pops throws his cigarette at Prophet's feet. Prophet sighs and continues to stare with a look that is impossible to categorize. Something like helplessness.

"Easy, man," he says. You can almost see the indecision in his face, whether to walk away or not. There is a real tension about and everybody is watching them. The only thing I hear is the birds and Callme nervously rubbing one boot through the dust.

"Fucker!" Pops yells, and suddenly charges Prophet. His head catches Prophet perfectly in the breastbone and sends him tripping over sandbags. They're both in the dust and rolling around at first, then apart enough to be taking short but purposeful swings. It is all real fast, too fast to react. They are rolling and swinging in the dust and

Prophet's knife falls out of its sheath, then they roll over on it, Pops on top. Prophet lands a roundhouse left from his back and it sends Pops sprawling onto the metal of the landing pad. He yells from the contact with the scorching-hot metal. His temple is bleeding now and the look on his face is one of determination—no humiliation. I know he is going to charge again. This time his head lands in Prophet's stomach and brings a yell from Prophet. He falls backwards with Pops's stocky legs churning up the dust until they fall again near the place we piled our rifles and rucks. They separate and get up. Callmeblack and a couple other guys have started to move toward them. He kicks Prophet's knife out of the way.

"Slow down, brothers."

"Hey," Pops says. He is breathing hard and the blood from his cut temple is now splattered all over the bridge of his nose too. Prophet doesn't seem to be breathing hard but he is slumped over partway and holding his stomach with one hand. The other hand is out straight in front of him, not pleading to Pops, rather threatening. It alternately tightens into a fist and opens up.

"Hey," Prophet says. "You're short, man. Tense."

"Yeah."

"Hey."

Pops doesn't answer.

"Sorry."

"It felt good, Prophet, can you dig it? I mean, man, I'm wound tight inside and it felt good." He wipes at the blood on his face with his wrist. "Maybe I should get a Heart for this."

"You should get at least an Arcom for being a good fuckin' dude," Prophet says. "I don't want you to rotate, I like you so much."

"Fucker."

"Fucker."

I feel the relief and all at once I realize I am smiling. It was a good fight, a plain old good fight. It is so out of place here on this deserted LZ in the middle of a jungle in the middle of a war, two guys fighting like that, but it seems so homegrown, so much a part of reality when nothing else does. There's nothing more manly these days than these two combat veterans who I like, but I want to giggle because they are calling each other names that don't have any meaning, like little kids.

I've got a lump in my guts that I know is the C-ration Tornado, so I head out to the slit trenches. The holes are on the other side of the LZ and I'm about halfway across when Pops yells at me. It scares me.

"Take your fucking rifle!"

"I'm in a hurry."

He meets me halfway with my rifle, and when he hands it to me he squints through the blood that is still on his face. "Dumb-ass, you forget you're fighting a war?"

"I figure it's gonna be a quick shit," I say, as a kind of apology.

"The dinks could hit us so fuckin' easy you wouldn't have a chance in hell. Don't be stupid."

Squatting, my legs hurting, I think: I had begun to forget, a little. I take his words to heart: I was stupid.

I think of taking a good solid shit. I am too nervous for my body to process like it should, and so about twice every day I squirt whatever I've eaten. I'm losing weight but I don't have any desire to eat. A couple times a week the Rear sends us hots, food prepared and delivered in canisters. The food is always spilled into the canister's tops and always running down the outside and it is usually hard to guess what it is meant to be, but none of us miss lining up to get it. Still, taking a solid shit is a pipedream.

In the weird light of the setting sun the jungle is about the same brown green that the food canisters are. The weak light makes black holes in the vegetation and I feel very vulnerable, squatting over this slit trench. Charlie could cut my head off with one round. The jungle rattles a little in a small wind. I can hear the static of the radio by the pad. There is the smell of gunpowder and burnt plastic. Flies swarm around the slit trench and create a constant drone. I can hear every pebble I drop. When I am done I realize all my toilet paper is in my rucksack by the pad. There are a few spare bundles thrown around me but they are soggy and muddy. I flash on a time ten years ago when I was at my mother's rural church and hiding in its outhouse from the sermon.

There's a piece of paper hung on the concertina wire that must be drier than the rest because it is square instead of a wad. So I retrieve it with my rifle, thanking Pops, and it is as dry as I hoped.

I'm sure nobody wants to stay on this LZ until dark. When I get back to the pad everybody is lying around or leaning against the lonely hooch passing another bowl. There is a cassette playing "Time Is on My Side" and a radio giving a newscast: heavy floods in Arkansas and Mississippi, and preparation for the World Series in Baltimore and New York.

Distance is accentuated during this time of day. There are heavy, thick clouds covering the range where there had only been golf balls in the sky before; it's as though a curtain was dropped so that all we can see in that direction is a painted backdrop. Every once in a while there's a crackle from one of the fires and we all jump. Finally, three Slicks appear in the valley below us, and we gather our stuff and stand near the pad. By the time we are in the air the only light left is in the west, and it feels safe to sit on the vibrating floor of the bird with our feet hanging out the doors for a few minutes while we ride through a flag-red sky full of popcorn clouds, closer to Cambodia. The perimeters of the new LZ are invisible until we descend to a hundred feet or so. I scoot up to the edge of the bird's floorboard, ready to jump.

LZ PANSY

THE SUN IS A HARD ORANGE BALL FOR AN INSTANT AS WE approach the new LZ; then, as we descend, it disappears behind the western range of mountains so that by the time we're on the ground the sky is Jell-O-and-cream. We're on a mountain with an oblong top and two fingers of gradual slopes on either end. One entire side drops off very steeply. The helicopter lands on one of the fingers, and it is a short climb to the center of the LZ. There is an hour of light left and everybody is using it to dig. A few guys are setting up trip flares but no claymore mines, because the hill is still almost as much jungle as it is landing zone, so no one knows for sure what is between them and the perimeter.

There is tension evident everywhere. Tempers are short and the approaching darkness seems like the enemy. I choose a certain spot for no particular reason and begin digging too. The only thing we have in mind is getting some kind of hole deep enough to get into. The top of the ground is a bitch: weeds and roots make digging difficult and I feel my temper mounting until eventually I am hacking angrily at the vegetation. It seems like all at once I realize it is almost dark.

Prophet gets through the layer of roots I am feuding with. He works his way over to my side of the hole, and together we soon have a six-inch layer peeled off an area five feet square.

"This move gives me the goddamn spooks."

"Why do you say that?"

I'm sweating despite the night and the sweat is aggravating the jungle rot around my balls, so I am leaning with one foot on the shovel and the air is moving through where the buttons of my barn-door have popped off. It feels good.

"Dunno," he says, still digging. "I never know why I feel anything, just do. I been right a *few* fucking times since I got here, anybody can tell you that."

"What have you been right about?"

"I knew we were gonna get some shit the night Greenwire got it. Were you here then?"

"Nope."

"Was a night like this that we went into that Z. Going into a new Z anytime but early morning is asking for it. That one was called Nicole. What's a name for this one?"

I didn't get the whole shape of the clearing from the air, but it had looked roughly like a pig to me.

"Pansy," I say, for the hell of it.

"Pansy!"

He stops working and is leaning toward me like he did the first time I ever met him. He leans so close I can see part of his face in the weak glow from the radio laying on top of his ruck between us.

"Pansy? Where the fuck did that come from?"

"I just named it after a pig we used to have."

"A fuckin' pig named Pansy. No shit? LZ Pansy Pig. I like that. But I predict this pig is gonna be butchered."

And he walks out of the hole and into the dark, like he knows where he's going. *But he can't. No way. He can't.* I keep telling myself he's crazy as I dig through the loam, which begins to work easier.

I sing to myself: *Pansy was a good ol' pig . . . good ol' pig . . . good ol' pig* we lashed to a stanchion and cold-cocked with a sixteen-pound sledgehammer one brittle morning. *Grandaddy swings once and Pansy goes down like a domino castle, looking at me. "Bring a hacksaw, Gabe." But I can't. I won't. Grandaddy is mad: "Your face is like a sunflower in October, boy; next time I'll have to tether you to a stanchion too."*

Prophet comes back with pills and we take two apiece. Maybe we'll dig all night. We are down to our knees when the Officer of the Day comes by and shines a flashlight at us for a minute.

"Hey, shut the fuckin' light out," Prophet says.

"At ease, Specialist," Eltee says. He is haughtily abrupt.

"I just don't want any goddamn mortar bein' zeroed in on my fuckin' hole. We're gonna catch some shit here and I ain't eager, y'understand?"

I wonder if Prophet gives a fuck who he's talking to.

"You two won't be in the hole anyway," Eltee says.

His voice is all there is to him, except I think his wrist-watch glows. The voice is hollow, like a telephone, and it comes from about six feet up in the dark.

"You're gonna pull three hours of perimeter, starting in half an hour. You get Nelson and Whitcomb to relieve you, got it? And don't forget your military courtesy, Specialist." He flashes his light once quick at Prophet, and for a minute I'm positive Prophet moves to go after him. When he leaves, Prophet sits down on the lip of our hole. I can only see the bottom half of his face in the orange radio light. His mouth is curled into a sneer.

"That newby fuckin' El-tee best watch his shit," he says. "He's forgetting where he is, I swear." There is biting wickedness in his tone.

In the weak orange light, I can almost read the anger in Prophet's thinking: That Eltee probably already has a hole and has it sandbagged but we don't. Prophet is sure we're going to hit some shit so he is scared. It is all unjust, and

Prophet is blaming that F.N.G. Eltee. I know what he is thinking, I've been here long enough. He is thinking of revenge. Not really revenge, or not *only*. It's like a game: The grunts can't let the Army get too far ahead, can't let the power structure work so very completely that the casualties get predetermined. . . . *I am cooking on that pill.*

"Prophet?" My voice feels childish. "Have you guys— our platoon—have they killed any lifers?"

I can see his mouth come open a little bit, but the light is too weak to show his eyes. He smiles, then, or smirks.

"Listen, asshole, you can't ask me that kind of shit. Not around here, anyway," he says.

"What'm I going to do, wait till we're home drinking in a bar, if we make it? Wait until then?"

"Jump back, for chrissakes." He leans closer and says, quieter, "Yeah, dammit. When the lifers get pushing us too hard we push back. Not many officers have been killed out there in the Bush, mostly guys like you and me. But there have been some officers that didn't leave their hole. That's all I'm gonna tell you."

I feel humble but not ashamed. For an instant my brain leaps back to when I learned a girlfriend stuffed toilet paper in her tiny bra. Whatever that pill is, it's coming on hard now. I begin digging vigorously. It is just as noisy as an hour ago. Everybody is digging in. The weird thing is, it is all sound; there is nothing to see. Higher on the hill there is occasionally a brief small light where Artillery is sighting in the guns. Their flashlights have red lenses to dim the light and you have to be looking to see it at all. But in every direction there are the sounds of shovels and some talking. Busy, things sound busy.

By our guard time I am beginning to slow down. The speed is wearing off and my muscles are beginning to ache. The hole is above our knees.

It's so dark we have to hold onto each other going out to the guard post. I keep stumbling over roots. Vines and bushes slap me in the face, and twice we come right up on holes we couldn't see. The second time Prophet steps on a guy sleeping and falls down. The guy yells and Prophet yells back. The yelling seems unattached to the night, which is quieter now.

One guy we are relieving is southern.

"Y'all keep the boogieman away, hear? My partner oughta have me a hole to crawl into and I got some reefer waitin' to have a LZ-warmin' party. What's the name o' this hill?"

"Pansy," Prophet says.

"No shit." And he is gone.

I wonder how Prophet even found this place. Maybe there is something I don't know. All I know is we came downhill on our way. I try to concentrate to get a feeling of where we are, but there aren't any reference points. I don't know what is ahead of us, don't even know for sure which way is "ahead." When I bang my shin on the ammo crate seat I am tempted to yell, to cuss every word I know. It hurts worse than it should. I can't see Prophet but I hear him pissing, and right then it begins to rain, barely.

Prophet sits down beside me.

"Fuckin' rain," he says. Too loud, it seems.

Night is *so* dark here. It's being asleep and knowing your eyes are closed but still wanting to see, not dream. Jungle dark. We can hear guys shoveling. Listening has to be the object of this guard because it is impossible to see anything. For all I know there is barely-cleared jungle on all sides of us. The engineers have only made one blow so far. They come in right after the first grunts and bring plenty of power with them. They wrap small sections of the jungle with detonation cord and plan as closely as they can to take out as big a patch at a time as they can, so what is left a lot of times is only thinned-out jungle. The grunts take over from there, clearing and digging, digging, digging. There are only two artillery pieces on Pansy now.

104

Tomorrow the others will come in, and that means helping dig the guns in and building parapets.

Meanwhile it is coal-dark night and Prophet and I sit in this easy, miserable rain. Listening. I'd like to have a cigarette and it seems so ridiculous not to, since Charlie has to know where we are anyway. Lighting a cigarette seems so harmless, yet Charlie could easily be sitting ten meters away waiting for it to pinpoint our location.

I feel like I am thinking just to keep myself awake. I flash on *sitting on a log in the woods at home and smoking a cigarette to keep the mosquitoes away, waiting until the squirrels move.* What will I be thinking a year from now, sitting on that log? Of this soggy guard? Of Peacock's bloody foot or of Pops doubling up the bandages on Bull? Then, like I am jabbed with a needle, it hits me that I've still got so long to go. I might get hit. I might get killed. I might see a lot more guys get hit or killed. Hunting squirrel is never going to be the same. All of a sudden thinking of home is as hard as trying to imagine this war used to be. But I can see the woods there, the trees. I feel like talking.

"Know anything about trees, Prophet?"

"I like aspens." Then he pauses before he says, "Just like pissing on any other tree. Nah . . . man, they're special. They only grow up high, probably about as high as we are now, and that's where I like it. I like the mountains."

"These are the first mountains I've ever seen."

"Ain't anything like I'm talking about. Y'know what's weird? Like, I thought this war was all fought in rice paddies, didn't you? Didja ever watch the news before you came over? Always fighting in paddies. I didn't even know there were mountains in Nam. And, ha, them news films of fighting seem like a movie made for TV, don't they?"

"Yeah. But you been through a lot of shit."

"Sometimes twice as much as anybody else, dig it? Because I see the shit before it happens, do you believe that?

That night you came, the night the other Effengee got it and Rogers got hit . . ."

He ends there, like he's asking me if I remember it or something. I say yeah, clear my throat, shift position so the ropes on the ammo crate don't cut my ass so bad. I'm uncomfortable; it's like Prophet is tuned into something else.

"I had it that night too," he says, in a different voice. "I saw that coming an hour before it happened. Never told nobody though, and since it was a direct hit it wouldn't have made any difference if I had."

I don't know what to say. I don't want to spoil the spell that seems to be here. It has stopped raining again and we can see, or I think I can, even though I don't see anything but shapes.

"Ever since I got hit the first time I been seeing things that would happen, do you believe that?"

"Yeah." I do. I believe it.

"I just wondered. I don't feel like I'm anything like I useta be. I think I'm goddamn nuts, some kind o' fortune-teller nut. I'm starting to think about being home. I'm short, and I wonder if this weird shit—being a prophet—will go home with me."

"Far out." That's all I can think of.

It begins to rain pretty hard so we tie ourselves into our field jackets and wrap up in our ponchos. We sit that way staring into the jungle I know is there but can't see. The rain first comes from my left, then lashes around and comes directly at my face, hard enough to sting. I've got my rifle underneath my poncho. Prophet begins to shiver beside me. Then I can tell he's opening a can of C's beneath his poncho. I can tell he's using his can opener by the way the seat bounces. I am hungry too.

"Prophet?"

"What?"

"Whattaya see for LZ Pansy?"

"I'm only gonna tell you part: Peacock will come back."

⦁⦁⦁⦁⦁⦁⦁⦁⦁

I SLEEP A COUPLE HOURS AFTER GUARD: WOUND INTO A ball in my field jacket, curled into the muddy hole we are digging, covered by my poncho, which serves only to channel the water to my feet. When I wake up my boots are soaked through, which must explain the dream I am having about pissing my pants in a dark cloakroom, the pee running down my legs and into my rubber boots.

"Hey, my man, eat this and you can go back to sleep."

It is the medic coming around with malaria pills. I take one but my wet feet keep me from trying to go back to sleep.

The sun is shining, reflecting off puddles of water here and there, and I flash on a junkyard full of broken windshields. Seeing the hill in the light for the first time I realize it doesn't look much like a pig. On the highest part of the hill is a big, tall rock. I am surprised that our hole is close to big coils of concertina wire; it would have been easy to get cut to hell in the dark last night. The engineers are preparing the area just below us. They have it wrapped in detonation cord.

Prophet is still asleep, his head lying in a mud puddle, and the way the red mud is caked on his coal-black hair would make a good picture of what Nam is really like. Pops and Chickenfeed are in the hole next door, and I can see Callme's hat bobbing around as he shovels out his hole farther down the slope. I have to shit but I decide to have some coffee first, if any stayed dry enough. I'm just getting the water to boil when Prophet wakes up.

"Jesus fuckin' Christ on a warped yellow-pine crutch, am I really here? Am I really goddamn layin' in a hole in the middle of a jungle with my million-dollar face in a mud puddle and my hundred-dollar hardon in my hand?"

He stands up, stretches, and walks over to Pops's hole, ready to piss. Pops is sitting on his muddy ruck eating. He is only wearing a pair of skivvies; his clothes are hanging on shovel handles to dry. Prophet looks his way, standing there like he is prepared to piss.

"Prophet," Pops says, "if you so much as dribble in my hole I'm gonna use the lid of my chopped-ham-and-eggs can to perform the operation that doctors in The World are getting big money to perform."

"It would get me out of the field," Prophet says before he turns downhill. "But I'm afraid that after I left, you guys would say I turned pussy. How'd you sleep last night, man? You leave your feather pillow somewhere?"

"I got it," Pops says around his chopped eggs, "but I don't wanna get it dirty, y'understand?"

Then instantly Prophet is silhouetted because there's a huge flash behind him where a round lands at the end of the jungle. Prophet is back in the hole as soon as I am, and I was sitting on its edge. More rounds come in and all kinds of shit comes raining down: dirt and rocks and parts of ammo crates, then some guy who was running by wearing only boots and a tee shirt. I was just turning around to peep over the hole's edge toward the perimeter and this guy was running low and blind. Just as he's at our hole something comes in that sounds like a rocket and lands down the hill near the patch of uncleared jungle that is wrapped in det cord. The runner takes a load of shrap and falls into our hole. His legs are on me and going crazy so his boot heels keep kicking me in the back and in the head. Prophet gets up enough to pull him flat into the hole. He is hit bad in the shoulder and neck or chest. Blood is pumping out and it makes me think of shooting cans full of water.

Prophet tries to hold him down but he thrashes around and pretty soon is sucking for breath through the hole in his chest. The sound is like an enema. Rounds are still coming in but landing up the hill. Prophet is trying to hold the guy down with his knee and at the same time trying to get his own rifle from underneath the guy. My mouth tastes like I'm eating rusty metal for a minute, my breath comes about as sporadically as the guy who is screaming between Prophet and me. More rounds come in, closer again, and that shit I never took takes itself. I'm not very afraid but *I don't know what to do*.

"Can you get to a frag?" Prophet yells.

I have one and he points toward the perimeter.

"Throw the fucker as far as you can."

I can't remember if anyone is digging a hole below us and I'm beginning to inch my way up to the edge of the hole to look when a rifle kicks up mud just outside the hole so I am definitely a scared muthafucker when I get up on my knees in order to throw the frag far enough. I'm only kneeling for an instant, but in that time I think of everything from praying to blow jobs. My mind is working ten times fast: I see me as a little kid kneeling to pray and I see myself kneeling to fasten the buttons on my brother's jacket...and I see me getting a clean tube through my head, as I wing the frag that sends back enough of a shock to jolt the mud I'm lying in, and I know I'm not dead yet.

I really didn't think of them being that close. There are M-16s firing steadily now, and Prophet pops up just enough to pump off about half a clip. When he is done I take my turn and fire off most of a clip on automatic. When I'm back changing magazines, scrunched against the side of the hill, I see Prophet look at the other guy; then he throws a poncho over him and almost carefully pulls it over him because he is dead now. Just before the poncho covers his face I see the look that is angelic except for the splattered blood and mud. The guy looked especially young lying there dead. After the poncho is over the body Prophet props it up a little to make more room in the hole. The bottom of the hole is patted smooth by our rummaging around and in some places the blood has soaked in but in other places there are small pools of dirty red water.

Prophet yells for Pops during a lull but doesn't get an answer. He pulls me up to his face then, at the unmistakable sound of an AK firing deliberate rounds.

"Listen," he says, "that muthafucker is sniping, and he is *close*! He's probably got a good look at our hole so keep your fuckin' head down. If he was close enough to frag us he would have by now, so just keep the fuck down and do what I do."

Another big explosion from around the hill.

"That's a GI frag," he says almost nonchalantly. Then he eases his rifle barrel up so it is on its forward mount, but just as he's shifting position the AK opens up again and we both try to burrow under the body between us from different sides. The rounds splatter into the wall of our hole opposite where we are leaning and the body. Three or four rounds *so goddamn quick*, and everything is the same color. *I am lying in my own shit beside a dead dude*. Spit dribbles out my mouth like simmering oatmeal, and suddenly there is an enormous explosion that brings me an inch off the ground. My expression must ask the question, because Prophet is almost laughing.

"That's Artillery," he says, "and some really big shit too. Maybe 105s or maybe even Navy guns—8-inchers, I don't know." Then there are five more rounds that land so simultaneously that it has to be something unconscious that counts them. Or maybe I just know from somewhere that artillery batteries come in groups of five. . . . I don't know. . . . I don't feel like I know anything. I keep thinking because I can't do anything else. Another battery comes in and is close enough this time that not only do I come off the ground from the shock, but a rock the size of a baseball lands at the edge of our hole and rolls in. Then another battery, and as soon as it's done Prophet sticks his head above the hole just enough to see out from under his steel pot.

"Well?"

"I think Charlie may be cutting out," he says. "Those rounds came almost up to the perimeter. Somebody somewhere did a hell of a job calling that support in."

"Y' think there'll be any more?" My last words are cut off by another battery so close I grab at the body's arm, thinking I might just fuckin' *bounce* out of that hole.

A couple minutes after the last explosions guys begin to yell from their holes. I don't recognize any voices and I can't hear them very well because I'm still pressing half my face into the mud and blood on the poncho. Prophet is crunched into the corner, smiling.

"Well, man, was I right about this LZ? What'd I tell you last night?"

"You told me Peacock would come back, that's all." I feel a little bit like a smart-ass.

Soon the colors come back: the red-brown of the mud wall is jigsawed by roots, the olive-greenness of the poncho over the body, the blue in Prophet's eyes. My arms and legs feel like I slept on them all wrong; all the nerves are tingling. There is now only a smell of gunpowder and something burning. I am still lying with my head on the body. There is slobber on my chin and in my mustache. And I get a whiff of my own shit.

"Hey, man, I shit my pants."

And he laughs. I laugh too but only briefly because of the dead guy. When I first began laughing it seemed natural enough that shitting my pants was funny, but as soon as I notice the poncho that lies there now like a discarded cigar my breath quits coming. I begin to tremble all over again. Guys are running every which way with their steel pots on and rifles loaded. I am all of a sudden as afraid as I ever was. I can't move. Prophet leaves the hole and I sit on its edge and go through some violent shakes. I can't take my eyes off the poncho. It shuts the rest of the world out. My eyes go over all the folds of the poncho, and I try to think what the guy had looked like. All I can remember is blond hair.

111

Pops comes.

"You OK?"

"Yeah. He ain't."

He gets down in the hole and uncovers the face. It has changed color now, it's bleached and paraffin-looking. All the bones in his head show like a chart: his blond-white eyebrows look like two caterpillars crawling over a knot in a beech log because the face is so white. It seems to have all drawn into its middle. It looks like a twisted rag. Pops looks at him for a minute then looks away, a look-at-nothing move.

"Did you know him, Pops?"

"He was in Alpha company. He was from New York and was gonna be a photographer. He probably had about as much time left as I got. I knew him a little. A little too much." His face looks tough. "Chickenfeed got hit. He's in our hole. Go on over there."

Fuck, no. Oh, fuck, no. I feel selfish or stupid or both; since I didn't get hit and Prophet didn't get hit I forgot to even think about the rest of them, the rest of *us.* Chickenfeed is lying in the bottom of the hole covered with a poncho liner soaked through by blood. Poncho liners are camouflage cloth and ponchos are rubberized nylon, and the first thought I have has something to do with comparing the dead guy being covered by the poncho and Chickenfeed lying there under this soft poncho liner; even though the blood comes through this, it seems right somehow. I don't know why.

Chickenfeed is crying. His black face is streaked in every direction like a football left in the rain. Tears come to me immediately. He is sobbing, and the sobs are as much like coughs as cries. His whole body heaves when he sobs and for a minute I stand there staring at him; then I get down in the hole and try to keep the blanket on him. His eyes are full of water and one is full of little flakes of dirt so I try to hold his head still and clean the dirt away from his eyes but I can't hold him still enough.

I begin talking to him like I was talking to a pet, just to comfort him—or me. "Easy, man, easy. Lay still. You're OK. You're gonna be all right. They're bringing you some morph before long. The Dustoff is coming. Pops is getting you something right now that'll make you feel better. Try to cry, Chicken, just cry. Don't let yourself stifle it and maybe you won't shake so much. You shouldn't move around, man. Easy. Lay still. Easy. Hold on, man, hold on."

And he takes hold of my wrist but can't hold on so I take his. *I don't want to be holding his hand if he dies. I got to see where he's hit. The bird has to be coming. How can the Dustoff not be here yet? Where did Pops go? I don't want to see his wound, there's nothing I can do and I don't want to see how bad he is. I know he's hit bad.*

I am welded to his hand. I wonder if I am squeezing too hard and he can't tell me. His free hand waves around in the air. Pain hits him and his hands closes into a fist. His fingernails dig deep into my wrist, and I almost jerk away. Pops comes back.

"How's he doing?"

"I don't know. Is he conscious?"

Pops is straddling him on his knees now, giving him water. Chickenfeed sucks the water from the canteen until Pops pulls it back.

"Chicken, can you hear me, man?"

Chickenfeed's eyes open and the eyeballs roll once, but that's all.

"He's losing a lot of blood. Why isn't the fuckin' Dustoff here by now?" He looks at me like I could know.

"I'll go see what I can find out." When I'm out of the hole I see a medic.

They undo the poncho liner and hand it to me to keep out of the mud. Chickenfeed's right thigh is shot in half. It is barely attached; the center of the wound is as big as a softball and the bone is plainly exposed, broken like a tree limb. I've never seen anything like this. I puke.

"Jesus," the medic says. He takes a shot of morphine out of his bag. It is a tube like toothpaste but only as big as a horse's tooth. It has a number, and the medic has to account for it. The tube has its own needle, and the medic jabs it in like he has done it a million times, then marks Chickenfeed's forehead so the Rear will know he's already had morphine. Immediately, Chickenfeed slows all the way down. When the medic and Pops move Chicken's leg enough to tourniquet it he seems to know it but the morph has taken the pain away. They tie the broken leg to the other leg.

"He's lost a fuckuva lot of blood," the medic says. "Keep him warm. I'll get him on the first Dustoff." He leaves and goes toward other shouts. Everything is in such slow motion in my mind that seeing him is like seeing a still photograph. He is covered by blood. Half the hair on his head is standing out, made stiff by caked blood, like a dirty paintbrush.

A staff lieutenant comes by taking names, and when he is gone Pops says we might be going out on a body count.

"He hardly noticed Chickenfeed."

"He noticed enough to know he can't send him out with us."

When we're loading Chickenfeed's stretcher onto the bird I get sick because there is a smell all around of, I guess, dried blood. Getting sick seems natural, and I feel like my head clears a little while I'm standing there dripping puke onto the helicopter's skid. Prophet has Chickenfeed's Bible and a Polaroid picture that Chicken has glued onto the cardboard end panel of a case of C's. The picture is his wife standing in front of their house trailer. There's a dog sitting on the iron steps. Chicken's face is so still it looks like a huge piece of licorice when Prophet shoves the picture and Bible under Chicken's shirt. His stomach looks like black leather but is spotted by blood. His legs are covered with a piece of green plastic that came on the Dustoff.

The next bird in brings ammo and body bags. From the side of the hill that took most of the shit comes a gruesome stream of guys, usually two or three, sometimes four, carrying the KIAs over to the pad. At least every other bearer is upset; some of them are crying too hard to be of much help, and one guy is wailing and won't let go of the body he helped carry. The dead guy only has half his head, and seeing the other guy crying and holding the body like it was whole makes me stiff inside. There can be no perfect description of the scene: the most obvious denominator is the blood. Some is still fresh and some is dried. The medic on the pad who is recording information off dog tags is shirtless, and his torso looks like strawberry pulp. I still feel fairly clear-headed and I help as best I can. I get chills of the nth degree when I see the medic put a dog tag between a guy's front teeth and shut his mouth. They told us about it, but I never believed it. It is true.

A formation of helicopters comes in two at a time. The first two birds unload about ten guys. I recognize Peacock even though the auxiliary pad, where they land, is halfway down the hill. He has on clean clothes. I see Prophet go up to him and I see Peacock slam his rucksack to the ground and I can tell he is weeping. Prophet stands above him for a few moments; then he leans down and picks up the ruck and helps Peacock to his feet. They disappear behind smoke from a still-smoldering fire in the middle of the hill.

The KIAs are all loaded so I drag back toward our hole. Pops is sitting down smoking a cigarette. His eyes look smaller than ever. Prophet and Peacock come up together. Pops and Peacock hug each other. Peacock nods at me. He has his dirty rabbit's foot on; in addition, there is a set of beads around his neck that looks a lot like mine.

We all sit quietly for a few minutes; in fact, the whole Z seems uncommonly quiet, like everybody is temporarily in the unkind grip of the same shock. The sun is getting high now and it has been raining off and on for an hour. When it rains nothing changes. We don't move, don't even try to keep anything dry, except our rifles that are all under a piece of plastic beside the hole: the black butts stick out from the plastic like shoes waiting to be shined.

Peacock is probably the most nervous. He keeps jiggling one leg. I can't remember which foot was wounded. He leaves a cigarette in his mouth, unlit, and is throwing and retrieving his knife. He sticks the knife in a sandbag between his feet. Pops and Prophet are lying almost head to head on the wet dirt. Prophet's eyes are closed but Pops is watching the smoke rings he is blowing.

"Where's Callmeblack?"

"The Eltee sent him out on security."

"Chickenfeed—" Pops begins,

"Is gonna be fine," Prophet says, too quickly, like he was waiting for Pops. "Chicken'll make it. He just got the ticket out forever, dig?" He straightens and rubs his neck. His hat is falling down his face but he doesn't rearrange it.

"He'll make it," Pops says, "but that leg is gone."

"They'll fix him up."

"C'mon, fucker," Pops whines, "you don't hafta tell me what'll happen. I ain't his mother or his wife. Tell me *why him*!" and he throws his helmet at the rifles.

"You're losing it, man."

"So fuckin' what?"

"Pops, man"—Prophet is sniffling now—"I saw it again. I saw Chicken get hit just before I went to sleep last night and you know what, man? I'm afraid. I'm afraid to go to sleep now." He must be six-two, but now he is curled up in the mud and he doesn't look big at all. I am thinking of my kid brother when I go over to him and squeeze his shoulder like Pops usually does. He has his head buried and is crying very softly.

When I look up, both of the others are looking at me. Pops looks down at Prophet with his small brown eyes, and Peacock gives me a clenched-fist sign—the friendliest one I've ever seen.

More birds come in, bringing ammo. After they leave, a Fire in the Hole is sounded so we all put on our steel pots and cram into the hole. The big patch of jungle just below us goes in a huge cloud of debris and black smoke. Little stuff rains down. When we get up and look out, the perimeter is farther away and already there is a detail ready to stretch concertina.

"Let's set some trip flares out there."

"I'll bet Charlie was right there on the edge. He sure as hell had a bead on our hole, but all we got was small arms. How'd Chicken get hit?"

"After the first couple of rounds he made a dash for his ruck, and as soon as he got to it, he got hit. An RPG, I think—something big."

"How'd he make it back to the hole? That guy who was sniping could've hit him again, seems to me."

"I went out and got him when the sniper was pinned down."

"Ah, maybe you'll get a Bronze for it."

"Fuck it."

"Somebody stepped on his dick in this move. They shoulda got us in here a lot earlier yesterday. Anybody I know ride a bag out?"

"That little guy from Alpha Company. Rhodes."

"If I remember right he nicknamed himself."

"What'd they call Rhodes?" I ask.

"Dead End."

■■■■■■■■■■

SOMEBODY IN THE MIDDLE OF THE HILL YELLS AND POINTS at an incoming bird, full of beautiful red mailbags. By the time the bird makes its approach to land there are probably forty dudes standing around the pad waiting. I don't expect anything but still I follow the crowd. Mail is magnetic; about everybody is swept by its magic.

"Hey, assholes, break it up!"

The red-haired lieutenant is standing on top of a water blivet, and even then he's not much taller than Prophet, who's standing on the ground beside him. The helicopter pulled up when the pilots saw the crowd, and it is circling now; the door gunner is waving his hands to break the group up. Everybody backs away from the pad and eight or ten mail sacks get kicked out; then the crowd converges again.

There is a letter. The stamp is on upside down. I recognize my mom's handwriting. The name takes up half the envelope. It is something like bad manners to open your mail before everybody gets his, so while Pops is passing out the squad's mail there is a joint going around. I try to imagine my mother writing. She doesn't usually write letters to anyone, but I can see her at the kitchen table with a cup of coffee doing bills. The kitchen table has always been all hers. I can see her writing very carefully and standing up to look out the window, every so often.

Dear Gabe. Everything is good here. It has been a beautiful fall. The road to town is as pretty as I've ever seen it, the oaks are just beginning to turn color. I pray God is watching over you. I pray every night. Grandaddy sends his love. We don't hear much from your brother, he is busy at work. But he got drafted. He is to report in January.

Oh, fuck.

118

He said last time I talked to him that he would write. So will your father, I know. He says getting mail over there is a mixed blessing. No one has heard from you, please write and tell what it's like.

"Gabe, y'wanna hit this?"

A big bowl of dope is coming around now. The whole squad is sitting on bundles of empty sandbags. Peacock doesn't have any mail and is whittling a vine into shavings that look like frozen noodles. The sound of a helicopter beating its way up the valley gets alternately loud and muffled as it flies through pockets of wet air. I take an extra-heavy hit and pass the pipe to Callmeblack, whose whole letter is written on yellow paper.

I made a big kettle of soup this week and we have been eating on that. My washing is drying on the porch and I've got another load to run so I better get to it.

Gabe, there is so much talk about the war being wrong, and I know you thought about it a lot, but I want you to know I love you. We all do. Gabe, your brother says he might not go if they send him. What do you think? (That's why he hasn't written you yet, but don't tell him I told you, please.) Gabe, please write us. Grandaddy would write if he could. He's always saying he would dictate a letter if I would write it but he never will.

"What should we do with Chickenfeed's letter?"
"Send it back on a bird."
"Maybe we oughta hold it for whoever goes in next. If we send it back to the Rear it'll take forever to get to him."

"He'll go to Japan. Yeah, save it. Somebody'll be going in in the next few days, and they can get his address."

I read in the paper where some boys (oops! I mean *men*) came home for a week on "R&R" is it? Well, I'm out of things to say and must get back to the wash (it's Monday), so God bless you. Everybody asks about you.

"Your mail musta got marked for the med, Peacock."

"Yeah, well, fuck it. They'll probably send it back with a note that I was medevacked and scare the shit out of my folks. Or I didn't get any because I'm too short."

"Just think, you guys, I'm too short to write anymore," Pops says dreamily. Then for the first time in a couple weeks, the look I love comes to his face. He just looks happy.

Mail is like finding one match when you think they're all wet. I vow to write home as soon as I can.

All of us take our time. Finally we mosey to our holes and start digging again. There is plenty of daylight left and we don't have any trouble getting deep enough to sleep in, but we don't have a chance of getting any overhead on before it gets dark. Prophet is digging and I am holding the bags. Instead of tying them I fold them and build the wall by laying them so the folded part is down. The wall around the hole is about a foot high on three sides now.

"What's in your crystal ball?" I'm mostly interested in talking.

"I only say this is gonna be a bad LZ," he says. "We haven't seen the end of the shit that we'll take while we're here."

"You've been hit three times, right?"

"Yup."

"Did you know you were going to get hit?"

"Once, yeah. When I took shrap in the shoulder."

"Do you think you would've gotten hit if you didn't think you were beforehand?"

"Yup."

"Why didn't you do something, or did you?"

"I did. I was hiding in a hole and the shrap was a freak. I was glad when I got it, because in my dream—or vision, if you want to call it that; I was awake when I saw it—I wasn't in a hole, and I got wasted."

Lieutenant Williams walks up. He's a good-looking black guy, and I like him better than any of the other officers. He's got a pretty smile, something like Ass's smile was. He sits down and spreads open a sandbag for me to fill.

"Sorry to hear about Chickenfeed. I didn't see him; how bad is he?"

"He'll live," Prophet says, "but I'd bet a year's pay he's gonna lose his leg."

"A fuckin' shame, real fuckin' shame. He was a good athlete, did you know that? Ah, sure you did. We came from the same high school. He was three or four years behind me, and he broke all kinds of track records—mine—and was a hell of a good baseball player. A fuckin' shame."

"Eltee, every fuckin' casualty is a fuckin' shame."

"I'm hip."

"Somehow even Charlie's hits are a shame, too. I mean, hell, man, right now if I had a chance I'd goddamn cut a gook's leg off for Chickenfeed, then cut his nuts off for Chickenfeed's wife, then his other leg for Chickenfeed's high school, but there ain't no sense to any of this, man."

"I'm hip."

"Let's quit. Let's goddamn call this war a draw and quit."

"You'll be home before long. . . ."

"Big fuckin' deal."

The scene doesn't seem to belong. I'm glad it's over. It

ends when Eltee Williams and Prophet slap a few fives and Williams gets up to leave. Somebody yells for him.

"The Captain calls," he says.

"Tell him we quit."

"What I came over here for in the first place is to tell you Two Squad will be going out in about an hour. I'll be humping with you."

"I advise you to get hold of all the ammo you feel like carrying," Prophet tells me. "I'm gonna get a few extra frags. I'll be back."

So I clean my rifle and make sure my ammo bandolier is full. I've got four frags and my string of ammo for the machine gun. I lace my rucksack together and tie the steel pot on. I settle down to spend a few minutes writing home, but nothing comes.

"YES SIR, YES SIR, THREE BAGS FULL"

THE SQUAD GOES OUT IN FILE, AND AS WE GO THE GUYS who are digging nod and give us mock salutes. It's brotherhood, not manhood. The brush thickens, and ten minutes outside the wire it's a different world. Prophet is walking point with his steel pot on, and his ruck rides high on his back. Peacock is next with the Sixty over his shoulder, its belt of ammo coming out the side like miniature ears of corn. I follow him, Eltee Williams is behind me, then Callmeblack and Pops. I can't look behind me, but I can imagine Callme carrying that grenade launcher like a toy.

We go downhill for a while and my legs soon ache from the strain. We're on a trail that is pretty clear, but a little slippery. I lock my eyes on our left side. Our pace is fairly gradual until we come to where two trails branch; then the walking gets harder. Once in a while I hear somebody slip or grunt but usually I can only hear my own steps—squishing sounds. After forty-five minutes, we get to the bottom of the hill, where Prophet stops and Callme and Peacock go out on security.

"Higher-higher said there oughta be a bunch of dead

dinks out here," Eltee says, looking at his map. From where we stopped we can see the tops of two nearby hills. We are in the saddle between them.

"I'm for going out as far as we can get. We don't want to be somewhere between the LZ and Charlie's mortars tonight."

"Dig it."

Pops has his map spread out too. He and Eltee are so completely opposite-looking it makes me think of a comic-book drawing. The lieutenant is tall, black, and thin. His face is smooth and handsome. Pops is thick, ruddy, ragged, and his face is rough and square. His eyebrows have grown together.

"This is just about where Artillery will be wanting to drop rounds tonight."

"And Charlie knows that the LZ is almost as fucked up as it was last night, so if we're close to one of his big supply routes or the main hospital around here, he's gonna keep fucking with us."

"Prophet, you see anything that looks like he was this close last night?"

"Not really. Hard to tell. It rained too much."

Prophet is on one knee, breaking chunks of mud between his hands. His deep-set blue eyes move slowly from Eltee to Pops.

"Want somebody else to take a turn on point?"

"Nah."

A fog that makes everything look like a fading photograph seems to come all at once, like there's a sheet of thin plastic on my eyes. What didn't stand out before now seems like all there is: the vines and leaves are erased by this fog and three tree trunks are straight and dark; it makes me think of charred logs after a fire has died. Besides, I hear something. We all hear it at the same time—footsteps.

It is two dinks carrying something, and everybody is so

surprised that the dinks see us just when we see them. There's not even time to react before they take off running. Nobody gets a shot off, it all happens so quick.

Eltee is up and runs in their direction but that's all that occurs.

"Goddamn, that was quick. They came right between our security."

They were carrying a body. It lies there limp now, no bigger than a ten-year-old American boy. The top half is face down and it is lying on one leg that's been shattered; there's only a day-old stump of the other one. Its clothes are a pair of black, bloody shorts.

"Why would they be carrying this body? So we wouldn't find it?"

"I've got a hunch," Eltee says. He pokes the barrel of his rifle into the shorts and I can't believe he is going to blow the guy's nuts off, but there aren't any nuts. His rifle barrel spreads the shorts apart just enough to show the pubic hair and the woman's cunt.

"I'll be damned."

"One of those guys' wife, or what?"

"I'd about bet on it."

"Jesus Fucking Christ."

"Call Higher-higher, tell 'em we found one. Don't tell 'em it got delivered to us."

"What about those guys?"

"They won't fuck with us. We're too many. Maybe they'll hide for a couple hours and sneak back for this, who knows?"

We make radio contact and report one enemy KIA.

"Let's move."

I feel like this fog is inside me, easing around my mind like it eases around the tree trunks in front of us, and easing around something foreign in my gut that lies there like this tiny tiny woman we leave behind, dead in the foggy jungle.

The new trail is narrow, slippery, steep. Prophet manages to keep pretty good footage, but I have a hard time. I go down to one knee a couple times and my rifle jabs into the mud once, so I am walking and trying to pick the mud out of the barrel at the same time. Eventually, we get far enough from the stream that the fog thins out a little, but there is still too much canopy overhead to let the sun through. Besides the dim light, the trail gets more faint. I see that Peacock is stopped a few meters in front of me so I stop too, in an awkward position but glad to catch my breath. Peacock looks back and flips me the bird, then disappears again around some vines that entangle so perfectly they look braided.

My legs and feet are hurting and I experiment with walking splay-footed, then pigeon-toed; then I try taking smaller steps but nothing eases the pain much. I am concentrating too much on getting rid of the pain because I dumbly walk up on Peacock, who is facing me. For an instant I panic, and my confusion must show because he chuckles and holds out his hand. Then I realize I am pointing my rifle right at him.

"You'd be so fuckin' dead now . . ."

"Man, my ass is dragging, ain't yours?"

Eltee Williams comes up. The fatigue shows on his face. He goes by us to Point to talk with Prophet. We are in a small glen that has a cuplike shape and will be full of water during the heavy monsoons. Callmeblack comes, panting, and bums a cigarette. His face is the color of dirty oil and spotted by sweat. His ODs are soaked and he stinks. He drops his ruck and sits on it.

We've been humping for probably three hours total. The glen we're in doesn't allow a view of anything beyond thirty meters. I wonder how far from the LZ we are, directly. Peacock is lying on the ground with his feet resting on low vines; the rest of us are in a rough circle, facing out. The fog is sparse now, but the light isn't very bright either. It's late afternoon. There are birds in the canopy. Once, when my eyes are beginning to close of their own accord, I think I see a snake hanging from a tree, but it's a vine. Callme is humming very softly.

"Let's ride. It's getting dark."

"Somebody take a turn on the Sixty, my neck hurts."

I take the pig. I haven't fired one for six months, and I look it over to remember what I know. It feels about four times as heavy as a rifle. There's a carrying handle mounted on top but it doesn't balance correctly when there's a belt of ammunition in. There are two legs that swing down from the perforated forestock. I inject a round and it tightens the belt up. The ammo belts are about four feet long and I loop them over my shoulders. Switching from an M-16 to this is like changing paintbrushes for bigger work; it takes some getting used to. Since the Sixty is longer than my rifle, the butt plate keeps getting snagged on my rucksack strap at first. Finally I give up trying to carry it in a ready position and flop it onto my shoulder, the way I'd seen Peacock carry it.

The trail evens out and gets a little bit more worn. It isn't as muddy but there are soft spots. The hardest part is stepping over the vines, which seem to be extra big here. We are about three quarters up a mountain and walking around a kind of horseshoe plateau that looks down into the thick cul-de-sac we've been coming through. We are going down as often as up for the first half hour; then it's a steady but gradual climb. We are headed west and the sun is low enough that the streaks it cuts through the fog are almost horizontal.

The M-60 works to my advantage. It is just enough heavier that, going uphill, I can use it to help stagger. I keep watching my side of the trail but it's hard to concentrate and instead I recall my neighborhood, the playground with its always-broken merry-go-round. Certain glimpses through the fog trigger flash memories of particular spots in particular woods. *Homesick.*

Prophet stops at a place where the trail curves around a rock face on the mountainside. Pops begins calculating where we are; Pea takes the M-60 and goes out for security. The rest of us begin setting up. Callme and I dig a shallow trench, trying to be as quiet as we can. Prophet and the Eltee set up claymores against the rock wall and aim them in opposite directions along the trail. There is trouble making radio contact, so Pops takes it up onto a ledge of rock face and calls in our position. When we're set up it is too dark to see more than five feet. Pops reminds me and Callmeblack not to leave the trench unless we tell somebody. I make sure I can lay my hands on my frags and I lean the rifle against my ruck with one bandolier of full ammo clips over the barrel. I open the first can I feel in my ruck; it turns out to be beef and potatoes. I'm glad it's too dark to see the grease that is always at the top of the can, but I can feel it make my lips slippery. I can't find my water so I borrow Callme's. It tastes like he put an extra purification tablet in it.

We'll pull middle guard and there is not jack-shit to do in the meantime and I'm not sleepy. Our trench is nearest the trail, and one of the claymore detonators is wrapped around a small root at the top of our trench. If we detonated it there would be a blast powerful enough to ruin a concrete wall two feet thick, six feet away. I think about that a couple minutes while I'm trying to get comfortable in my poncho liner. We've got our ponchos stretched over the trench to shed water, and as soon as I'm comfortable it begins to rain, but softly, so instead of claymore blasts I'm thinking of lying underneath a tin roof. It works: I'm almost dozed off when Callme accidentally kicks me. I give him a little more room and now the water runs down the poncho and right on me.

Fuck.

Callmeblack begins snoring, plenty loud, I think. I lie there for another hour I reckon, trying to keep from lying on my hardon. Then I begin thinking about the whore in Cam Ranh, and about some little Vietnamese girls we saw at the convoy point who were eating lice out of each other's hair, then about the dead woman today. Then I'm not hard anymore. Even though I deliberately try not to, I begin figuring how much longer I'll be here. Peacock rolls over in the trench next to us and makes some kind of pained grunt.

From our position, the LZ is over the mountain on the other side of the gully. They are calling in Artillery illumination around the Z to set up Night Fire positions. The illumination rounds come down on their parachutes, to plot heavy explosive rounds. *Dinks can mark where they land and could plan routes around them.*

It's sure different to be out here, so much easier to understand how a few men can invade a complex Army outpost and get away with it; the jungle and the night are allies. The illumination rounds cast eerie patterns through the canopy. Shapes and shadows dance around. The rain is sometimes plain to see. It is still soft and steady. Other than the soft *pffts* it makes, the only sounds I hear are the distant thuds of artillery and Callme's gentle snoring.

It seems so fucking unreal. Once, when I must be on the verge of sleep, I feel like I am *seeing* it all. Floating between wakefulness and sleep, my mind roams like there's no difference between what is real and what is imaginary. It's pleasant, but I can't quite relax.

I'd like to get up and walk but that is impossible. I'd like to get that redheaded lifer into a gunnysack and beat it open with a tire iron. I'd like to call ten or twelve rounds in on the peace talks in Paris. I'd like to go home and paint a house. I'd like to be nine years old and playing hide-and-seek along the railroad tracks instead of hiding in the jungle somewhere in Asia. I'd . . .

A rifle burst, an AK, not very distinct, and for a minute I'm not sure if I'm awake or dreaming; then there are explosions in pairs, and machine-gun fire, more explosions. I know the LZ is getting hit; I roll over on my stomach, not quite sure what to do other than waking somebody up, but everybody is awake.

I hear Peacock jamming home the machine-gun bolt. Prophet comes down the trail repeating "New York Yankees" over and over.

"OK, they're getting hit again. Everybody know which way the trail is from here?"

"Which claymore is which?"

"That one is the one looking up the trail."

"Come with me, Gabe. You guys stay here. We're going down the trail a ways. Don't panic. I'll take the radio with us. Stay cool, it'll be Chevy Supersport if I come back. If you hear anybody going by and they ain't namin' cars, blow the mines."

The action seems far, far away. I think of the first night we got hit, the RPGs everywhere, the impact of the explosions, the smells. Pops and I are going uphill, climbing around on the ledge of rock where the radio reception was good; Pops is using a flashlight, but very carefully. I try to be quiet but Pops is mostly in a hurry instead of worrying about noise. When we get to our position he sets the radio up and dials it to the emergency push. The LZ is calling in guns and before the voice is done transmitting there is an explosion. The push goes dead.

From up here on the ledge, we can see a little of the LZ. There are all colors of explosions, red and yellow and blue and white. It is awesome from this distance. There are hand-held flares up everywhere and plenty of M-16 fire putting tracer rounds in every direction, but most of it toward us.

"Muthafucker, they're getting hit hard."

"Listen," he says, "the dinks are probably working in

130

waves. They'll send a squad in and then another one to cover their ass, then maybe another one to keep the confusion going. Unless there's a shitload of 'em, they'll hit hard and fast, then they'll scatter in every direction. I'd say there's a damn good chance they could come this way, and if it happens to be the first wave who come this direction, it could happen soon. So don't be fuckin' half-stepping."

"Chevy. Supersport."

It's Lieutenant Williams's voice, below us.

"Whatsa matter, Eltee?"

"I'm coming up. Nothing wrong. Not yet."

Pops shines the light once just as Williams is climbing over the last small cliff. Somebody is with him but I can't tell who. This all seems rehearsed but dangerous. A script would call for somebody to stumble and fall, but instead it's all so smooth. This is a safe place to be, as far as ambushes go, backed up against a stone wall and higher than the trail.

"What's up, Eltee?"

"I was looking at the map, Pops, and it shows a trail that must be right on the other side of this." He knocks the end of his rifle against the rock. He brought Peacock with him, and he is setting up a claymore.

"So what're you saying?"

"We oughta cover it."

"C'mon, Eltee, we can't cover it. Unless we climb over this sonofabitchin' rock right now and get all set up and —"

"Yeah, let's go. You and—"

"You're crazy, man!"

"Pops, I noticed, when we were coming up, that this trail was going up faster than the slope. We were cutting up at a sharp angle. And on the map there's a little trail meeting a big one right up above us. I thought we were on the big one, but I think we're on the little one and the big one is right up there."

"Fuck, we can't climb up there now."

"The claymores down there will cover that little trail, no matter what. Even if some shit hits, we're still right above it."

"Right over our own guys, and it's night."

"The dinks aren't gonna stop and fight; they're just interested in getting the fuck out of here."

"What if we're smackfuckindab in the middle of their staging area or something? We're fuckin' sitting ducks when it gets light."

"So all the more reason to cover the other trail. They'll sure as hell be using the speed trail."

"Unless they know we're up here. Those guys this afternoon with the woman . . . maybe there *are* a bunch of 'em around here. So we can play it cool, just sneak the fuck back out of here tomorrow."

"We don't know anything, Pops. We must play the odds."

"We don't even know if they're coming this way."

"Dammit, I've thought of all that, and we're going up there."

"This is stupid, man. Stupid. This is my squad."

"Pops, don't make me order you. I respect you to the utmost, I just feel I'm right."

"All right, fuck it. What about the Sixty?"

"Peacock is set up so he can see down the little trail, and if that other one comes up right at the top of the ridge, he's within range of that side too."

The top of the ledge is closer than I thought and we're there in five minutes. Since we're even higher now, the base camp is more visible, but there's no time to watch right away. We scout the section out with flashlights and rig up two claymores. There isn't enough space to set them both up in opposite directions and still compensate for the back blast, so we set them in tandem about ten feet apart. We're shielded from the back blast by a rock the size of a coffin. Callme and I get set up on one end of the rock and

Pops sets up with Eltee on the other side and down the trail a little. It's necessary that we know where the other is, as much as we can.

There are illumination rounds hanging all around the LZ. It looks like a distant sports arena, from the blimp. All the sound from the Z is mixed together. Artillery is coming in in groups now, awfully close to the Z. Those flashes are red and yellow. Evidently, there are two different batteries firing, and their patterns crisscross, then work around the Z. Most of the defensive fire is directed toward our side of the Z, so apparently the attack came from this side. I hope the dinks run the other way. The action has been going on for more than half an hour now. The illumination rounds have come from artillery, mortars, and hand-held flares. There are probably fifty bulbs in the air now, hanging at different heights. The only thing it illuminates from here is the smoke and fog. As we watch, heavy explosive rounds land in purple flashes. The flashes are walking away from the Z, beginning to comb the surrounding ridges, so maybe the offensive is over for tonight.

Callmeblack is huddled beside me, his poncho wrapped around him with the hood up. He is shivering, and his M-79 is rapping against a rock. The sound annoys me. I am so soaked through that the rain doesn't seem to stop at my clothes; it's like I can feel individual drops hit me on the shoulders.

Gunships are coming. At first their sound is steady and soft, a medium-range and constant sound. They come in twos, two pair of blinking lights, red and green. The Cobras strafe all around the base of the mountain the Z is on with rockets and miniguns, and there's no way to describe the sight. Even though only every seventh round is a tracer, the air and ground are lined like a neon screen door. It is such a visual show I have to hold my breath. I'd like to know the number of rounds and what the rounds are hitting. Thee pattern of the artillery has moved into a wider circle now and some are coming closer and closer to us, walking our way in giant purple steps. Pops comes over to our side.

"They're throwing everything we've got at Charlie. If anything happens, be damn sure you don't forget where we are. Callme, use that launcher careful, you hear? Gabe, fire short bursts if you fire. We'll all wait on Eltee. If this is really a speed trail, they could be getting here soon, might even be riding motorbikes. If they come down the trail Prophet and Peacock are covering, you guys come around this way, behind us, but don't fire down there unless there's all kinds of shit coming our way."

"Muthafucker, I ain't ready for no goddamn ambush," Callme says, his voice as deep and black as the jungle. The gunships are still working out and Artillery is firing illumination rounds again.

My nerves are hammering my insides and the rain is drilling me in the face now. My muscles are all hard. I think of hiding underneath a car and hearing the cops run by five years ago. I can feel myself sweating. My legs ache but I can't move. I can smell Callmeblack's BO, like goat piss.

The Cobras quit firing and are only motor sounds now, above the clouds and smoke. The smell from the illumination rounds has drifted to us. Rhythmically, illuminations pop above the smoke and drift into the canopy and make the whole sky somehow look like a petticoat, just before I see the flashlights.

They are coming up the hill like cow eyes coming across a pasture: lights, then voices. The voices aren't clear. I'm in a daze. I feel Callme move beside me. I hear the voices like I am listening to a television from a different room. I flash on opening the kitchen door to a Chinese restaurant I used to have on my garbage route: quick, chatty sounds. They are even with us, twenty feet away. They are half-running. Eltee opens up. The Sixty chatters.

Callme launches one. I fire a quick clip. The claymores burn a momentary swath through the dark, like a flashbulb.

The claymores start something on fire for a minute, and I can see spastic movement like a chicken with its head gone. Then it is dark again. There's a thrashing sound, then nothing but quiet. *Dead silence.*

I hear either Pops or Eltee puke. I can smell Callmeblack's goat-piss BO. The rain sounds too perfect.

There's a rock behind me to lean on. Callmeblack is lying down, I think. There is not much sound from anybody: some rustling around, once a stifled sneeze. I am wide awake. Every sense is acute, although it's so dark now without the illumination rounds drifting it is hard to see anything. Still, my eyes won't stay shut. The scene that stays with me is that last bit of scrambling after the claymores went off. It was brief, instantaneous, but I'm positive I saw flailing. No screaming, at least none that I heard. Twenty or thirty feet away are some dead gooks, caught in our ambush. *Why don't I feel more than I do?* I get my bootlaces untied. My feet stink. I'd like to have a cigarette. I run my tongue around the inside of my teeth until the tip is sore. Light can't be more than a couple hours away.

What does it look like down there? When I imagine it, I think of a painting from a history book. I think the picture I keep seeing is from the Civil War: soldiers in the foreground and bodies behind them. Clean, old-fashioned battle death. A claymore has something like 150 pellets in it. The pellets are a little smaller than rabbit turds. We blew two claymores, so there's not going to be anything clean about these guys. They'll be full of holes.

The canopy creaks in a wind and it starts raining harder. I've been wet for a week. The way I'm sitting, water catches in my lap. Nothing matters, so I piss in my pants. The piss is warm and feels thicker than rainwater.

The rain is so steady I can imagine every single leaf

getting a drip at the same time. I want to count something. I try to count every drop that hits me. Then I try counting the drops I can hear land on my steel pot. Then I try to quit counting but my mind keeps on trying to count something, just measure time, measure these slowest minutes of my life. I feel like beating off. *There are 3,600 seconds in an hour. Light must be 5,000 seconds away. One thousand one, one thousand two, one thousand three. Shit.*

I wonder if Mom still shuts the bathroom door now that nobody's there.

Movement. From where Eltee and Pops are comes a sliding, dragging sound. The rain is constant. The movement is careful and very slow. It can't be more than twenty-five feet away, but if I didn't know where they are I couldn't have estimated the distance from the sound. It is going away from us, toward Peacock. He must be crawling. I try turning my head different ways to find the angle I can hear it best. While he's moving across the underbrush the sound is more muffled than when he hits rocks. Only once does his equipment make noise, a metallic noise, and it enables me to get a better fix on his position. The movement stops and there is whispering; then the movement begins again.

No, more than one movement. One set of sounds goes back toward the other position and the other sound comes toward us. I strain my eyes to see, but nothing. There must be no moon whatsoever. Whoever is coming is walking instead of crawling. He is sliding his feet along the ground. He isn't very far away when he bumps something and moves to my right. I don't know whether or not to say anything. His sliding steps stop.

"Ford Mustang." It's Peacock.

"We're here, to your left."

Our voices aren't any louder than the rain, but the rain doesn't do anything to cover them up either. His steps begin again. I guess he is twenty feet away. I try to figure out if he is coming at the proper angle. I count his steps. At twelve, I whisper again and his direction changes toward me. Twelve more steps, but he doesn't seem much closer. I wonder if there are rocks that fool us.

"Hey, dude," Callmeblack whispers.

"I'm fuckin' dizzy from trying to see," he says. It sounds like he may be facing away from us.

Callme taps something against his rifle four or five times, then Peacock's slow steps start again. He kicks a loose rock and it rolls a few feet and stops with a *sploosh*. He is close now, homing in on Callmeblack's steady clicking. Seven more steps.

"Who's making the noise?"

"I am," Callme says.

"Where are you, Gabe?"

"Here."

"OK, I'm between you."

So now we three are the highest up. The ambush site is downhill in one direction and Pops and Eltee are downhill in the other, our left. Prophet is farther below them. Peacock is setting up the Sixty. I wonder which way he faces it. I hear the bipod snap into place. I have to reset my eyes even though I haven't been able to see anything.

I think of Chickenfeed crying and I can see his pewter thigh bone tied to his other leg. I wonder if he is in a hospital in Japan and if they had to cut the leg off. I purposely keep my eyes shut until I count to one hundred, rushing the nineties. I hope to see a trace of light when I open them. I try again to foresee the scene downtrail.

The rain sounds like a giant wadding paper.

"Pea, what's the plan?"

"Wait'll it gets light and take it from there. Eltee sent me up here to you guys in case there's dinks up above us. The Sixty is good for covering our ass."

"Think there's much chance of more dinks?"

"Hard to say."

"Sure as hell a lot of medevacs going to the Z."

"Charlie poured shit onto that hill for a good twenty minutes before they got any support, and Charlie makes a lot more rounds count than we do."

"Especially when there's no sandbags on the hooches."

"We'd better shut up."

So it's back to waiting for light and listening to the rain: *dif-da-datta-dif*. There's still the drone of distant helicopters. They could be Cobras standing by, probably above the rain clouds, or there could still be medevacs going into the Z. From the other direction come barely audible thumps of artillery rounds walking guard over other mountains. My saliva glands are working hard to stem my wish for nicotine. The small of my back is sore, and periodically I catch myself gripping the stock of my rifle so tightly that my fingers go numb. I've been sitting crooked so long my lungs feel like there would be a crease in them.

The very first light that shows resembles wax paper. The canopy, even though we're partway up the mountain, is still fairly thick and the light seems to seep through it slowly at first so that straight above me it looks like a black roof with very light frost on it—just the minutest change of color. When I first see it I expect to be able to see around me, but ground level is just as black as it's been all night. I suppose my eyes are playing tricks until I look up again and it is still there, changing. It must have something to do with the cup of land we're in. There is nothing ambiant about the light. I swear this stuff that was frost color, then movie-screen color, is now as dull as chalk above us but only finally reaching the ground. I see Pea and the Sixty in silhouette, then Callme beyond him.

Gradually, I can see farther. The jungle comes in jigsaw pieces that are edged by the dark trees and vines. Everybody lies completely still and looks around, weapons ready. I can't see over the cliff but I hear somebody moving down there. As it gets lighter Peacock adjusts the machine gun so he can swivel it almost 360 degrees. I don't know where to look or what exactly to look for. The spot where the dinks are is over a ridge from us, so we can't see it. I look mostly into the trees—for movement, I guess.

Suddenly a huge bird flies over us low and we can hear it beat wings to a stop, then a throaty *caw-caw* that sounds like an enormous crow comes back from where the dinks are. It is the weirdest, coldest sound I have ever heard. It sends chills down my already-cold backbone. I am aware, too, of the sound of other birds in the trees.

Another vulture comes from the other direction and the two birds begin talking to each other. I look at Peacock and he makes a face full of disgust.

"Goddamn, that's gross, man."

"Fuck it, it's only dinks. I don't want to look at the sonofabitches anyway. Let the buzzards eat 'em up."

I hope, almost pray, that there aren't any dinks still alive but wounded so bad they can't move. Watching a bird eat your buddy when you know there is somebody watching you would be the utmost punishment. I'll never be that hard, never think of anything that awful without remorse, of . . . *shit! Quit thinking, Gabe.*

The other three guys begin coming toward us. First Prophet, his Boonie hat low on his forehead and his rifle held high in one hand so he can claw up the cliff with his other. He is mean-looking, soaked through by the rain. His shirt is half undone and the beads around his neck swing silently as he takes giant steps up the trail now. Behind him is Eltee, still good-looking, a red streak of mud covering the front of his ODs, from crawling. He is carrying the radio but its weight doesn't keep him from walking unbelievably erect. Pops comes last, dumpy and rugged. On the way, he picks up a clod of dirt and heaves it and the vultures take off together.

When I was very young, Grandaddy used to make me cry because he said the buzzards would be back for me someday, that I was left on a buzzard stump: *"Lookin' for mushrooms one day and scared a big ol' buzzard outa the creek bed. Said to m'self, 'What would a buzzard be eatin' on down there?' and when I went on down in the creek I see a ol' sycamore stump there and whattaya know? Gabe, you was laying there suckin' your thumb, naked as a buzzard baby. Them buzzards'll be back to get you someday unless you get strong enough to fight 'em off."*

Am I strong enough to fight the buzzards off now? These real ones?

"What do you think the dinks are worried about around here, Eltee?"

"Probably a hospital."

"How close are we to Cambodia?"

"Close."

It is light enough now to feel a little confident. We can see a hundred feet in every direction. We're at a kind of summit. This is the first time we can see the big trail. It doesn't look that much different from the trail we followed up, but most of it is rock instead of mud. There are two sets of boulders between us and the ambush point, instead of one. The rocks are the color of old telephone poles and they're mostly smooth.

"What did Higher-higher say to do when it gets light?"

"Said get a count and call 'em."

"It's light enough to count."

"No, it ain't," Pops says. "If them fuckers were booby-trapped we don't wanna be fuckin' around in this much light."

"How could they be booby-trapped?" Callme asks.

"When they go on these raids, a lot of times they booby-trap themselves, so if one gets wasted and some dumb-ass GI rolls him over, boom, they're even."

"Of if we didn't get 'em all, the other guys might have fixed 'em up last night."

"Shit, we woulda heard 'em."

"Bullshit, you know how good Charlie is, man? Those little fuckers have been ambushing here for twenty years, and their old man before them, fuckin' et cetera and *ad infinitum*," Pea says. He has his professor look.

Even though we're all subdued, Prophet seems especially so. He very often sits a little apart from everybody else like he is now, but he has a kind of nervous energy that usually keeps him doing something. Not this time. He is sullen-looking. His face is colorless, and his gaze wanders from the circle we're sitting in to the jungle without any change of expression. There is something so charismatic about him that he is a kind of spiritual leader of the squad, even though Eltee and Pops outrank him, he's the one we trust; since he is so quiet everybody seems dumbstruck. As if to underscore what I'm thinking, he bums a cigarette from Pea by hand signals and sits smoking it without ever taking it out of his mouth.

The rain has slowed way down but it is chilly. I am debating whether or not to unroll my poncho; it seems like a tardy thing to do since I'm already so wet. There are a lot of bird noises now, mostly high in the canopy. The light is still uncommonly dull, as though there should be fog, but if there is it's so evenly distributed I can't see it. Maybe my eyes are just that tired.

Callmeblack and Peacock are huddled together under one poncho, the grenade launcher sticking out one end and the machine gun out the other. Pops is curled up at my feet. He has his poncho on too, snapped all the way up with the hood tied tight and his hat on top of the hood. It's a classic hat: the brim is shaped like a dried-up leaf. He has all the LZs he has been to written on the hat, probably thirty or more. There's also a calendar that I can't make any sense of, though it's apparent from all the ink that he's been here a long time.

"How long you got, Pops?"

"Jesus Christ, what a thing to ask me. I don't wanna

remember because it'll just make me nervous to think about it. You asshole."

I didn't expect him to jump into my shit and it hurts my feelings, but I had it coming; it was a dumb thing to ask at a time like this. It's hard to think what it'll be like after he's gone.

It is harder to think of what it will be like when *I* am as close as he is. Deep inside of me—no, maybe not so deep —I don't believe I'll make it. Even when I first got orders for Nam I never thought I'd make it if I ever got here. All along, I thought something would happen and somehow I'd get out of coming here.

"Pops, man, I'm sorry, I'm scared, man. I'm an ass-hole."

"Hey, fuck it. Just because you're scared doesn't mean you're an asshole."

"Shut up, you two," Prophet says. There's no insistence in his voice.

"Let's see what we got out there," Peacock says. "The sooner we get it done the sooner we can get back to building our hole."

"I am not ready for this," Eltee says.

"Man, you're the boss. If you ain't ready, what about us?"

"What's the difference?"

"Hey, you're an officer, that's what."

"Back off, Prophet. I'm just a man. I make more money than you do and I've had different training than you guys, and I guess I'm a little older, but I'm muthafuckin' queasy. I grew up in a neighborhood that might make some guys tremble to walk through at night. I've seen bad street fights. My friends have beaten up cops and been beaten up and shot at. . . . I should be one bad-ass fucker. But, listen: I escaped, y'hear? I made it out of the ghetto, I went to college, the whole fuckin' success story, but all that has not a goddamn thing to do with right now. I'm worthless. For

142

two hours I've been trying to keep from screaming. I don't know for sure what I'm afraid of but, dig it, I am fuckin' scared of something, and . . . well, fuck it."

"Sounds like a regular guy, don't he?"

"The way I see it, all we gotta do is get a count and get the fuck outa here so we can get totally fucked up and forget it when we get back to the Z, so the sooner it's over the sooner we can pretend it didn't happen."

"You guys are counting chickens we don't even know are hatched."

"Peacock, what does that mean?"

"Fuck if I know."

●●●●●●●●●●●●

BLOOD.

Like cottage-red paint shot from a fire hydrant, blood everywhere: sprayed all over the leaves and rocks and running in the rainwater that trickles off the rocks. *Jesusfuckinchrist.*

"Oh, muthafucker, they're dead."

"We musta got 'em all."

"Let's go. We're lucky this didn't draw a tiger last night."

As we came up, some rodents scampered away and as we are standing there I look away and meet two little eyes looking at us from under a rock. I feel like I hate the goddamn rodent. I hate everything. There are four dinks. Two of them were cut in half by our claymores. *How goddamn much blood is there in a person?* I might faint. It seems like everything should be still but there are flies by the hundreds and the birds in the canopy are squawking. There must be an animal in the matted grass behind the bodies because there is noise there too. At first I can't identify the other sound I hear; then I realize it is the static of the radio.

I have been breathing fast and I'm sweating, but I can't turn away. The rain is drizzle now, but it seems like it would have washed more blood away. I smell something besides wet jungle, but it doesn't smell dead. *Does blood have a smell of its own? Is that what the vultures smell?* I feel faint again: like my mind is swinging up there in the canopy, like *I'm a vulture seeing us look at the bodies. I see Pops break the silence.*

"Four of 'em. That's all we want to know. Let's go back to the top and call it in. I don't want to stand around here. Pick up the rifles." *And I can see me pick up a gun. When I feel it* my mind comes back to earth. We go back up where our rucks are.

The rifle is an AK. I can't forget the sound after the day Chickenfeed got hit. The rifle is beat to pieces. It only has half the original stock; the back half is a piece of wood with twig marks on it still, carved on the end to fit a shoulder. *Which of the four did it come from?*

"Greenleaf, this is Titbird. How's your copy?"

Pops has the radio up on a rock, and the way he is standing there talking makes me flash on a cop, *downtown Cincinnati*, calling in from a beat box. I feel fuckin' drugged. OK, *this is war, man. This ain't Cincinnati. You're part of this, Gabriel.* Everybody looks the same— empty. Muthafucker, *can this be*? I smell the rifle to see if it was fired last night but there isn't any smell but metal. This ain't the fuckin' movies; you ain't John Wayne. I wonder if it had shot any GIs. It's heavier than my rifle. The ammo clip is curved. The more I stare at the gun the more it looks unreal, toylike. No, it actually looks more real than my plastic M-16 but there is something childish about it. *The fucking thing looks homemade. That carved butt piece, the way it's wired together. Homemade.*

Pops is scooting the radio up the rock now. It occurs to me that I haven't been watching the bush. Eltee gets up and goes to help Pops. He seems to have regained his composure but his face is tightlooking. Peacock is picking his nose with one hand and toothbrushing the feed mechanism of the Sixty with his other.

"We got four rabbits out here. Coming back to your position. Over."

"Titbird, Greenleaf."

"Stand by."

"Them dinks caught our claymores letters-high," Pea says, to nobody in particular.

"Think of how much dinky damage they musta done to the Z."

"Titbird, how's your copy? Over."

"Good copy. Go ahead, dammit."

"Titbird, Higher says cut a chimney, they'll be out. Over."

Prophet angrily slams his hat on his thigh and Pops bangs the microphone with his free hand.

"No way," Pops says to Eltee. "Fuck those lifers. You tell 'em, we can't cut a chimney through that canopy. All they want to do is make sure we counted right, and I ain't fuckin' doing it."

I can't imagine how we could cut a hole, big enough to let a Loach down, and I can't imagine why.

Pops reads my mind.

"They wanna bring a Chieu Hoi out here and see if he can tell what unit the dinks are from."

"There isn't enough left of the four dinks to tell anybody jack-shit."

"Eltee, tell the fuckers to walk out here. We did," Prophet says.

Lieutenant Williams is standing up with his arms folded across the radio. He is rocking back and forth on his heels and toes. He never looks our way. The radio is low-volume static. If I can read Eltee's mind, I know he is torn, tortured, confused. He's going to be caught in the middle.

"Well, do something, for chrissakes. We can't cut 'em a

hole, and we sure as fuck don't want to stay here much longer. Charlie is gonna be looking for these guys."

"Greenleaf, Titbird. Code name William."

"Go, Titbird."

"Greenleaf, too much canopy, too high. We'll bring captured weapons to your papa. These rabbits are in parts. Repeat, in parts. Not enough left for ID. Copy?"

"Code name William, code name Beaver. Wait one."

Pops flips through the code book.

"It's that short red-haired fucker, Billingham."

I didn't know his name, but I figured that's who it was. He's some kind of aide to the colonel and he carries a Car-15. A few days ago I saw his radioman taking his picture. He had a flak jacket and helmet on then, and the asshole probably hasn't ever been to the Bush. This is beginning to get real shitty. I'm becoming afraid again. We blew these guys away and their pals must be around here somewhere. If we don't get going we'll be sitting ducks. I feel my anger and fear mount together. I have a quick fantasy of taking a swing at that fat little fucker.

"Titbird, Greenleaf."

Even the radio seems alive and against us. It must be my fear that makes me think that way all of a sudden. Unfuckin' fair to be out here in the middle of nowhere and scared, talking long-distance and visualizing Billingham sitting in a sandbagged conex telling us to do something we already told him we can't fuckin' do.

"Titbird, it is essential that you provide us a way of identifying your rabbits. Many lives may depend on it."

"Many lives! Our lives are the only ones relevant to them dead dinks; where does he get off giving us a lecture like we're still in The World? This ain't practice. There ain't enough of them dinks left to tell anything. Make the fucker understand they're using us for bait."

Peacock is standing beside Williams now, struggling to keep his voice under control. Eltee looks at him blankly, puts a hand on his back, then pushes his own helmet back on his head. Eltee looks five years older than he did yesterday, and he looks confused.

"Oh, fucker . . ." Callme moans.

Prophet has been sitting with his elbows on his knees, looking away from us. Now he looks up at the canopy and shakes his head.

"Greenleaf, code name William, over."

"Go."

"I repeat. No can do."

"Titbird, that's affirm. Transport your rabbits to Checkpoint Bravo. Out."

No! *Bullshit*. I'm dreaming. Or is this a movie?

Peacock slumps down into the mud and begins stabbing at it with his knife. He is soon using both hands to stab with. He's nuts. I feel crazy too. Everybody else *looks* crazy. Eltee lets the microphone drop against the rock and stands staring at us. He looks like he's trying to get his mind to work.

"OK—" he starts.

"OK, so let's go to Bravo and they can fuckin' walk back up here without us. We'll tell 'em right where the ambush is."

"Listen up," Eltee says. "This is some real bullshit, but there's no alternative."

"No alternative? Let's just fuckin' refuse to do it."

"Pops, you're a short-timer. If we don't do it we're all guilty of disobeying a direct order and we're all going to get court-martialed. You know that. Not just me. They'd bust us, send us all to jail, then send us back out here, and that jail time is bad time. You won't rotate out of here until *next* year. Think about it."

Pops's face is stretched round with red anger. He looks like he's ready to explode. I expect an outburst, but instead he slumps down to his knees and turns his face upward to let the silent rain hit him. He sighs.

"Eltee is right," Peacock says.

"If we're gonna do it, let's do it. We'll get even with them fuckin' Higher-highers," Prophet says.

Lieutenant Williams looks at him and opens his mouth but doesn't say anything.

"You never heard me say that, Eltee, for your own good. We like you and I know what you're thinking, but just forget it. You're one of us, for now."

Jesus, this is escalating. I don't know for sure what Prophet is saying, but his tone is severe and he isn't about ready to back down from anything the Eltee can offer.

"I won't hump no dead guy," Callme says.

"Dinks don't weigh much," Pea says.

Callmeblack makes his big black hand into a big black fist and drives it into his wadded-up poncho. Then he half buries his face in the poncho and either sobs or sighs.

Dear Dad: You won't belive this. Dear Brother Bob: Go to Canada. Dear President Johnson: Could you do this? Dear God: For my mother's sake, numb me. (Fucking jail! . . . Everybody knows the horror stories about military prisons, especially in The Nam). There's nothing fair about some Army officer three kilometers away telling us to obey this insane order or go to jail. But why should I expect fairness? I'm in the Army, and the Army is in a war. It's simple. I don't have any choice.

So I'm the first one to move. I stand up and unroll my poncho. I'm conscious of the rest of them watching me but I don't look at them.

"Are we supposed to call 'em when we get there?"

"Yeah," Prophet says, "call 'em and say send a taxi after we dragged the muthafuckin' corpses all the way through this damn jungle while they meanwhile sit back there getting dug in, then fly out to meet us."

He stands and is talking loud but not yelling.

"Then, goddammit, then they'll turn that helicopter around and we'll goddamn have to walk back too!"

"Those hardcore Shake-and-Bake officers don't even think about us killing these poor bastards, let alone have to haul around what's left. They probably *can't* think of it, just have wet dreams about being a hero when they get home."

We're psyching ourselves up. Everybody but Peacock is getting ready now. Eltee already has his ruck on. He goes over to Callme and squats alongside him. They don't even say anything but I can see Callme's courage—or whatever it is—coming back. I feel a little jealous of Eltee right now. I'm ready. My ruck doesn't feel so heavy and I'm not as tired as I was before it got light.

"Pray for luck," Peacock says. "If Charlie is around here close and sees this mess, you know he ain't gonna goddamn worry about big guns out here. He's gonna have our shit on a stick. He'll be hawking my goddamn watch in Hanoi if he knows what we're carrying and just happens to see us clod-hoppin' American boys here in his jungle. Them lifers think about the wrong things, that's all. They call the war by numbers. They're gonna say them four dinks only had one arm anyway, so we really blew eight away."

"Peacock," Pops says, "I never heard you be so right."

"Man, I'm just talking to keep from seeing, because seeing is believing."

"That's more like your old self, you asshole. That doesn't make any sense."

Jesus the flies.

We have two sets of ponchos snapped into pairs and are going to gather the bodies onto the ponchos, then split the weight up so four guys can carry the two slings. Even then, two guys will have to hump the radio, the machine gun, and the extra weapons, so really we'll be fuckin'-A useless if anything happens. Prophet goes to look for the best way by himself; we want to keep him as light as we can because he will be walking point. When he leaves, the rest of us go back to the site together. The flies are so loud I hear them from behind the first set of rocks, ten meters away.

We spread the ponchos out. Nobody talks. At first we all stand still. Then Callmeblack begins humming "Swing Low, Sweet Chariot" and Pops drags most of a body onto one of the ponchos. The guts drag along between the body's legs. The flies swarm in one extra-loud sound and land again when the body is on the poncho. Pops goes off from us a bit.

Right at my feet is an arm. It's short but it looks like what there is is almost all of what there ever was, like it came off at the shoulder. There are green flies around its bloody end. Callme is still humming and has tossed a couple pieces onto the poncho. I pick the arm up by the unbloody hand and it is like shaking hands with a snake. I'm careful not to touch the fingers. I fling the arm onto the pile that must be most of two guys now. Or women. Pops is back, white and old-looking.

Callmeblack sits down and spits a lot between his boots, but doesn't puke. The head that had been hanging by a thread of skin onto the body Pops carried is between Callmeblack and me and we both see it at the same time. It is most of a face, but half of it is turned into the muddy trail so it looks like a mask except for the flies. Callmeblack and I both look at it and then at each other and he looks back between his boots and half spits, half retches. I kick the head good; the face sails a foot off the ground and lands at the top of the pile, then rolls over the top. I'm glad it doesn't end up looking at me.

Eltee and Pops are about to fold the poncho over their pile and tie it shut.

"Let's be damn sure they're about the same weight."

"I pretended I was splitting a hundred pounds of Cambodian Red weed, man. I eyeballed it like I didn't know which half was mine, I—"

"OK, OK, OK. Shut up."

Peacock looks hurt. His tattoo is showing. I don't think it's raining. I think what is coming down is dripping off the canopy. Peacock's face is an eggshell color. In fact the light is all like that, the color of a dirty white dog.

●●●●●●●●●●●

I TAKE AS MUCH AIR INTO MY LUNGS AS I CAN. I WALK second, behind Prophet, who is carrying one of the captured rifles. Peacock has the other end of the poncho; then Pops and Callmeblack carrying the other sling, and Eltee is walking last. We tried slinging the weight on vines, in hopes that it would be easier carrying, but that didn't work because the trail is so sharp in places that the vines were too long to turn without the lead guy having to stop and turn around. So I twist the corners of the poncho together and use both hands to shoulder my end. Prophet helped me sling my rifle with shoelaces so it at least hangs in front of me and will be possible to get at, if it comes to that.

Eltee stays quite a ways back from the rest of us. Incredibly, he has the radio, the Sixty, and an extra rifle, and he has to pull rear security. I can't breathe normally—it's more like taking a gulp of air in and walking until it's used up, then gasping again, like I've swum too far away from shore. The going is slow and seems noisy. For a while we walk on a fairly level trail and our footing is solid, but the weight gets to us and we have to rest. When we set the poncho down the flies all seem to catch up and swirl into the holes between the snaps on the ponchos. The blood still isn't dried, so when I pick up the knot that makes my handle the blood squeezes out, and some runs down my arms.

After fifteen minutes my back begins to throb. Trying to walk mostly downhill now and still trying to keep the poncho fairly level to make it easier on Peacock strains my muscles and makes me aware of the spots I slept on last night. I'm constantly gasping for breath, and the bag keeps swinging, so I have to struggle to keep my balance. I come to the edge of my endurance. I want to cuss and throw something. I want to destroy. Finally, the slippery knot comes out of my grasp and the sling falls. Without looking back, because I am so goddamn out of touch, I keep walking, dragging the poncho behind me. It slides easily enough through the mud and makes a small sound like a brake rubbing against a bicycle tire. We don't go on like that very long before Prophet stops us and points at a swale below: Checkpoint Bravo. I simply fall down, gasping so hard I wonder if it's possible to catch up on the air I'm missing. I lie there with my eyes closed, listening to the others catching their breath and the buzzing of the flies.

It is almost as though I am asleep momentarily, because the sound of the flies begins to sound like a song. Honest to God: song. I hear snatches of nursery rhymes, and church choirs and classical music, and the ditty that is the commercial for life insurance. . . . When my breathing gets closer to normal the smell of reality fights its way back, and once again the predominant sound is that of the blood-thirsty flies swarming. I could puke in my own lap and it wouldn't make any difference right now.

From a sitting position I can see cleanly through the foliage. Checkpoint Bravo is a small, almost round, hollow. It looks marshy. Instead of jungle it looks like tall grass. I wonder how deep the water is. My breath has come back now. I see that one of the arms has worked its way partly out from the bundled poncho. I'll be damned if I'm going to touch it again to shove it back in. I don't care if it gets lost.

Eltee is making radio contact; otherwise there isn't any sound except for the goddamn flies. It takes skill to use an Army PRC-25 radio so that it isn't like hearing a super-market speaker, and Williams is good enough that I can barely hear the transmissions from five meters away. I semi-want to smoke a cigarette, but my hands smell like the blood that is drying black now. I try to think of what it resembles, having squeezed out of the poncho, but it doesn't look like anything but what it is. Thinking about carrying these pieces of dinks to a helicopter landing in a small clearing makes the fear come hard, but who is there to tell I'm scared, and what good would it do?

"Wait till we hear the birds coming," Eltee says. "Pass it on."

We whisper it ahead and Prophet nods. His face is rock-hard and dirty. The way the light is hitting his face I can see the rivulets of sweat running over the wax we use to camouflage our faces. He must have mostly used the stick of green. I used brown. The camo sticks are precious; it is one more thing the Army never has enough of. Prophet sits quietly looking around all 360 degrees, spitting silently between his teeth. I'm glad the rain has quit, at least for now; I'm still cold, or shivering from fear. It isn't long before we hear the helicopters coming. We don't want to give our position away any sooner than we absolutely have to, so we don't move until the birds are in sight. As high up as they stay, their sound is no louder than the noise of the flies. Everybody chambers a round, ready to pick up the ponchos for the last time.

"Pray, baby," Peacock whispers. I nod. I do. I breathe as deeply as I can.

The clearing is a shade different in color than everything else around, darker green. From this distance, it looks like briars, but I've never seen briars over here. I can tell the grass is too tall for a bird to come down in, that we'll have to hack some of it away. My question is what we're going to do with these fucking bodies in the meantime.

Eltee is working his way up the line, whispering to everybody as he goes by. It strikes me as absurd, although not stupid, for him to be whispering. I don't know, maybe he isn't whispering: it's as though all I can hear are the goddamn flies, like a radio station off the air for the night

—a low *hummmzaat*. As Williams moves up he walks hunchback to carry the weight of the radio and his ruck. My ruck straps cut into me all the way down the trail but I didn't notice the ache much until now. Fuck it. All we have to do is get these slings another thirty meters, cut a hole, and catch a ride back to the LZ.

Before I know it Eltee is at my side.

"We're about ready to move," he says. His face is like a clock, so exact is the intensity of his expression. I notice his nose looks wider on one side than the other. I listen to what he says, and it seems to echo through my mind even after he's gone. We'll be up and move fast. We're dropping the ponchos on signal. Three of us go out for security and the other three hack a hole in the weeds, good enough for a bird to come down long enough to pick up the pieces; when that bird is gone another will come in to get us. I'm going to be one who cuts.

My mouth feels like I've been sucking a rubber band. The nylon pads in my shoulder straps look freshly painted, and I feel conscious of every one of the five hundred more seconds we sit there. Eltee is still up front with Prophet. I can see them both through a hole in the trees. Eltee is talking on the radio some of the time. First one of their faces shows in the hole, then the other—like watching TV.

We're up. I get the signal from Prophet and pass it on to Peacock, who passes it on. Now we pick up the sling. Heavy. This time I'm very conscious of my rifle swinging in front of me. I've gotten used to having it in my hand when I want it, and right now I want it.

We hustle. Everything hurts—my back, my head where the steel pot has bounced, my arms from having the sling behind me, my feet, my chafing asshole, even my goddamn eyes from sleeplessness. I hurt inside too. I feel like a piece of shit, like nobody. But on we go. In five minutes we're into the swamp. The water is quickly up to my shins, finally up to my balls. It doesn't feel warm or cold, not thick or clean, just wet and one more thing to fight against. We drop the poncho and it half sinks. The flies are there, like they're pissed off. They swirl in a wave like paint flung off a roller. I *hate* them. Air escapes from the poncho and comes to the surface, and the water turns the color of aged leather from the mud we stir up and the blood.

By pure luck, we stumble upon a hard bottom so we can stand up and hack away at the bushes exactly at water level. It's me, Prophet, and Peacock. We don't speak. We give it hell, our machetes swirling. The bushes are mostly easy to cut, and it doesn't take long to hack a ten-foot by ten-foot hole down to the waterline, and it isn't long after that that the bird arrives.

It comes over the tree line like a hotrod cresting some country hill, then settles over us with the motion that only helicopters have, a gliding sort of motion, with its tail swerving from side to side. The machine gunners give us a long peace sign. We half carry, half float the ponchos over. It takes four of us to get them out of the water and into the bird. As we're loading the second, trying to keep the chopped-up grass and water out of our eyes and struggling to keep our footing, rounds begin pelting the windshield of the helicopter and either the pilot or the copilot gets hit. I dive into the water and weeds and futilely try to keep my rifle up.

Rounds begin to richochet all over hell. The gunners open up, firing directly over our heads into the tree line. The shell casings come off the gun in a perfect arc, and some of them land on the grass we have cut that floats on the water. I'm disoriented and afraid to fire because I don't know where anybody else is, but I get my safety off and try to be careful to keep the barrel pointed up while I work my way, staying oh-so-low, away from where the bird is. I glance quickly at it and I can see the gunner taking the vibration of his gun with exact concentration. There is scurrying behind him and either the other gunner or a crew chief is leaned into the cockpit, probably aiding the pilot. I catch sight of Peacock, who has his Sixty at shoulder height. He is pouring rounds out toward the tree line.

The helicopter gets up and hovers for only an instant before it banks slightly and takes off away from the tree line we're facing. It circles and comes back over, low, stirring up the water and cut weeds. It passes over the tree line and both gunners fire continually. Then it comes back again and keeps a steady stream of rounds slashing into the tree line.

Eltee is yelling and signaling to make a circle. He has the radio mike in his hand. His rifle is slung downward and the AK is strapped to the radio. Prophet and Callme come out of the weeds behind him and run as best they can through the water until they reach the edge of our cut. Pops and I begin making it toward the cleared spot from opposite sides. Pops's face is covered with blood. I can't tell if he has been hit or not. Just as I get to where I intend to stop there is an explosion a few meters on the other side of Peacock, then another one, then two more. Mortars. The bursts hit the swamp in tandems now. First, two beyond us; then two in front of us. Peacock is trying to move back to our position but he has to get down every time a mortar lands. They bracketed, and have the range on those tubes now, so I expect the next rounds to come right on top of us. The helicopter is still hanging above the tree line, blasting it.

Four more mortars. The first two are off target but the second ones land almost right on top of Lieutenant Williams, maybe twenty meters away from me on the other side of the clearing. He screams. The wave of water from the mortar's concussion passes by me and there is still shit in the air. Pops slips out of his ruck and begins to work his way toward Eltee. Everybody else begins to pump rounds into the tree line. I fire about where the helicopter is working out because I thought I saw a muzzle flash come from somewhere near there. As I am looking I see one for sure, a few feet off the ground. I squeeze three or four rounds off at where I saw it, then have to change magazines and when I look up again, the spot is being torn apart by the bird's Sixties. I cheer to myself. *Kill the fuckers*. I expect more mortars any time.

Pops is coming back toward us. He has the radio in one hand and is dragging Eltee behind him in a sort of backward-walking fireman's carry. Eltee is no longer screaming. A second helicopter comes over the opposite tree line. Eltee is dead.

The first helicopter continues working on the tree line and the second one comes at us rapidly. We all make a break for it. I go to Pops to help him. Together, we manage to get to the bird with our gear and the body. He didn't live past the scream. More than half of that handsome black face has been ripped back toward his skull. As long as the body was in the water the blood didn't show much, but when we are loaded and drag the body in after us, a pool of blood the color of fire spreads across the floor. We're all in, we're up, we head away from the tree line, high above which the bird with the ponchos full of bodies now hovers. Exhaustion hits and my body feels like a wet paper bag.

Jesus, there's no way to describe the ride. We get up fast, over a set of mountains, then up again. Riding along on the vibration of the bird is like being wind-rocked in a hammock. The five of us are sitting toward the front. I am leaning against the aluminum wall that defines the cockpit; the machine gunner is between me and the open door; past him I can see a patch of sky and beyond that mountains, mountains, mountains.

The sound of the rotor is steady: *rum thump thump rum thump thump*.

God, I stink. I've been sweating into these same clothes for at least ten days; I've been wallowing around in swamp water.

My mind just roams around like my eyes. The door gunner on my side is dark-complexioned and stocky. His mustache is trimmed and just a dab of black hair shows below the headset helmet. The back of his helmet has something painted on it but I can't read it. Across from me, against the wall on the other side of the doorway to the cockpit, Pops is slumped in a heap. He's filthy. There is a line of mud that runs from the top of his head, over his face and through his mustache, through the hair on his belly, and down to his pants. His shirt is unbuttoned and his flak jacket isn't hooked. Just a trace of a paunch hangs over the belt loops. He looks thinner now than he did just a month ago.

The others are leaning against whatever there is to lean against, and toward the back is Eltee's body. I stare at it, and it doesn't seem like he could be dead. I can't see his head that is half mincemeat now and I can't really believe he will never move again. Dead. Goddamn dead. It could've been anybody. He got a mortar; the dinks weren't going for the radio and they weren't going for him because he was an officer. They were just going for anybody and trying to disable the helicopters. I wonder who will have to write a report up on this mission, and I wonder what Lieutenant Williams's family will find out.

Thump rump kathump kathump. We are descending. I have to sit up straight to see the Z below us and I feel so tired. As we come down we scoot toward the door. It isn't easy because the bird isn't level and the ruck seems to weigh more than ever. I'm so tired. I just want to lie down. It seems like there should be more waiting for us than this goddamn hill full of holes. This, my man, is home for now. Eltee doesn't even have this.

Fifty feet up, then thirty. It's like working on a high, high ladder. The guys on the ground all move away from the pad and cover their eyes. Parts of C-ration cartons whirl up as high as we are and dive through the crazy air currents like bats going after insects in a porch light. All the dudes on the ground are wearing flak jackets, and a lot of them have helmets on. The landing pad is built out of sandbags, and from a few feet up it reminds me of a caned chair seat. We settle between two big slings of ammunition. After the bird shuts down to a low speed, guys start again at unloading the slings and carrying the ammo away. Most of it is for our mortars and artillery. The rounds come in wooden boxes about two feet long.

Over by the big guns are stacks of ammo crates, and guys are carrying these empties away to fill full of sand and build hooches.

The CO comes over to the bird with his face down. He is a stern-looking guy, maybe thirty years old. His expression isn't meanlooking but it sure as hell isn't joyful. He reaches up and helps us off the bird, just puts his hand under our rucks. When he helps me off he is already looking at whoever is behind me.

"There's coffee over there," he says to all of us. "I want to see the whole squad in a few minutes."

We all drop our rucks as soon as we're far enough away from the pad. Getting the ruck off is like taking a good shit. It's cloudy and there's dust in the air from something. Since we've been out, there have probably been a couple thousand sandbags filled. Some are laid into flat parapet walls and some of the hooches are getting to be deep enough for roofs. Ammo crates and full sandbags make squat, solid walls.

Most of three companies are on the Z now and it has spread out like a carnival parking lot. When we started to dig in, we were on the outside of the perimeter but now the perimeter has moved out in all directions.

There are two guys sitting near the coffeepot smoking and waiting for us. They have been humping ammo from the pad.

"Hey, what it is."

"It is a muthafucker," Pops says. It seems like a long time since I have heard his voice.

"You guys the squad that got some dinks last night?"

"Yeah, four. How bad was it here?"

"Bad, man. Mostly incoming, but they almost broke through on the other side of the hill. Over there." The guy points to our right.

"Charlie put some shit in here last night," the other guy says. He emphasizes "put" by pounding his rifle's butt plate against the ammo crate he has his feet resting on.

"Eighty-twos?"

"Mostly."

"He was keying on that side of the hill. We were over there, the other side, and everything went over us, wounded one guy out on LP. Alpha Company got it the worst. I heard six KIAs and twenty wounded."

"Our Eltee ate an eighty-two round."

"Dead?"

"Fuckin'-A dead."

"Anybody else get hit?"

"Nope. Freaky. We were loading those goddamn dinks and Charlie walked about a dozen rounds in."

"Bravo Company is going to move out that direction."

"You guys from Bravo?"

"Yeah. We aren't even dug in, but they keep trying to stick us on ammo detail."

"Well, man, Charlie's out there. Even though it musta been bad here last night, I'd rather be here tonight."

"Dig it, but at least our whole company's going out."

I'm surprised the coffee tastes good. C-ration coffee sucks; this came from a big urn shaped like a fire hydrant. There are some shit-green food cans lined up behind the coffee, but it looks like the food must have come in sometime yesterday because some of the cans have shrapnel in them. After I get my coffee I sit down on a pile of sandbags that have been filled but not tied off yet. I can see the bad side of the Z, where there must be twenty shallow craters. The thing I didn't expect to see is the shrapnel holes everywhere and even a few pieces of shrap. There's none nearby but I can see it glint in the sun in a few paths.

Big guns sound somewhere. I wonder what time it is. The sun is still a little above the west ridge of mountains. I'd guess it will be dark in four hours. I wonder if these guys from Bravo are going to try to get dug in tonight. I look at them and try to see the fear that I know is somewhere in their faces.

One guy is Italian-looking. He is sitting on one of the melomite cans, sipping coffee from his canteen cup.

"Eltee didn't have a shot at it," Callme says.

I don't feel like saying anything. I helped float his body through the water. I flash on the body over there in the bird in a pool of blood. The CO is just starting back from the pad. Even though there isn't any dust flying now, he still walks with his face down. Somebody is leaning into the helicopter. Slowly, the rotor starts to turn, and when the CO gets to us the bird is starting off. We all have to shield ourselves from the shit that flies around. When I look up, the CO is looking at Peacock, who's still looking down. So the CO looks right at me.

"What's your name, soldier?"

"Gabriel Sauers, sir."

"Tell me about it."

"About the patrol?"

"Yeah, from the time you made contact."

"Well . . ." I don't know what to say. Talking to an officer always bothers me. Eltee was an officer though, too. "Well," I say again, "it all happened awful fast. We were set up on a trail, and me and Callme were pretty close together and the rest of them were spread out. Peacock was ahead of us with the Sixty. We heard them coming and somebody blew the claymores. I could see the explosion

161

and action. I emptied a clip and reloaded. That's all I know."

"Did you hear anything afterwards?"

"Nothing, sir."

"Who's the squad leader?"

"I am," Pops says. He doesn't add "sir."

"What's your name, Sergeant?"

"Pops," he says. He has undone his pants and is standing there talking to the CO with his dick out, rubbing one finger all around the jungle rot on his balls. I notice the CO has rot too, on his neck.

"You have anything to add, Pops?"

"I don't think Eltee Williams should be dead."

"What are you saying, soldier?"

"I think somebody fucked up back there. Those dinks were in pieces no bigger than these damn sandbags and there was no reason to bring 'em back here, but we hadda goddamn carry 'em down the fuckin' hill and into that clearing. Any-fuckin'-body woulda known the dinks were gonna drop some shit in there, but if we coulda got right in and right out of the edge of it, then Eltee wouldn't have gotten fuckin' killed. They walked 'em right in on us."

"Sergeant, your squad killed four enemies who might be responsible for killing ten GIs. That's what you have to think of. And"—he puts his hand on Pops's hand, which is still on his nuts, and looks around at all of us—"I understand how you feel. There's nothing I can do about it. Echo Company didn't make the decision, you know that. Listen, I *know* how you feel."

The way he says it, the way he looks around at all of us with a tiny little frown, the way he gives Pops's ball-handling wrist an additional shake . . . something makes me think he *does* know how Pops feels, and probably how I feel even if I don't. I feel something in my throat. Prophet spits, Callme spits, Peacock spits. The CO turns to leave and spits. I spit.

POINT

Isn't there something about pride on all the recruiting posters? Or is that the Marines? Well, maybe the Marines would look proud now somehow, but our squad doesn't, walking to our section of the hill. Pops can barely drag himself along ahead of me, his ruck hung on one shoulder, his rifle skimming along the mud, held by his bloody hand. Me, I feel like I weigh more than I should. My legs are rubbery; it's hard to breathe. A medium rain is falling, and it is cold. Everywhere is red mud and puddles of ugly water. Anything that can glisten glistens—the wet side of the pile of ammo boxes, that part of our metal equipment that isn't covered by mud, Pops's neck.

Nothing has changed since we left. Our holes are still only knee-deep, and there are still bundles of empty sandbags tied together. Most of the bundles are haphazardly scattered in the mud. The hole that Prophet and I started digging has water in its deep side. The water is clear except for where part of the bank is caving in, forming a red-brown rivulet. We drop our rucks almost simultaneously and sit on them, nobody saying anything, digging through our rucks to find a cigarette dry enough to burn. We're all dumb and tired and slow; we've been too close to the bullets. Our platoon leader is dead. *Godammit*, I keep telling myself, everything that has happened has happened.

Four dead gooks—but no pride. I want to go to sleep and wake up to find out it was a dream.

The sun peeks through a little. The radio is on low. I sort of nod out and, although I can hear everything, I float back to sometime in my life when I was sick. When my mother's boys were sick they slept in the sun-room, underneath a special quilt that was sewn out of pretty feed sacks, the "sick quilt." When I come out of my reverie, looking over the jungled mountains that are patched with shadows reminds me of the sick quilt. The feeling I have is something like *waking up in the sun-room with the quilt over me, not knowing whether I like being sick or not.* I am mostly grown up now, Mom. I've been in snatches of a war. If I get it tomorrow, you can cover me with a flag.

The static and low-volume traffic on the radio irritates me. It isn't necessary to have it on anymore. I get up and turn it off. The radio has been pierced by shrapnel; there are holes through the canvas bag around its bottom, and a piece shaped like a church key is stuck near where the aerial comes out, pointed end down. I wonder if shrapnel ever sticks halfway into a person's face, or if it always burrows out of sight.

Our side of the LZ is opposite the landing pad, so the helicopter turbulence doesn't reach us. Without moving my head, I can see three of them circling the hill, waiting for an opening on the pad. One is a Shithook with ammo slung beneath it, and the other two are Slicks. Their sound intermixes and the noise is like standing next to a bulldozer engine that isn't running right. I let myself fade off again and the sound softens—more now like something electric, maybe a milling-machine motor.

Prophet gets down into the hole but doesn't do anything. He simply stares into the jungle. He is a little hunched over and turned away from me. He has on his flak jacket and fatigue pants and only one boot. The other red boot sits beside his rucksack with an ammo bandolier stuffed into its top. The boots should be bronzed. The one by his ruck is torn alongside the strip of leather than runs to the heel. Originally the leather was black and the canvas was OD, but now the whole boot is the same color, the color of wet old wood, but redder. It is appropriate that the bootlaces are brand new. One thing the Army has lots of is bootlaces. My rifle still has its bootlace sling. Prophet is wearing half a dozen laces around his neck. I'm still fascinated by how *everyone* wears something around his neck; Prophet wears all those bootlaces, one dog tag, and a peace symbol. His other dog tag must be tied to his left boot; I can't see.

"Pops," he says, "what say we all work on one hole again tonight, try and get one deep enough that we can get something over it and a couple-three of us can stay in it."

"Yeah. You and Gabe dig and we'll fill sandbags."

With all five of us working for a straight hour we get the hole down to our waists. The first few shovels are a hassle because of the water and mud, but once we get to drier dirt we move steadily down. We all seem to find a second wind and it lasts about an hour. Since the hole is waist-deep and the sandbag walls are a foot high I can stand in the hole and lean on the wall. Artillery or mortars are burning up spare powder charges and the smell is raw. It stings.

Three Squad is digging on the other side of a bunch of rocks. Four Squad and One are out on humps. Every so often somebody from Three will pass by on his way to the water trailer and they all ask about last night, but the facts are enough. Nobody wants to hear the whole story. The news has gotten around. A couple of guys say something about Eltee Williams. Since he went out with all four squads at times, everybody in the platoon knew him.

Peacock and Callme are digging now and throwing the dirt up to Pops, who is quietly filling sandbags by himself. He keeps a cigarette going all the time and his head is tilted away from the smoke; he holds the sandbag with one hand

and uses the little shovel like a trowel. His Boonie hat is wet from sweat, perched on his curly hair like a bent-up kettle lid. I wonder what will become of the hat when he gets home. Prophet is coming up the hill with two bundles of sandbags. He has taken his flak jacket off and put his other boot back on.

The rain has stayed steady. The trail Prophet is walking is mud to the top of his boots, and more than once he goes down to his knees. I walk fifty feet and take one of the bundles. Walking through the mud is like going through a pile of leaves, except it sucks at my feet, so my legs are worn out by the time I get back. I let the bundle of bags drop off my shoulder and it half buries itself with a sound like a quart of paint turning over off a ladder.

I expect us to get hit again tonight. The sun is down to the top of the western range of mountains and the sky around it is very yellow. There's a cloud like a banana peel. We have three ponchos stretched across the top of the hole and the other two laid on the bottom. Our only night duty will be pulling an LP about fifty meters straight downhill: easy walking, easy duty. Callme and I go down with an empty ammo crate and dig a trench. Since there hasn't been as much activity downhill it isn't quite as muddy, but still, as we dig in the last light, the uphill side of the trench keeps falling in.

Dark comes fast, like it always seems to over here. When we get back to the hole we have a sort of roof-raising party. The rain has slowed down just a little, and the sound of it hitting the rubber poncho is like that of a hundred little Ping-Pong balls. Pops has saved some chocolate fudge from last time we got mail, and he breaks it out as we are all five sitting in the hole with a sealing-wax candle going, a couple of bowls of dope in us. The fudge is wrapped in wax paper and shaped like a pile of dog shit. It has been wet and crushed and wet again. Water runs out of the wax package when he opens it but we cheer anyway. He cuts it into five equal parts with his bayonet.

"I couldn't eat all this myself before I go home," he says.

"If I was going home in three weeks, fatman, I wouldn't eat *any*."

"The fuck you wouldn't."

"You know, that pussy back in The World is used to good ol' draft-dodgin' dick by now. Clean dicks."

"I'll worry about it when I get back there, homes, and I'll send you a picture of the first woman to get hold of this starved but sturdy hurdy-gurdy."

"What's a hurdy-gurdy?"

"An *organ* grinder," Pops says. His eyes are full of life and a long-gone smile makes his face look cherubic in the candlelight.

"Pops, you made out your souvenir list?"

"Yeah. I ain't leaving nobody nuthin'."

"What you gonna do with that beat-up ol' ugly Boonie hat in The World?"

His smile comes fast again, and he takes the cigarette out of his mouth like he is Franklin Roosevelt.

"Troops, when I get back home I'm gonna take my GED, and I'm gonna pass, and I'm gonna go to the school prom in May, and I'm gonna wear this here hat."

He will, too.

The night comes and goes. No incoming, not even much H&I from our guns. The next morning I can't believe I've been asleep so long. I pulled middle guard and fell asleep outside the hole before our relief even got up to go downhill, so I slept on a bed made from my ruck and a bundle of bags. When I woke, at first I had one of those moments of disorientation, small panic. It was still early, and about the only activity was a few guys shaving down by the water trailer.

I draw water into my steel pot and splash a little over

my face and neck. There's a guy standing behind me scratching around his rot.

"Morning."

"Yeah."

"You with Two Squad?"

"Yeah."

"Hit some shit, eh?"

"Yeah."

"I'm in Artillery, call me Snake." He is thin but broad-shouldered, about as tall as I am. He has a big-city accent. When I move away from the water buffalo, he moves to the spigot and takes just enough water to fill his canteen cup. Then he dips two fingers into the cup and all he washes is around both eyes. He sees me staring.

"All I give a shit about most of the time is keeping the dust out of my eyes," he says. "I spend most of my time sitting up there reading or sighting in the guns, so I figure all I need to take care of is my eyes."

"Dig it. By the way, how'd you know I was in Two?"

"I didn't, just guessed. But I did notice you come from that direction." He points, and the upraised arm releases a smell like spoiled beans.

I've got my mirror propped up on the wall of sandbags around the trailer and I take a few swipes at my face with the razor, just to get the rough stuff. "Keep your head down," Snake says. "You guys come on up the hill and party with us some night."

After everybody is awake a shower comes, so we sit in the hole and wait it out. It lasts about an hour. The water runs down the walls, and before it is over there is two inches of water in the bottom of the hole again. We play some cards and listen to the radio, but mostly we huddle as best we can to try and stay dry. The worst thing that happens is that I lean against the wall and get a sizable chunk of the red mud down my neck. My shirt is hanging outside on a shovel handle, and I had put my flak jacket on to keep warmer. The mud pisses me off; part of it runs down my back to my asshole, but the small rocks and sand stay up on my neck where my flak jacket rubs. The best thing that happens is Pops wins fifteen dollars in a game of In Between. Playing cards with MPC is like playing Monopoly, but for a guy who soon goes home, the MPC is the real shit.

"Nineteen days and a wakeup," he says, scooping in the money, "and this funny money will be greenbacks. If I do say so myself, it couldn't happen to a nicer guy."

"Fuck you, short-timer."

"Man, dig it: I am so short I'm going to need a circumcision just to keep my dick from dragging on the ground."

When it quits raining the sun comes out. The ground steams. First it is cool but in another hour it is hot. The medic comes by with our malaria pills and a whole bottle of salt tablets. If everything went right, we could have some of our roof beams on before dark. I feel pretty good. I wonder how long we're going to stay on this LZ, how long before we hump out again.

We dig all day. The hole gets to be five feet deep and the double-thick walls get five layers high, so Peacock, Prophet, and Callme go out after overhead and Pops and I begin to cut in the stairs.

All Pops has on are his OD shorts and his hat. He's been smoking dope all day and does some dumb-ass things; he makes one step two feet high. A runner comes to say there is a squad leaders' meeting with the CO, so when he leaves I start at the outside of the stairs to make one more step and reduce the big one. Callme's cassette is going; it's in the hole, sitting on an ammo crate, wired to the radio battery: the Beatles, "Happiness Is a Warm Gun." I feel OK. The other guys come back with a log that is twice as long as it has to be, so I quit on the steps and start cutting the log in two while they go out for another one.

A little guy comes walking by with clean fatigues on. He asks me if I'm from Two Squad and pulls out a letter.

"I just got back from R and R," he says, "and I met a guy in transit who told me to give this to you guys."

"Big guy? Hit in the shoulder?"

"Yeah. Partying dude. I met him down in Cam Ranh. I guess he was on his way up to another hospital. He seemed OK but he's all bandaged up."

"Great. Thanks, man."

It is written on USO stationery.

Hey, fuckers. Nuthin' but round-eyed pussy here. They're sending me to the hospital in Qui Nhon. I'm fine, but I'm going to sham away all the time I can. If I get down below thirty days there's no way in hell I'm coming back out there so I'll let you know where I'll be and you can look me up when you come through for R&R or whatever. Right now I can't move my fingers, guess it got some nerves somewhere, but the medics say there's a good chance it can be fixed. Hope you guys ain't hittin' any shit. I read *Stars and Stripes* to see if there are any names I recognize in the KIA section. Peacock, you can have my white underwear. Prophet, keep my extra waterproof (which I know you were going to anyway). Pops, I'll see you back in The World—I got your folks' address. One thing you might not know, they cut Chickenfeed's leg off. I ran across a guy who knew him. He said Chicken busted up a ward in Japan. You ain't gonna believe this but I kinda miss it out there, it's all chickenshit back here, like Stateside Army. But I won't be back if I can help it. Keep your heads down. Bull.

I bump the bowl when I go down into the hole to flip the cassette over and it makes me lazy immediately. The music sounds good. My mind wanders and an image comes of school kids walking home with their lunch boxes. It is a curious thing to be thinking about but it is very pleasant to sit in the cool dark hole and imagine being high above the sidewalk, painting a soffit, seeing kids come home from school. Already, I can't remember my phone number. Eight and a half more months. In order to avoid the home-sickness I go back to hacking the log in two.

I give Bull's letter to Pops when he comes back, and he reads it without saying anything. Then he pulls a brown bottle out of his fatigue pocket.

"What's that?"

"Peroxide. Got it from the medics."

"What's it for?"

"It's a short-timer's trick, man. I'll wash my face with it every day from now on and whamo—Mr. Clean. Zit re-mover." It foams when he pours it onto a piece of C-ration toilet paper.

"Any news from Higher-higher?"

"The fuckers are gonna send the squad out either tomor-row or the next day. Right back where we were. And they're gonna bust me."

"Say what?"

"They're taking a stripe, but I could give a shit. I told 'em how fucked up it was to bring them dinks back."

"Fuck it, man. So you'll get out a Four instead of Five."

"Three. I ain't going back into the Bush, so they'll probably take another one."

It's going to be different out there without him. It's going to be different, period. He looks at me with his face cocked sideways, as though he's waiting for me to say something else, and he gives my shoulder a squeeze.

"Pops, you're a good grunt. It's gonna be different without you."

"Can it, man."

"It's canned. I said all I've got to say."

He gives me the peace sign and drops his pants. He winces when the peroxide hits his rot, then he starts whistling.

"Man, there were a few times I didn't think I'd be sitting here like this, so close to being back on the block."

"Out there in that swamp yesterday?"

"No, not really. I worried we were gonna hit some shit, all right, but during most of that I felt calm, like I knew it wasn't me who was gonna get it. The ambush was worse, even though we had our asses covered. I think there's something in everybody's gut that triggers fear, you know? It's like a clit: if it gets rubbed, something happens."

"Never heard it put like that before. But I know what you mean."

"You know, because you've been in combat now. I think that's the difference, and I wonder if that difference is always going to be with me. Dig it, what I'm saying, man, is that I feel weird about going back to The World. Does that make any sense? I mean, I'm fuckin'-A *ready* to get the fuck outa here, but for the past coupla days I've been trying to imagine being back on the block and it's as hard as it was to imagine coming over here. I already know I'm gonna play hell fitting back in."

I'm looking at a guy who is about to go back home, who as been in The Nam for a year, a guy who has been partly responsible for my life. There are *tears* in his eyes. He looks extra short and thick. He isn't handsome. He is totally covered by puppy-shit mud. There would be no way to know he is a GI unless it is the look on his face. It is that look that I'll probably remember him by: a sort of confused, vacant stare. I wonder if I'll have it in eight months, if I will be ambivalent about going home. Then something rubs the clit in my gut and I'm afraid. I'm afraid I might be next, or that I'll get it in seven months. A spasm goes through me. All my muscles shimmy. I take a deep breath and before I know it I put my arm around him, give *his* shoulder a squeeze. He makes a fist, I make a fist, and we slam them together hard.

That night is solid dope and Kool-Aid. The Red Cross, or somebody, sends packs of Kool-Aid to the field and nobody usually drinks it, but halfway through the night Prophet takes his helmet and goes outside. He comes back with the helmet full of water and digs into his ruck. He brings out maybe five packets of Kool-Aid that are all hardened, dumps them into the helmet, and begins stirring it with his bayonet. Then he takes Callme's helmet and gets more water, dumps in another handful of powder, and stirs that. With the pride of a winemaker, he pours the helmet-fuls back and forth carefully. It reminds me of mixing paint. One by one we pass him our canteen cups—it might as well be wine. Sometime in the next couple hours I fall asleep, and when I wake up there is rain hitting the poncho roof. It is light outside.

The rain is not very hard. The valley that our side of the hill looks at is full of fog and the whole sky is gray. It is impossible to guess what time it is by the sky, but since there seems to be quite a bit of activity going on around the LZ it might be a couple hours past daylight. I mix up a cup of C-rat coffee. I'm beginning to hate the rain. Prophet comes from the direction of the top of the hill, wearing his poncho. His mustache has snot in it.

"Morning."

"Yup, so it is. We'll be moving out in about half an hour. Go over to the pad and get two cases of C's."

There haven't been any bulldozers into the Z since we first got here, so now the cut they made for a garbage dump is overflowing. It is downhill from the pad and there is a meager line of guys taking garbage down. One guy begins shooting at rats just when I get to the pad, and even though I am watching him, the shots make me duck. I wonder if he is doing it officially or just for the fuck of it. When I get back to the hole, everybody except Peacock is awake and making coffee. I cut the wire around the case of C's and begin looking for something that might taste good tomorrow. I snarf the two meals that I know contain peaches and pound cake.

When we saddle up, Pops shakes our hands and gives us each one of his patented shoulder squeezes. I don't want to get tears in my eyes; I'm glad for him, but I will feel the loss. I can imagine what it must be like for Prophet. Just before I get into the Bush I turn around to wave at him and he is standing where I thought he'd be, rubbing peroxide on his face. There's a chance we'll get back before he leaves, but not much of one. I won't see him in The Nam anymore. Maybe in The World, maybe never. He souvenired me and Callme short-timer calendars that he made by erasing parts of a picture out of a *Playboy*. My girl is white, Callme's is black. The calendars start at 205 days so in less than a week I can start marking the days off. He gave Peacock a glasses case that he used to keep his dope in. He gave Prophet his from-The-World knife that is almost as big as a machete. They said their good-byes privately. The rest of us could see them but we couldn't hear. Prophet came back and strapped the knife onto his leg without saying anything and without looking at us.

Prophet walks point; I walk second; Peacock comes behind me with the Sixty; Callmeblack pulls rear security. We don't have to go very far. We're supposed to set up a daytime OP on the other side of the river. Three Squad is going to make a circle and meet us there.

Every time a bird takes off from the LZ I wonder if Pops is on it. He said all he was going to do until we got back was dig on the hooch and stay in it. We walk down to the river without much concern, but when we get to it I get nervous. A four-man patrol is dangerous. I am carrying the radio. With it, the ammo I carry for Peacock, and my ruck, I must be carrying eighty pounds. Prophet is the squad leader now and he is supposed to be traveling light, but he has a whole shitload of frags strapped to his ruck and flak jacket.

The trail is wide and easy to follow as far as the river. The river is a dividing line—Charlie wouldn't be between it and our LZ, at least not in daylight—but beyond the river is no-man's land. I flash on going out at night when I was a kid; only so many street-lights belonged to me and my neighborhood. Where we come upon the river it is wide but there's an easy crossing on rocks. We set up our side of the river in a thicket crisscrossed by spoors.

I'm hungry already. I've had the same pair of pants on for a month and they're crusty: dried mud, spilled C-ration grease, and Eltee's blood. Either the trousers stretched or I have lost weight because the pants fit a lot better when I got them; I have to wear a belt made of shoelaces to keep them up. I keep the bottoms tied off just above the boots so river leeches can't sneak in, and to prevent the pants legs from snagging on stuff along the trail. Above where the legs are tied off, the utes are torn, and though I covered the tear with Army OD tape it is beginning to come loose.

I'm tempted to eat my peaches and pound cake but instead I munch on cookies out of the B-2 unit. They taste like shit. Peacock is staring at a beat-to-shit book that he never turns a page in. His face is full of pockmarks which are full of grime. His mustache is ragged as hell. One of his nervous habits is shutting half his nose with the biggest knuckle and he is doing it now, looking sometimes at the book and sometimes into the jungle. He squeaks out a fart, and as though that was what he had been waiting for, he opens a can of C's that looks like chopped-eggs-and-ham from where I am sitting.

Higher-higher calls. We are supposed to cross the river

and walk alongside it until we meet Three Squad. The news doesn't mean much. We had to cross anyway, and meeting another squad is something to look forward to. Nonetheless, we don't get up to move right away. Everybody finishes eating. Right before we saddle up to cross, Prophet comes over: he says I am going across first. Then he tells me I will be walking point when we get there. He tells me to get onto the first trail I find that heads north and go.

Walking point is the hardon. It means you're first out there, that there is nobody else to rely on. Somewhere inside of my ego, I take it as a compliment.

When we finish eating, Peacock lights a big bowl. I debate a minute whether or not to smoke it because I already know I'll be walking point. I take one big hit. It relaxes me, but as I sit there I begin to think the leaves look pasted onto the limbs. I strip the radio and give it to Callmeblack. He shoulders it and its antenna waves back and forth. While I'm looking at him to see if he needs help adjusting the straps, Prophet waves me on and moves away. So this it.

The An Loa flows east, so when I get to the other side I turn right. The crossing was pud. The water never got deeper than my thighs. I'm so into my own challenge—point—that it seems necessary to forget about the rest of them. I begin to act as though I am all alone. I look for the trail and find it and head north. All the time I am walking, I know I'm on a fine-tuned stone, but it feels so good, so brash, so much like the movies. It is an absence of fear that I've never felt before.

Something unusual is working on me. There is an intoxication to walking point. Part of me keeps hoping for something important, like footprints. Even though it is a gradual incline, I don't notice the slope until we've been walking awhile, and during that twenty minutes or so I feel like the leader. From somewhere comes the knowledge that

I *will* be the next leader. Pops is gone now, Prophet only has six weeks left, and Peacock only has a couple weeks more. Somehow, walking down that red, rutted trail—without ceremony, of course—it dawns on me that it won't be long at all.

I'm careful. And slow. I walk one foot at a time. A power thing comes to my mind. Nobody can walk faster than I walk. My rot bothers me once in a while, but I beat the aggravation of it by saying "rot" to myself every time I put my right foot down.

I think of being able to tell someone about this someday, someone who never did it. Shit, what will I say? There isn't anybody ahead of you. *You* are responsible. Point man, shit! I'm wearing my steel pot and flak jacket and these beat-to-shit, tied off, bloodspotted jungle utilities. I've got an M-16 locked and loaded with the safety off. I'm walking down a jungle trail the color of new bricks, looking for movement ahead of me and footprints. I'm high.

Next time I take a half look behind me, Callme signals to stop. We aren't at a good place because the trail curves uphill just ahead, so I go that far. We get off the trail and sit back to back so we can see all four directions. Prophet is looking at the map. I smoke a cigarette and try to sit so my rot doesn't rub against my flak jacket; it burns where the camouflage grease got into the sores.

"Goddammit," Prophet grumbles. "It looks to me like we should've come to the intersection of a little river by now. These maps are old, but not so goddamn old that a river disappeared. Maybe we ain't where I think."

"What's new?"

"Get hold of the Z and find out where Three Squad is."

"Sounds like a good idea," Prophet says, "except it ain't gonna do a lot of good if we don't figure out where the fuck *we* are."

"We could have 'em shoot a smoke round and take a trajectory."

"I don't wanna do that yet."

"Let's pick up the pace and hump hard until we come to the Blue Line."

I am hoping to be in a trench big enough to stretch out in when it gets dark, and I'd sure as hell rather be with the squad we're supposed to meet than lost. In another hundred meters we come to a place where another trail branches off. I stop us again and we decide to take the small one because it gets us into the bush a little, away from the main river. There is probably three hours until dark. The logic is simple enough: We'll either come to the Blue Line and be able to set up our rendezvous, even if we have to shoot a smoke to get together, or we'll be uphill a little, off the main trail, and not so likely to be where we'll have to set up an ambush. We aren't interested in making contact with Charlie. A couple times since the ambush, we've talked about the shittiness of it. They were strange conversations, a combination of slapping-ourselves-on-the-back and simple fear. Pops was the most pissed off. He said he would write his congressman.

It gives me the chills to think about the ambush. Walking point, it is still too close. Prophet changed. Ever since I got here, he has been the coolest one: wounded three times, always walking point, his eyes constantly blank but confident, he was the guts of the squad, our mascot. But since the ambush he has become less dignified, or something. His eyes dart around a lot more. His hands shake in the morning. He won't talk about it to anybody who isn't in the squad. Me, I feel different too. I've been through incoming mortars, I've seen dinks alive, and now I'm walking point. Anybody who has ever done it will know what I'm talking about: combat warfare, The Nam.

The high from the bowl has worn off to some degree,

but as I walk along and think of Pops, his indignation, and Prophet's new distance I am suddenly afraid again. I feel too far away from Callmeblack. I feel like an inadequate point man. I glance back and he is where he should be. He flips me a quick peace sign. It helps. It must be the hard downside of the dope, a paranoia, but I deserve it. I begin to concentrate hard, looking for movement and listening for anything that isn't coming from the squad and listening as far ahead of me as I can, being so goddamn trustful of my rifle with its full clip in, its selector switch on rock-and-roll.

I walk into a giant cobweb. The web spans the whole trail, which is two feet. When I break the web all kinds of bugs fall onto me and the web itself gets snagged around my right ear. Fuck it. The bugs all fall off or fly away, and my concentration doesn't get broken much.

I know the woods and fields that I hunt at home, at least most of them, so I know where the creeks are. Besides, I can tell when I'm coming to a stream by the plants that grow nearby. I am pretty shocked when I hear a sound I know I should recognize, an undisturbing sound, and yet walk almost stupidly up to the brink of a small cliff that heads down to the river. The sound I heard was the water. Fast water. The confidence I had ten minutes ago might as well float downstream. I feel plain stupid because I wonder if I should have come up on the water more slowly. I wonder if anybody else heard it before me and I wonder if anybody else feels the panic creep in to replace the confidence. I stop the squad and they all come up to move out in both directions along the riverbank. This being point man is a drug all its own and it has its own way with you. If I walked us into an ambush—and goddamn I know it's possible—and everybody but me got hit, I'd kill myself.

●●●●●●●●●●●

179

I WISH I HAD A CAMERA; THE STREAM IS BEAUTIFUL. IT IS probably fifteen meters across and runs pretty much unbroken. The vegetation on the other side is totally tangled trees and vines. Below the tangle is a two-foot embankment that is almost brilliant red; it shows the height the water has risen to so far this year. Yellow roots jut out of the mud, and in one place downstream there's a fresh backwash. Soon after we arrive, a big section of the bank caves in and a tree as big around as a lamppost falls in, sending a signature of blood-red mud toward the middle of the stream.

Every year, when the monsoons come, this stream gets wider. There are sure as hell no dams on it anywhere, and how much of the bank it eats away depends entirely on how much it rains during the season. The jungle is as natural as a desert: big, unique, and powerful. There is nothing close to a jungle in The World. Even though I wish I had a camera, I know I couldn't take the kind of picture I'd need to, the picture couldn't show the dynamism. A picture couldn't even show how hard it rains here.

Prophet is using the radio.

"Anybody think Charlie is watching from the other side?" Peacock asks.

"Dig it," Prophet says. "I called in, and we're goddamn near where we're supposed to be. Three Squad is upstream about a klik."

He makes sure his ammo clips are full and stuffs his toilet paper and matches into the band around his helmet cover.

"Callme, you want somebody to go alongside you?"

"Yeah, boss, this here river looks wicked."

"I'll go with him," I say.

"OK, then let's do it this way. I'll go about halfway across and then you two start. That leaves Pea with the Sixty on this side. I'll take the radio."

"I wish Pops was here. Four guys isn't enough to cross

a river this fast and wide. Man, this would be shitty if we get hit."

"We ain't gonna get hit."

Prophet starts out. I know he's got a dozen frags on him, and when he gets out to waist-deep he leans over just enough that he looks like a turtle. The grenades bang against each other because of the current, and the sound seems a lot louder than I would have guessed. When he is halfway across he is dog-paddling. He turns and signals us to begin. Callme looks grim. His sweaty face is stiff and he is chewing on the inside of his cheek. He takes a deep breath and we go in.

Our last river crossing was a cakewalk compared to this. The current is very strong. We started out probably ten feet apart, Callme upstream, but the current seems to carry me faster than it does him, because he is heavier, and within a few moments I have to struggle to keep upright and it is a definite bitch to swim. I try to keep looking around me but it is almost impossible. I see, though, that Prophet is probably twenty yards downstream from where we started out. Callmeblack is scared shitless; it's all over his face. He is trying to keep his M-79 out of the water and trying to stroke with one hand. So far I am able to move myself with my rifle ahead of me, in a kind of crawling-baby way.

Then Callme goes under. He either hit the channel all at once or he panicked, because when I look his way I see everything but the top of his helmet and his grenade launcher disappear. The weapon is waving above the water like it alone is calling for help. Then Callme's helmet and face come up. He begins to flail and tries to *climb* out. He gets a big breath and for an instant I think he is under control but after a few strokes he goes under again and this time lets go of the weapon.

Muthafucker! I begin swimming toward him but it is rough because of the current and because of my rifle. My rifle hits something solid and his grenade launcher pokes up out of the water, stock first. I grab it by pure luck, but now I have more than I can manage. I am within a few feet of him because I have made some progress against the current and he has floated down on it. He is scared to death by now. Maybe his fear works in the long run, maybe it saves him, because he starts trying to go back to the shore we left and makes enough headway that he floats into me.

As if I practice it, I wrap my legs around his waist and put one arm around his neck. At first it makes us both go under and he struggles against me and against the water and almost knocks my hold loose, but I am squeezing with all my strength.

"Callme, goddamn it, I've got you."

Maybe he faints. He gets limp. I've still got both weapons in one hand and I am growing tired, so tired, but I am able to go under and—*I don't know how*—push him up a little. I am just ready to ditch the guns when we bang into something that knocks my helmet off. The helmet disappears immediately and I grapple for whatever it is we hit. It is the tree that fell off the bank half an hour before. Callme gets hold of its skinniest branches and they break, but he claws his way to some that are more substantial and hangs on to them, breathing deep and spitting water.

"Hold the fuck on," Prophet yells now, from the bank.

And we do, goddammit, we hold on.

Peacock comes across with the Sixty held above him and I think of a dog I used to have coming back to me five years ago, a pleasant thought—so pleasant that, sitting on the bank watching Pea come with his glasses stuck straight up in the strap that holds his cover on, I cry just a little bit: a pleasant cry that has been inside me since the ambush.

We wring our pants out.

"Man, oh, my mammy," Callme says. "How does a nigger learn to swim?"

"In a city pool, with women lifeguards, is a good way."

There is a small breeze, probably the forerunner of a

shower. The sun is just about ready to pass over the top of the trees on the other side of the stream. The stream doesn't look as pretty as it did before.

"Next time we're gonna have to tie ourselves together," Prophet says, "and I'm here to tell you fuckers it was a dumb goddamn thing for me not to think of it this time. Some fuckin' squad leader I am. Pops woulda thought of it."

"Hey, Pops ain't even thinking about any of this—or us—now, man. He's not a troop anymore."

"To Pops."

Peacock raises his canteen cup, but since nobody else is drinking anything we raise our hands, fists, in the toast.

BAPTISM BY FLARE

THE RAIN COMES LIKE A COMBINE MOVING THROUGH A wheat field. At first it is bunched up above the mountains in a dark cloud the color of asphalt; then, as fast as a window shade rolls, it forms into a gray curtain that hangs high but too quickly comes at us like that combine. There is no time and probably no reason to do anything about it. It is cruel and cold and bangs down onto the jungle around us like a slamming door, like a million rubber bands hitting me in the face. And there is plenty of sound to it: a sound as loud as thunder as it pelts the trees around us and the dirt that soon turns into pizza sauce.

Only the tiny space afforded by the brim of my Boonie hat allows me to see when we get up. Peacock takes point and I take the Sixty and walk last. I feel distinctly vulnerable without my steel pot but my Boonie hat feels more familiar, if not as protective. We start walking alongside the stream but we move miserably slow because Peacock has to hack the trail with his machete in some places. It is a complete bitch to keep my footing and I am swearing half aloud after twenty minutes, cussing the rain, the mud, the jungle, the Army.

When we stop we all stay standing up except Prophet, who leans over in order to shelter his radio code book a little. He adjusts the radio to a different push.

184

"Owlshit, Titbird," he says.

"Titbird," the radio says back. Then, like a telephone call, so casual, "Where ya been, over."

"On a picnic," Prophet says, just as casually. "Anybody tell you we're coming for dinner?"

"That's affirm. When's your train due? Over."

"Coming from the Sierra, maybe half an hour. How's your copy?"

"Good copy. We'll have you a hole with a custom rut for your hardon."

"Make the rut a foot long."

"The rain's in your brain, chump. Bring the wine. Over."

"Out."

"A foot long, eh?" Callme's spread of piano-key teeth pinholes the curtain of rain.

"It's for you."

I mean the rain is hard and loud. The trail is mostly moss, and the moss is full of water. At every step my foot sinks and the water oozes up and into the air holes of my boots. We walk steadily but slowly. I'm in the rear again with the Sixty, its barrel resting on my shoulder and its ammo belts banging me in the breastbone as I walk.

A dab of worry spots my thinking after we have walked more than half an hour. It would be plenty easy to miss another squad out here, to be just enough off course to pass them by. I know the stream is the reference point, though, so I assuage the worry by knowing Prophet might have only miscalculated the distance. Maybe walking along worrying is a defense against the rain. I am miserable and my body begins to ache all over. I flash on crossing the water earlier, on Callme's close call; I feel a bit of pride. It will be another story to tell in The World.

Compared to when I got here, I'm in good shape. I am carrying a lot of weight and we're going uphill. I ache, I'm tired, but I have found a way of walking that overcomes all that. I feel like I can walk as far as anybody. I'm able to take a drink of water from my canteen without breaking stride, and that isn't as easy as I would have thought. We keep slicing through the rain, me keeping a good eye on our left side. We're pretty quiet.

Still, I am surprised when we get to Three Squad's camp. The vegetation has been alternately thick and less thick, and just after we enter a thick part we come upon Three. They make me think of hoboes. There are shirts hanging on vines at the perimeter of the camp and there is a twist of smoke coming from what was once a small fire. Just as we arrive the rain slows considerably. All four of us bunch up at the edge of the camp, like cows in a storm. There's a guy leaning against his ruck, underneath a shelter half stretched across some small branches. The shelter half won't cover all of him and his legs stick out into the rain, so his pants legs are wet from about his knees down. He is barefooted, and I see a pair of boots beside the fire. He has sunglasses on and a joint in his fingers that's as big as a fifty-cent cigar.

"Hey, GI, you guys waiting on the bathroom or what?"

"Simpleton," Prophet says, "I didn't goddamn see you, so laidback there. You're completely camouflaged with them shades on, man."

"They blur everything, too," the guy says. "Makes it easy to pretend I'm in Hawaii and any minute now some dancing girl is gonna drop her grass skirt. . . . Need I say more?"

There are shallow trenches dug into the high ground with a single layer of sandbags around each of them. This kind of encampment is something between the permanency of an LZ and a one-night stand. Evidently the rest of the squad is around somewhere, pulling OP. Simpleton is a cool-looking dude. There is something about him that assures me he's been here a long time. I guess that he is the squad leader. He and Prophet are something alike. Simpleton is tall and thin and has a solid mustache and hasn't shaved in a few days. I think his shades are black, or close to it.

It feels plenty good to drop the ruck and squat down, even though the extra bandolier of ammo jabs me in the kidneys and reminds me I need to piss.

"Where you guys been since Clitoris?" Peacock asks. He has dropped his ruck too but doesn't sit down. His glasses are far down on his nose. He swings his elbows behind him to stretch.

"If you can goddamn believe it, we've been right fuckin' here for almost a week."

"Sounds dangerous."

"No shit. They dropped us in a couple kliks from here before they moved the Z. Then we heard 'em take big hits for two separate nights, so they might have meant to be using us for bait but baited they-own-selves instead. Where's Pops? Where you guys been?" He lights the joint.

"Pops is on the freedom bird. He rotated. Gone mutha-fucker. His last hump was a bad ambush. Four dinks, and the lifers made us hump 'em to a pickup; Eltee Williams got wasted trying to load 'em onto the bird."

"Jesus. We heard part of it on the push but didn't know it was you guys."

"Where's the rest of you lazy assholes?"

"We're pulling one-man OPs all around here. You passed by Clemson. They'll be coming in pretty quick. How come you guys are out here with only four guys?"

"This is Two Squad, complete. Ain't it a bitch?"

"Man, they oughtn't send a four-manner out here. No wonder they hooked you up to us, but still, that's some bullshit."

"Dig it. I'd rather go out with just a partner. Easier to hide."

"Who're the Effengees?" Simpleton says. He tilts his shades down and looks at Callme and me.

"Back down, Jake," Pea says, "these guys ain't Effengees. They've *seen* some shit. You've been gone too long. How was Hawaii?"

"Too good. Too short—the days are shorter over there, so I took twice as many as I was supposed to. Lost a stripe and I could give a shit. I almost didn't come back, but my wife made me. Hey, dudes, I didn't mean to insult you guys, calling you Effengees. I just never met you before, and I've known these assholes a long time."

The three of us shake hands. Simpleton's eyes are muddy-green and bloodshot. He reminds me of what I think Ichabod Crane would look like. Another guy comes walking in with his rifle across both shoulders. He's wearing his poncho.

"That hillbilly fucker there is Scratch, from Tennessee."

Two more guys come in off OP. One is from Queens and the other from Alabama. They're black and really loaded. They look a lot alike: both are tall and thin and have oval faces. One guy has long sideburns.

It is fairly dark now and somebody kicks dirt over the fire, even though there isn't any color to it. I move near to one of the trenches and fish into my ruck for C's. Ham and muthafuckers, which at one time I probably thought were impossible to eat cold. It's like a mouthful of wax. I have fruit cocktail for dessert and I'm still hungry. I smear myself with mosquito repellent and take a couple hits off a bowl. The guys at the trench nearest me have a cassette going, very softly: Isaac Hayes. I simply lie back with my ruck for a pillow, my rifle beside me, my Boonie hat over my face to ward off the mosquitoes, my hands down my pants. I hope it doesn't start to rain hard during the night.

Callme shakes me awake. I don't want to get up because I am dreaming, but as soon as I wake I forget what the dream is about. There's another guy with Callmeblack. He has a flashlight with a yellow lens, and the three of us follow the guard we're relieving in the direction we came from this afternoon. There is a very little moonlight. Peacock is on the team of guards we are relieving. They're smoking dope when we get to the position.

"Cover our ass," Pea says.

The sound of the stream comes from our left, and we set up back to back. There are night birds, and a small wind is blowing. Before it got dark, Simpleton pointed out a small grove of bamboo trees, and the wind is coming from that direction. The breeze makes the bamboo trees clatter against each other, and the sound makes me think of a chain rattling against a flagpole. There is a musty smell around. I can't tell if it is coming from one or all of us or if it is from the vegetation.

This is the last guard shift of the night, and we agree that if anyone wants to doze off, it won't hurt. It's always eerie, sitting there without knowing what is around. The air is slightly cool but I might not notice it if I hadn't sensed how comfortable it is to lean against Callme and the other guy. The small wind and the coolness makes the warmth of their bodies cozy.

I flash on about exactly one year ago when I was with Rita Wilson. We spent most of the night in a sleeping bag on a small beach and took a night swim to a raft. We sat on the raft with our feet in the water for an easy two hours. Her body was warmer than these GIs, but still, it somehow feels a lot like that to lean here in the blackness, feeling their every move, listening.

I am homesick—again—but I get the feeling that comes every once in a while, that this is one of those moments I'm going to remember if I get home alive. I am thinking consciously, and I shudder involuntarily because the thought skates through my mind that I might *not* make it. It is only a fleeting thought, and a small shudder, but the other guy must feel it.

He says, "Cold, dude?" in a whisper.

"Just a little."

"Hear anything?"

"Nah."

"It's not smart to keep a conversation going, but my name's Pantsload."

"Gabe."

"Messenger of God, eh?"

"You know your Bible."

"Nah, just remember a few things."

"Gabe," Callme says, "you're the only guy here without a nickname."

"He'll probably get one. I went four months. I'll tell you the story: I shit my pants in a firefight." He chuckles, and it sounds like a chipmunk.

We're quiet for a few minutes and I'm totally surprised when Callme says, and I can tell he turns toward Pantsload when he says it, "Gabe saved my sweet black ass this mornin'."

"There's a lot of that going on, over here."

Yes, this is one of those moments I'll remember.

It might be getting light, very slowly. It makes me think of the morning of the ambush. There are no new sounds, just the talk of birds that seem satisfied to stay where they are, calling back and forth: smooth, gentle sounds.

Once in a while there is the sound of artillery hitting somewhere but nothing to indicate that the firing is necessary; rather, there is a pattern to the soft *wahooomps* of the guns, then the *barummb-mum-bum* of the rounds landing. We never see any of the flashes. Most of the explosions are in the west. Only twice during our guard do the rounds come our direction, and I guess that they are aimed somewhere near the big river.

Just when it is light enough to see into the bush a little, something scampers out of the moss and runs across my feet, then turns enough to run across Pantsload's too, and it causes a quick adrenaline rush. We giggle at ourselves and get up to head back to camp. Maybe I got extra-good sleep last night; my nerves aren't so bad. I feel like a kid who's just spent some time at a secret fort in the woods.

To be out with this many guys is weird, like being at a reunion with cousins I don't know much. Some of us are sitting in the part of the clearing that is lit by the sun, others are out on OP. Simpleton and Prophet are by themselves in one of the trenches, smoking dope.

"Hey, dig it," Clemson says. "As of today I am a double-digit midget, ninety-nine days to go."

"Six months, two days," Pantsload says. He looks at me and I gotta answer.

"One ninety-eight."

"Your next step is figuring when your replacement gets drafted. Mine gets drafted this week, the way I see it."

"Maybe the war will be over by then."

"Maybe chickens have lips."

"That's no way for a hero to talk," Clemson says.

"Hero?"

"Tell 'em the story, Pantsload."

"Hey, I shit my pants in a firefight, am I a hero?"

"This fucker is too, too modest," Clemson says. "He shit his pants just after he dragged a guy in who'd been shot up bad and the sniper was still pouring it out. And Pantsload got the sniper, no less. He's in for a Silver Star."

I like Pantsload and he looks embarrassed.

"Probably a lot of that going on, over here," I say. It makes him smile. The Silver Star man is cute-looking, chubby like the Pillsbury Doughboy.

Then Simpleton comes over, chewing on one side of his mustache and with his glasses up on his head. He walks with big steps and keeps his arms away from his body because he has just salved the jungle rot around his armpits. Everybody is expecting him to say something and he looks at all of us, one at a time, then begins humming, still looking at us.

"Hey, dork, what's the word?"

"Thunderbird."

"I'd drink to that."

"Drink to this." He pulls his glasses down, and now it is impossible to tell who he is looking at. "I just called in, and we're all headed to where you guys sprung that ambush."

"Say what?"

"Say yeah."

"Say fuck it. There's likely to be dinks around there."

"That's what Higher-higher thinks too."

"Say, man, have 'em CA somebody else in there."

"I thought Bravo Company was supposed to be there already."

"Bravo's got SRRPs all around. We're coming in the back way."

"Fuck me, man. I only got enough food for two more days."

"Dig it. Prophet and I were talking. When we get back to the Z, we gotta find out who is laying all this shit on us and do something about it."

"If we goddamn make it back to the Z."

"What's on the breeze, brother?"

"Well, Prophet—all you guys in Two, probably—is extra pissed. He's wanting to waste that red-haired Billingham. We agree that that chump is expendable. I think maybe we oughta warn 'im first. I say we pin one, and that should get the message across. Think about it. We'll decide when we get back. Meanwhile, saddle up. We're heading out in half an hour."

It will take us all day to get to the ambush site, and a ten-man patrol makes it that much easier for Charlie to see us, hear us, track us, ambush us.

Before we get out of camp the sun disappears and rain comes like a waterfall. The trenches fill up with water and mud.

WE WALK ALL DAY. IT RAINS ALL DAY. THE HUMP IS ABOUT seven kliks on a straight line, which is only a little over four miles, but we can't go in a straight line, and even when we can the walking is ass-breaking in a lot of places, because we are going up to the ambush point from the other side of the mountain, directly opposite the side that faces the river, and this side is steep most of the way. It is a miserable-ass patrol. Three or four times, one of the ten of us falls backward. We have been walking on a difficult incline for half an hour, and although we're on a trail, it is a poor one, and it's gotten worse fast because of all the rain, and it's worse yet for those of us toward the rear because the guys going ahead of us have helped make the mud slippery. When we come to a washout that cuts the trail with a three-foot-wide creek, the guy from Three hands me his rifle and throws his ruck across. He's a tall, thin guy. The other side of the washout is probably two feet above our side. He jumps and tries to grab hold of a tree, but it's too wet to hold on to and he falls in the water on his back and rolls out. I can see right away that he isn't hurt, but he's sure as hell mad. He takes a Y. A. Tittle posture at the edge of the water and stays kneeling like that for half a minute. Then he swipes his rifle out of my hand and plugs through, scrambles up the other bank, and kneels again to get into his ruck. I don't try the jump and simply wade through the fast water and mud, then climb up on the bank, but it wears me out.

We take a few breaks, and it helps heal the body, but standing, kneeling, sitting, or even lying in a downpour fails to mend the angry washout in my thinking that separates the *concept* of ten guys humping through the mud and up a mountain to an ambush site from the *reality*. In six hours or so I have grown mean. I am more self-pitying than I've ever been in my life when we get to the top of the climb. Out of ten men, there aren't two who could fight, but if I am at all representative of those ten, there are ten who could kill. I think about the fragging we halfway discussed early in the morning, and it dawns on me that I have done a complete turnaround. Instead of wanting to be silent about my indecision toward a mutinous warning, I would drop the fragmentation grenade in a lifer's lap if I knew it was him who had us out here.

In addition to being mad, I get scared. The trail we came up meets another trail just below the top of the mountain, and a feeling of recognition runs from my nuts to my eyes: this big, hard-packed trail is the one the dinks were using. The ambush site can't be more than half a klik away. I don't know who is walking point, but we stop when we hit the hard trail, so I suspect it is either Peacock or Prophet, and I suspect that the main reason we stop is related to my fear. The rain is coming straight down, hard, like it has been all day. There is no talking. There is a weak hour of daylight left. My ankles hurt.

I can see Callmeblack, Pantsload, Clemson, and two other guys from Three. The black guy who was in front of me, Clemson, Pantsload, and I set up in a back-to-back circle and watch it rain. There is another four-man circle on the other side of the trail. Simpleton and Prophet huddle underneath their ponchos with a map and a radio. I can hear the squelch breaks, but that's all. After a few minutes, Prophet comes to our circle and Simpleton goes to the other side.

With his poncho covering the ruck on his back, Prophet's body is formless except for the hump where the ruck is, and he looks like a circus monster. His expression is as monstrous. One side of his face is covered with the red mud, where he wiped it with his hand. His teeth look particularly yellow, and he is scowling like I've never seen him scowl before. He squats on the downhill side of the four of us and sighs.

"This is it," he says. "We're gonna spend the night here and get into an ambush posture. It'll be a double setup.

You four guys will have this side of the hump up there, and the other four will go up the trail toward the top a little. Set your claymores up so they crisscross the trail; send out an LP down the trail a little. Clemson, set your Sixty up to face uptrail. If you can, rig a trip flare as far down the trail as you can see. We've got to hustle. Higher-higher says Bravo Company is down at the bottom of this hill and that they've had constant movement. The theory is that we're right in the middle of a dink staging area. Everybody goes on lock-and-load from now on, so be careful. If any shit hits and you gotta use frags, be damn sure you don't throw 'em far enough to get the other guys. I'll be back with the code words as soon as I can. Everybody all right?"

"That's a stupid question," Clemson says. But he holds his fist out and Prophet slaps it. Then Prophet holds his out, and we all slap it in turn. I think there is some kind of collective sigh.

"What's your name?" I ask the black guy.

"Ollin G. Harding. But for the next two months it's plain ol' Hardon."

"Gabriel Sauers."

"No nick?"

"Nope."

"Got a trip flare?"

I don't, so he gets one out of his ruck. Clemson lights a cigarette and moves closer to the trail to set his gun up. I take my rifle, a bandolier, and the trip flare and sneak my way down the trail. When I get twenty feet away it's hard to see back to where the others are, so I set the flare up there, stretching the black wire across the trail about eight inches off the ground. I always have a pessimistic vision of the sonofabitch going off in my face when I rig one for release, and this time is no different. It doesn't, and the wire seems about the right tautness. I pray I don't see this fucker pop tonight. I count my steps back to the position so we know where it is.

On my way back I help Hardon set up two claymores facing the trip flare. I set mine up against a rock the shape of a lamp a little old lady would have in her living room, and unwind the detonator back toward Clemson. Hardon sets the other one across the trail from mine and takes the detonator up to his position. Pantsload will be LP. He goes downhill at an angle so he is a little past the trip flare. When he comes back, the four of us sit in the rain. We all eat, I think just because we know we should, not because we're hungry, and sure as hell not because it tastes good. It is getting dark fast now. None of us will sleep tonight. I'm beat to shit and I ache, but I couldn't sleep even if it weren't raining so hard.

Just at dark we take our positions. There is absolutely nothing to do except to try and move enough, ever so quietly, to keep from getting sore, and to desperately keep as much of myself as I can underneath my poncho. I deliberately try to imagine being home again, but thinking of a sunny day is impossible. It seems like all I can remember are days when it rained, when I was little and wanted to play outside but couldn't because of the rain; of days in the summertime when my baseball games got rained out; of mornings when I had begun to paint and got caught with half a house side done; of November days when the rain kept the briars wet and the rabbits sitting tight. But I've never seen it rain like this for so long. I wonder if the dinks use the word "monsoon." *How many more times before DEROS am I going to be sitting here like this, almost wanting to yell or cry?*

When half the night is gone I feel like if I don't stand up I won't be able to use my legs when it gets light. It is still raining hard and colder than ever, but the *sound* seems less. I begin to yawn so I take the chance that I can be quiet about it, and I stand up. I am about to stretch with my rifle over my head when Pantsload opens up. His rounds might as well go through me, they so thoroughly stop my heart. And immediately afterward the trip flare goes up.

"*Chieu hoi, chieu hoi, chieu hoi.*" It is a scream so sudden and frightening that I involuntarily say it aloud myself: "*Chieu hoi.*" I have brought my rifle down and stand there now with it pointed at two small men who throw their guns down in front of them. The flare casts a light like the light from a sparkler, and twelve steps away from me are two faces. The faces are all I see. My finger tightens on the trigger and I gasp for air. These poor sonofabitches are alive and more scared than I am. I, Gabriel Sauers, have eighteen rounds in my finger and two enemy prisoners now on their knees.

"Hey," Hardon shouts, "get to them before the flare burns out." But it burns out before I can, or do, take a step. The next five seconds are an hour. I honestly don't know what to do. I know if I hear them move I will burst the darkness with eighteen quick sparks, but that is all I know.

"*Chieu hoi*, muthafuckers," I order, although it doesn't mean anything. But I don't hear them move. Then they are exposed by a tiny bit of red light that comes from Hardon's flashlight as he comes walking carefully toward them, and me.

Pantsload's voice comes from the darkness at about four o'clock from where I am facing.

"Watch those bastards. Be goddamn careful. Kick their guns away and don't either one of you guys quit looking at 'em."

The vast-ass jungle is full of the noise of rain, lit only by a small red flashlight beam. Two black-haired dinks in black, soaking wet, are saying "*Chieu hoi*" over and over, but softly, and crying.

In the opposite direction I can hear Clemson whispering and I can hear my heartbeat like a jukebox a block away. I can't hear it rain.

Simpleton brings a rope and ties them unmercifully, and

for the next three hours four of us sit across from the dinks, our rifles always so near their faces that a fat dog couldn't pass between. When, periodically, we turn the flashlight on them as though we could tell why they were crying if we could see, the rain falls like Christmas tinsel. At daylight I begin to shake, a shaking that will not leave me for months, if ever. An hour after daylight we get our orders to bring the prisoners to Checkpoint Bravo. Prophet refuses and they give us another site to go to. We walk through the rain and mud, toward Checkpoint Charlie, two kliks away.

Maybe God is walking point. The shaking that came during the night is still with me while we ten GIs and two prisoners fight the mud uphill along a steep trail that is often exposed on the cliff side. The shakes seem both the result of fear and a cause too. I try as staunchly as I can to rein myself in, to relax enough to breathe evenly. I'm positive we're going to be seen and get hit. Whether or not I am authorized to, since I'm in the middle of the file, I keep my clip up tight and a round chambered. The rain keeps on coming.

Maybe Moses is flying the helicopter. The checkpoint is at the top of the hump, and it is rocky and clear. And—it couldn't have been timed more perfectly—when we get there the rain almost quits, so the birds can come in and get us, and they do. No grass to hack down, no hostile fire, very little rain. Two birds, six of us on each, and there is a gunship flying circles around us all the time. Once we are above the clouds and the jungle looks half a world away, a breath comes and I can feel so much tension leave me that I simply close my eyes and smile. The helicopter's steady cadence and gentle rocking is as effective as a bassinet; I feel a million miles, a hundred years away from last night, until the struts of the bird hit the landing pad and I see rain like a sprinkler being blown around by the helicopter's blade.

We go to our hooch and crowd in, waiting on the CO to come.

"Man," Peacock says, "I am goddamn *done* with this war. My nerves won't take any more."

"You shoulda been with us, man," Pantsload says. "I heard those fuckers not five seconds before they hit the trip wire, and I knew it was too late already, so I pumped off half a clip. Man, you know? I'm glad I missed. And I'm glad they *Chieu hoi*ed." He laughs a little and looks at me. "And you, my man, I see you standing in the dark there, above 'em, saying, '*Chieu hoi*, muthafuckers.'" Everybody laughs.

Peacock has his shirt open and is tracing what he can see of his tattoo. He stops and looks at Pantsload and me. Then he says, "I believe we oughta christen Gabe, troops. I believe I'll call him Chieu Hoi from now on."

Maybe my Angel Gabriel tells me to do this: probably the only dry spot on my utility fatigues is underneath where the pocket flap is, and I write my nickname there in black waterproof ink. I think about the beech tree.

LZ RAIN

"CHIEU HOI, MUTHAFUCKER."

I am cramped into a corner of the hooch and when I first hear it I panic and go for my rifle, but then I realize where I am, and that it is Prophet yelling. Me, the guy who thought he would never be able to sleep again, is the only one left inside the hooch, the last one awake.

"The sun is shining, Chieu Hoi."

"Does that mean we're humping out, or what?"

"No hump, but we're moving."

"Are you shitting me?"

"No shit. The whole fucking battalion, and it starts in half an hour."

"What if it starts raining?"

"Hey, man. It *will* start raining. This has been an extra-wet year, and the real season is just beginning. It seems to rain off and on all year up here in the mountains—the seasons aren't as distinct as in the Delta. The difference is the mud. The mud won't dry up, like it has been, for months."

It does start, about an hour after we get to the new LZ. The site is farther west and there is an enormous force of engineers on the hill when we come in, so our first job is to go down toward the bottom of the hill and pull security while the engineers blow the mountain's top. We were brought in by Slick and there were probably twenty other birds with us, full of GIs. Echo Company and Alpha Company are completely here. Bravo and Delta companies are partly here and Charlie is on the nearest hill. The move is well planned, and every available helicopter in the division must be working for us. Shithooks bring in slings of ammo, artillery pieces, conexes, water trailers, demolition materials for the engineers, and pallets of sandbags.

It isn't raining very hard. The new Z gets named LZ Rain. It is the highest mountain around and is in a valley made from three other ranges that must be ten kliks away at the closest point. All afternoon the four of us sit in a small enclave made by wet green rocks. We have fun, smoking dope and listening to the cassette player. Up above us the engineers are blowing huge charges and the sky is constantly filled with very black smoke. There is a charge set off about every twenty minutes and the concussions always reach us.

But Prophet drops the bomb, when we're all completely fucked up on the dope. He is sitting against the wall of rock without his shirt on and using a handkerchief to rub the back of his neck. He giggles, and Prophet doesn't very often giggle.

"Anybody wanna make book on whether Billingham shows up on LZ Rain?"

"Sure, he'll be here," Peacock says.

"I'll take that bet," Callme says, laughing now too.

"What'd you fuckers do?"

"Now, I don't know anything for sure," Prophet says, "but I heard that somebody scared him off."

"I heard that some nigger who couldn't swim put a hole in that lifer's boat," Callmeblack says.

Callmeblack threw a pinned frag into the officer's hooch last night, and just before dawn this morning Prophet tossed a smoke grenade through his doorway.

"Shoulda seen that fat little fucker come out of there,"

he says now, "swatting himself and cussing and trying to wipe away his tears. I thought I was gonna give myself away laughing."

Then Peacock stands up and pulls the pin on a frag. He heaves it as hard as he can into the bush and we calmly sit there when it busts, throwing a spattering of branches and stuff, the sound like a cap pistol compared to the gigantic dynamite blast that echoes it almost immediately from the top of the hill.

Man, we're high.

For four days in a row Two Squad gets good duty at the bottom of the hill. The Army ain't what it used to be a week ago. We are only responsible for keeping a watch on the part of the perimeter directly in front of us, and it seems ungoddamnly safe, so we don't keep all that good an eye. Instead, we sit around under ponchos, take turns emptying the water out of their middles, play cards, write letters, read, smoke dope, and have grenade-throwing contests. We've probably thrown fifty grenades in front of us, and the spot where most of them land is now minced-up leaves and vines. When we get bored cleaning our rifles over and over—oiling them with WD-40 until the metal is black again—and tired of throwing grenades because we have to go all the way uphill to resupply ourselves, we take turns working out on the Sixty, mowing down the jungle little by little. In two days we've gone through more ammo than I used up in Basic Training, and that was a lot. The whole hill is like that: small units of grunts scattered all around its base, busting uncountable amounts of ammunition at nothing. Once, the word comes down to cool it and there is quiet for maybe an hour, but as soon as somebody on the other side of the hill starts, everybody gets in on the action and pours it out, like the teacher had turned his back.

Meanwhile, bulldozers get slung in and they charge the top of the hill as if there was a highway coming through.

What is left up there is solid mud and rocks. LZ Rain is going to be our monsoon headquarters. It is a safe-looking place: I don't think Charlie has anything to reach us, except from maybe one point where the valley narrows down and the hills there are almost as high as ours. Certainly, this seems like the safest place I've been since I hit the Bush, and that's fine by me.

The four of us tell a lot of stories and smoke a lot of dope: about all day and all night there's a bowl going. Peacock resupplies us the second day with a bag the size of a baseball cap that he got by walking a quarter of the way around the hill. He left early in the morning and didn't come back until the middle of the afternoon, totally fucked up.

"We're celebrities," he says, when he dumps the bag out onto a C-ration case. "All I did was start walking and begging. When I told 'em we were Two Squad, Echo Company, thank you, everybody opened up. I told and retold the story of the ambushes, so if I got some of the facts mixed up and it comes back to you, think not a thing of it. Remember the cause."

Toward dark one day three guys come down the hill. I allow myself to smile when I see them. They are brand-fucking-new. They all have on clean utilities and their rucksacks are tidy-looking. One guy looks like a Mexican. I'm the one holding the bowl when they stop and stand awkwardly outside the shelter of the poncho. When I see that the Mexican is a second lieutenant I cup the bowl in my hand.

"You guys Two Squad, Echo Company?" the Eltee asks.

"Who wants to know?" Prophet says, always the wise-ass.

"Charlie wants to know. He heard you were bad-asses."

Prophet gets up off the ammo crate and sticks his hand out.

"I'm the new platoon leader," the Mexican says.

"I'm the old squad leader, call me Prophet. This here's Callmeblack, call him Callmeblack. This is Peacock, an asshole, and that guy over there is Mr. Chieu Hoi."

"My name's Rodriguez. These two men will be in your squad. Omar Smith. Charles Murphy."

We shake hands. Theirs are all clean. Omar is black but lighter than Callme, and Murphy is about the size of Pops but better-looking. It seems so long ago now that I was this new, and so long ago that Ass got killed. I swear, these guys even *smell* good. Their Boonie hats are fresh out of the box.

"I've got to make my rounds, Sarge," Rodriguez says to Prophet. Then, to me, "How about a quick bump off that bowl?" It catches me by surprise and I spill it trying to get it out of my fatigue pocket, but Callmeblack has one packed and we hit it around once. The F.N.G.s take small hits.

"Welcome," Peacock says, after the new Eltee leaves. Then he unpins a frag and holds it out to Murphy, who doesn't know what the hell to do. Pea whirls and heaves it into the Bush and gets an air burst. I'm watching Murphy and I feel sorry for him because his surprise and fear show.

"We ain't all that crazy," Prophet says. "Or at least not all the time."

"Where you from?"

"Chicago," Omar says.

"Pennsylvania," says Murphy.

"You guys came at a good time. This is sham time. We been sitting down here on our ass for four days and the monsoons just started, so we won't be doing a goddamn thing for weeks."

"We heard you were in a bunch of shit last week."

"You heard right."

"How long you got to go?"

"Son, I'm glad you asked that," Prophet says. "Peacock, he's got over a month; them two guys got so many days they won't tell you how many. Me, I got thirty-five days."

"Jesus," Murphy says. I know how he feels. He looks like he might be older than the rest of us. His hair is the color of coffee and he has blue eyes and kind of a double chin. There is a scar alongside his right eye that is still fresh enough to be pinker than the rest of his face, shaped like a quarter moon. He's nervous and pulls his shoulders up every time there is a rifle burst or a grenade explosion. The bulldozers are shutting down for the night. The engineers are making fewer and fewer blows every day and the dozers are mostly pushing the cut-up vegetation into piles that get burned and send a mostly pleasant smell into the air. By now the mud around our area is up to the top of our boots and it rains all the time—monsoons.

We sleep sitting up, drawn into our field jackets, two each against the rocks. The other two guys pull guard. Peacock wakes me up for the middle shift. Omar is my partner. Pea and Murphy take our places against the rocks and we move down the hill to where another poncho is rigged up over an ammo crate. It's raining and I can't quit yawning. Omar is wide awake and sits on the ammo crate. I know he is looking hard into the dark rain, and I know he can't see anything, and I know that is a shitty feeling.

"Ordinarily," I say, lighting a smoke behind my hands, "we don't smoke when we're pulling LP, but there's absolutely nothing out there tonight. So smoke if you want to, but keep it sheltered."

He doesn't say anything. For the first ten minutes we sit beside each other and listen. The rain is steady. Artillery is firing from on top of the hill, Night Fire Programs aimed in the direction opposite us and Night Fires that land down in the valley in front of us. We can't see them hit. There is a sound of helicopters way up high, above the rain, and that sound is steady, like a small electric fan.

I feel like I need to shit but it isn't so urgent that I can't wait. I hope to last it out until daylight.

Omar is quiet all night long. At first I try to make him comfortable, try to make conversation, but he never answers me with more than a few words and finally it makes me uncomfortable, so I quit trying. I don't know if he is that frightened or what; maybe he doesn't like white guys. *Fuck him.* Toward morning I light up a bowl and sort of half-ass offer it to him. He shakes his head, so I sit there and smoke off it, get stoned enough to enjoy the dawn, which isn't spectacular but keeps my attention. He sits without moving and without speaking, looking into the Bush. I figure Callme can get the lowdown on him. If he ends up being an asshole, it'll be tough on him.

I only nod my head when I'm ready to go back to the rocks and for an instant, a very quick instant, I see something besides a mask on his face—maybe relief. He follows me. Charles is awake, Peacock is sleeping with his feet higher than his head, Prophet and Callme are huddled together in the narrowest part of the rocks. They remind me of puppies. I feel like fucking around, so I get the bowl going good and go over to shotgun Peacock. He first pulls his face away, then opens his mouth to take the smoke in, and never opens his eyes until, sitting up straighter, he opens one eye at a time and pulls his glasses out of his ammo can.

"Beautiful morning," he says, spitting into the rain.

"We're one day shorter, my man."

"Us too," Murphy says.

Peacock and I laugh with him. Omar doesn't react. Since nobody has emptied out the middle of the poncho during the night, the water has accumulated to the point where the poncho sags a good foot in the middle. If we stretch it tight and at an angle, then the wind catches it and shakes it like a sail. It is better to let it catch water and empty it periodically, which is the first thing Peacock does.

I flash on folding up wet paint canvases, and like any memory of The World I think about it as long as I can.

We get the word to move up the hill later. We're going to build two hooches simultaneously. The spots are side by side, on the edge of a mud cliff left by the dozers, and one hooch will back up against the other, the doors facing opposite directions. Prophet scrounges an extra shovel, so we have three now.

We cook. Everybody seems plenty satisfied to be digging in and we all work hard. Omar is working beside me and he is extremely strong and tireless. Even though it is raining hard it is stifling hot and the sweat burns my rot. The scabs have begun to spread fast. It started under my arms and beneath where my ruckstrap rides on my shoulders, but now there is a constant streak of open sores down to my waist from my armpits. The sweat makes it sting so I wipe mud onto it. The mud takes the sting away immediately.

The Z is a city of activity. Everybody is digging in. The mood is light. There are radios and cassettes going everywhere. Even after hearing the station all the time since I got here, it still seems odd to me that there aren't any commercials. During "Satisfaction" by the Stones, the work almost stops. I could have counted a dozen guys standing on piles of sandbags, on piles of wooden ammo crates, on maybe only a rucksack—anything remotely like a stage—playing imaginary guitars, screaming "I can't get no . . . satisfaction" loud enough to drown out the sound of rain hitting the lifers' steel conexes. I'm the guy on top of a rucksack. I feel fuckin'-A mighty. Jagger never had a more sympathetic audience, and I've never sung better.

We dig all day long, then most of the night. We work by the tiny Christmas tree bulbs run by our radio batteries. It doesn't matter that we can't see very well. We dig. Man, we dig. The hooch will be enormous. There will be a wall about three feet thick between the hooch we are digging and the one next door. We've considered a tunnel between them, but for now it isn't in the blueprint. It keeps on raining. Occasionally a mosquito destroys a notion I'd always had that they wouldn't bite during a rain. Maybe jungle mosquitoes are different. The small lights cause our shadows to gyrate across the muddy walls. Once I get out of the hole to piss, and standing in the darkness looking back at the hole gives me a strange feeling, like standing at a bus stop looking into a manhole when a crew is working all night.

The fucking rain. The light from the small bulb is weak but the night is so dark that the light stares upward and illuminates the rain, which comes down as if trying to put it out by force. I have on my Boonie hat and a pair of utes, and now I take my hat off to wring it out. I don't know why. I like the feeling I have now, this sense of removal. I wish my time was done, that I could go home.

When I wake up lying on my side, in the posture of someone sitting on a tractor, I regret not covering up with a poncho but it wouldn't have made any difference because I was wet to begin with. It is still raining solidly, and my first question is whether or not I can find a dry match. A guy is walking by me with nothing but his boots on and he has a cigarette going, so I bum a light. It is just beginning to grow into day and makes me think of the morning of the ambush. I wonder if I'll remember that morning a thousand times before I die. This time I only think of the daybreak; the memory shuts off before I see the blood and guts.

Peacock is sitting on a pile of mud, rubbing his ankle. The scar from where the shrapnel went in is balloon-pink and the skin of the wound stands out in a fold. The rest of his ankle—the rest of him, period—is covered with mud, so much mud that it is hard to tell where his utes stop and his hairy bare legs begin. His glasses are crooked on his face and his dark, curly hair tangles out from under his Boonie hat like broken rubber bands. He has water in his helmet and the helmet is sitting on a frame made from wire he took off C-ration cases. Underneath the helmet is the purple glow of flame from a can of Sterno. He tests the water with a finger and it suits him, so he lathers up his face with a gun brush.

"Pea, anybody got dibs on your water?"

"All yours, Chieu Hoi." He leans over and rips a loud fart. "Catch that and paint it green," he says, pulling down the side of his face toward which his crooked glasses droop.

"You'll settle for olive drab, eh?"

"Good morning," Murphy says. He slept in the hole last night and is now standing in it and stretching. He stretches and does toe touches. When he bends over to touch his toes he disappears, then reappears, and disappears again. It makes me think of somebody hunting night crawlers. His back is lean and the backbone is prominent, like a woman's. I wish him a good morning when he next pops up.

The rain is softer than it was last night but still steady. The eastern sky is the color of an old furnace filter. I am oozing mud between my toes and scraping designs into the ground like I was finger-painting. My rot is somewhere between itching and aching; I'm going to salve it after I shave.

Prophet is coming along the side of the hill with his rifle over a shoulder, and his canteen is swinging from the carrying handle.

"Something happened last night," he says.

Peacock points at the helmet full of water to tell me he's done.

"What happened?"

"Somebody shot a flare into some lieutenant's hooch and they had to dust the Eltee off for burns."

"Which Eltee?"

"A red-haired guy, name of Billingham. I just came

from a squad leaders' meeting, and the lifers are upset about it. If they find out who did it, the guy will be charged with mutiny or something."

Prophet's cowlick is exaggerated because his head is soaking wet. His deep-set blue eyes are deadly expressionless. He should be a bartender listening to some whining drunk, so stoic. The first surprise is that Billingham is on the Z. More surprising is the fact that I have no idea if Prophet knows who did it. I immediately think of Three Squad, of Pantsload or Scratch. I feel no compassion for Billingham; I am thinking of Eltee Williams, as dead as a duffel bag.

"So what's coming down?"

"There's an investigative committee going to be coming around asking questions."

"Let 'em ask," Callme says from the hole on the other side of the wall. We all look at him at the same time. He shrugs. A feeling of love goes from me and I'd bet it reaches him. His face unzips into a smile of beautiful teeth.

The helicopters haven't started flying yet. Small wisps of cold clouds go by at our altitude, and when the sun works its way through the haze I can see thick fog, the color of cement, in the valley below us. My shave didn't do much more than skim the dirt off my face. The ache of my rot is dull. I get hold of a shovel stuck in a mound of mud and jump into the hole that has an inch of water in its bottom. I wonder how those guys slept here last night. The first shovelful causes a sound like the last bit of water leaving a bathtub. My shoulder aches when I lift the shovel and I can feel some of the scabs of my rot break loose. The rain is almost friendly.

■■■■■■■■■■

BY THE MIDDLE OF THE AFTERNOON THE HOLE IS AS DEEP as I am tall, and instead of throwing the dirt out of the hole before we put it in sandbags we start filling the bags in the bottom of the hole. Peacock sits on a pile of full ones with an empty one on his head for a hat. Charles, Peacock, and I are working in this hole; Callme, Omar, and Prophet are digging next door. Every so often we'll start fucking around and throw our mud over the wall and into their hole. Once, Callmeblack sneaks up over us and dumps a whole helmetful of mud that's like baby shit down on top of Peacock. It coats his head and his glasses and I have to sit down because I'm laughing so hard at him when he takes his glasses off and starts eating the mud off the lenses. The afternoon is all fun. We smoke just enough dope but not too much, so that we don't get completely worn out. The four of us are in better shape than the F.N.G.s. Charles looks like he is ready for his nap when we sit down to eat.

Just when I have my C-rats open and am pinching off C-4 to get the food hot, we hear the first bird of the day coming, but we don't hear it much before we see it and when we do I stop what I'm doing because the bird is a Slick with doors on it. It's somebody pretty high up, I know that.

The weird thing about all this is that the F.N.G.s don't know what's going on. This is the first time I've seen a Slick with its doors closed. *But a lifer ain't what they don't know anything about. They don't know that two guys sitting beside them can be convicted of some crime like mutiny. And they don't know why those two guys did what they did. And they don't know I know and Peacock knows.* The two of them aren't paying any attention to the helicopter; Pea, Prophet, and Callme are all watching the pad with expressions that aren't usual. Prophet's eyes keep scrambling from side to side. Those steel-blue eyes that welded me to the ground when I was an F.N.G. are moving now like shooter marbles in an empty kitchen drawer.

Callme quits looking first. He digs a cigarette out of his ute pocket and backhands Omar's shoulder, then points to his smoke. Omar fishes him a pack of matches and goes back to eating. I didn't even know Callme carried cigarettes on him; I've only seen him smoke a couple times since we got here, but now he drags on the cigarette until there is an inch of orange. I wish he'd look at me. I don't know what I'd do; wink maybe. His eyes are whiskey-colored and those whiskey eyes and the bouncing blue ones finally meet. Callme stops dead instantly, and he looks at Prophet like a cat looks at a dog. Prophet makes a vague gesture with his hand, something like an umpire calling a strike.

The new guys can't know, can't be told.

The rain gets whipped around in the whirl of the bird's blades. A big guy gets out when the door first slides open, then a man whose rank is written all over him. His uniform is as dark as ours but ours are wet and his isn't. Seeing him makes me remember that I am wearing a uniform, an Army uniform. My boots are like waffles, my socks are stiff with blood from the scabs of the rot on my legs, my utilities are something a painter would throw away, but I'm in a uniform. This guy makes me remember it. Everybody remembers it; the first sergeant sends a guy from Four Squad to tell us to get shirts on. The uniform is a two-star general.

"Murphy, Smith," Prophet says. Then he stutters, he's so nervous. "You t-t-two guys, you—you go over in that hole, that hole there, and dig. Now."

The F.N.G.s seem baffled. Murphy looks at us momentarily, his eyes rolled toward the scarred side of his face; then he is up and over the wall with a shovel. Omar drags ass and I wonder if I am being unfair thinking it might be intentional. Callmeblack is pacing around in a small circle, and he stops beside Smith and stares down at him.

"Go, bro," Callme says, not harshly but not matter-of-factly either.

Smith looks up fast, then back down at his C's, then gets up and drops over the wall into the hole. Callme paces the top of the wall like he is a prison guard walking the catwalk. I know it's just nervousness, but I bet the F.N.G.s don't know what to make of all this. I forget how big Callme is. Up there on the wall, pacing around the mounds of dirt and piles of sandbags, with just a touch of sun behind him, he looks like a goddamn tight end.

Now the nerves hit me and I have to pace. I get down into the hole and attack its bottom with my shovel. I dare the mud to resist me and this adrenaline-fueled strength, but the mud submits in hunks the size of a gallon can and I lever them up to the hole's edge, even with my shoulders, and challenge the pain that comes when my rot scabs break open. Within three or four minutes my uncustomary shirt is splattered like an old dropcloth and there is more sweat on my face than there is rain.

●●●●●●●●●●●

THE FOUR OF US ARE IN THE HOLE, BY DESIGN, WHEN THE lifers come around. From the bottom of the hole the neat uniforms which are full of creases are what I see; the faces on top of the uniforms are erasers on the end of pencils.

"Attention," Prophet tells us in a voice just loud enough to sound like an order but not loud from practice. We come to a kind of attention, and Prophet snaps a quick salute. The general keeps his hands behind his back and nods the salute off.

"As you were," he says.

"Sergeant Theodore Ramsey, sir. Two Squad, Echo Company, First Battalion, Twelfth Infantry, Fourth Division."

A fucking general. A two-fuckin'-star-fuckin'-general. He is as tall as Prophet and Callmeblack. His face is smooth except for three or four prominent creases across his forehead. Everything about him is straight: his helmet liner is parallel with the ground; his back is perfectly perpendicular; the creases in his uniform are precisely centered; his shirt-pocket flaps are as even as drawer pulls; even the creases on his forehead look like somebody inked them there with a T-square. His lips move like he operates them from strings he holds in his hands behind his back.

"Sergeant, is this your full squad?"

"No, sir. There are two other guys in the hole next door. They just joined our squad, sir."

We can hear them digging, but I can tell by the sounds that they aren't working steadily. I wonder if they are trying to listen to the conversation. I want to scratch the rot around my balls. I'm so nervous that my legs are shaking.

"Men, you're part of the United States Army. The United States of America is the greatest nation in the world, and its Army is the greatest Army in the world. The strength of that Army depends on a great many things, soldiers, and one of those things is respect and discipline between the troops." He takes his hands from behind his back and locks his two index fingers together in front of him, and in front of us, for such a long quiet time that the shaking in my legs becomes so bad I begin to think I'll fall down. He looks at every one of us singly, and when he looks at me I feel like pissing my pants. I can feel water ooze into my boots when I shift my weight after his gaze goes on to Peacock. A major and the first sergeant are with him. They stand behind him a little, but their eyes seem to travel with the general's from one face to the next. Only the First Shirt looks remotely kind.

The general unlocks his index fingers and his hands swing down to his sides; the thumbs point straight ahead. I prefer looking at his thumbs to looking at his eyes.

"Where were you last night, son?" he is asking me. *Me*.

"We were down the hill, sir." I'm surprised how steady my voice is. I'm surprised I have any voice at all. I'm surprised I don't blurt out that I wish it was me who they're looking for, instead of . . . "Pulling perimeter. We just came in off an ambush the day we moved here." *Fuck, he knows that.*

"Soldier, I know you were on an ambush, and I know Two Squad ambushed and killed four enemy personnel. And I know you men know there has been a heinous crime committed against an Army officer, and that that is the reason for this investigation. We will find the guilty man, or men, troops, and there will be suitable punishment administered against the perpetrators. The backbone of an Army is dignified respect, and anyone who does not honor that respect will break the back of this Army."

Does he know what it is like to carry those four dead guys, in pieces, to a helicopter, then watch the only officer you feel accountable to get blown to hell? Does he know what it's like to be my age, a house painter a year ago, and to have seen Chickenfeed get his leg blown off or that guy I didn't even know breathe for the last time while I am trying to hold him down in my hole and the shit is still flying? Does this fuckin' guy who rides around in a helicopter with closed doors understand how miserable this rain is after two straight weeks of seeing my jungle rot eat toward the inside of my balls? This guy, and his two stars —how'd he get 'em?—is trying to tell me to honor that little red-haired wimp who never crossed the wire with us. I expect something like the lecture they used to give us in Basic Training about protecting America. I don't think this guy could convince my *mother* of anything. The rain comes harder, and the First Shirt humps his shoulders up against it, but the major and the general ignore it without struggling. We are still basically at parade rest, and the rain is as cold as snow.

"Men, all of us are here for the same reason. We are here to do our duty for our country. That duty begins with obeying orders. I obey my orders, troops, and I expect every order I give to be followed. It is not up to us to

215

question orders, nor is it likely that your judgment is more perfect than the judgment of those who give you orders."

The general is so rigid, even standing at ease, that I know we aren't in the same Army even if we do have the same kind of uniform. My confidence gets a boost of some sort. I am determined not to let his Army shame me into betraying mine. He should know that Billingham is a dead man if things go wrong. *He has to know that. He isn't stupid.*

He gives each of us a long, hard stare. His expression never changes. When he comes to attention Prophet calls us up, too. The two of them exchange salutes, and the investigators leave. They go from hole to hole. While they are on the Z, about everybody who goes by us gives a sign of some kind, mostly clenched fists. We keep digging, in our shirts.

Maybe an hour after they were questioning us, they go to the pad, where the padman slides open the bird's door, and they climb in. The Slick is as professional as the team was. It ascends perfectly straight, then chugs away like it wasn't used to wearing its shirt either. I'm not surprised that nobody says anything. I feel relieved, nothing more.

LZ Rain is beginning to look like a small village. A tall communications aerial stands on top of the Commo hooch, which is buried under sandbags at the top of the hill. There are four 105s, each corraled by a parapet the size of a big swimming pool. The parapet walls are as thick as they are tall and the artillery-men have their hooches already finished, because their roofs are made from metal Air Force pallets, with ammo crates filled full of sand on top of the pallets. The gun crews build their A-shaped hooches by digging down three feet and bagging two sides other than the parapet wall, so they can get to their guns as fast as possible.

Bravo Company is the line company closest to the guns. They came to the Z a few days before we did and have their hooches pretty much done. They are still filling sandbags from a pile left by a bulldozer and are piling these bags alongside a trench that runs around the mountain between the guns and the hooches. In case of heavy incoming, the trenches will serve as paths. Most of the hill is cleared and muddy, but there are some patches of scattered vegetation and there are piles of underbrush that haven't been burned. Water runs down the hill because there isn't anything to slow it down, and little by little the water begins to form distinct channels. One of the channels comes directly toward our hooches so we dig a crooked canal to divert it past us, and the guys below us have to dig one to divert it around them, and so on, down the hill.

Our company is about halfway between the top of the hill and the slings of concertina wire that mark the perimeter in piles that look like bent-up bedsprings. The holes below us aren't as deep as ours and the guys there are still working, even though it is getting dark. We are ready to go out for logs for our roof but can't go tonight. We've got shelter halves rigged over our hole, and it helps but doesn't keep all the water out, so we have one corner dug deeper. The deep hole is as big as three five-gallon buckets. It takes the water that gets in past our shelter halves about two hours to fill the hole; then we take turns bailing it out with our helmets.

I take the respite from work to clean myself and my rifle with four or five of the little towels that come in Red Cross packets. They are moistened with alcohol and something that smells good. The first one comes off my face the color of a red bandanna but after three towels my face feels dry and clean and tight. I haven't taken my shirt off since the lifers were here. My neck isn't used to a collar and the collar rubs the rot there, so I tuck the last towelette between the collar and my rotted neck; it makes the sores sting at first but is finally cool and soothing.

Peacock and Murphy are trying to sleep in the uphill

side of our hole and the space downside is used up by our rucks and the sump hole, so I take my rifle and cleaning stuff into the next hole. Omar and Callmeblack are there, sitting on their rucks listening to jams. When I jump into the hole I splash mud onto them.

"Thanks, Chieu Hoi," Callme says. "I just fuckin' got these utes back from the cleaners."

"Here, man, wear mine. I haven't shit in 'em for a week."

Omar looks up at me, then away, toward the muddy side of the hole. I'm hit with the feeling I've had since he came that he doesn't like me or any other white guy. I break my rifle down and spread the parts out on a piece of ammo crate. Instead of being the color of a Zippo lighter, like it should be, the firing pin is a dull but slimy green, the color of a lily pad. The forestock and barrel are spotted with mud and there are weeds caught in the perforations. Even though it is filthy there was no more chance of it jamming than if it had been clean, because the slime-green in the action is from oil. I can't remember the last time I cleaned it. I wipe it all down and oil it, reassemble it, and check it out with a dry clip in.

I wonder if Callme has talked to Omar about the investigation.

"How do you like the The Nam so far, Omar?"

"I wish it'd rain a little more so maybe they'd call this war. They'd call it in Comiskey."

"You go to a lot of games?"

"Beaucoup. They drafted me during tryouts."

"No shit?"

"No shit."

"A pro ball player, eh? Now we got me, a painter; Callme, a truck driver; Peacock, who's a college professor or student or something; and Prophet, who . . . Christ! What'd Prophet do before he came in? You know, Callme?"

"Nah, I dunno, but he'd make a good gangster."

"Shit, he'll be leaving in a month, can you dig it?"

"I'll have to."

■■■■■■■■■■

IT RAINS ALL DAY EVERY DAY FOR THE NEXT THREE WEEKS and the mud gets thicker and thicker. The channels that the water comes down the hill in get deeper. Our walls keep caving in and the sandbags begin falling apart and our roof sags. Every day we have to do what we can to fight against the monsoons. My rot gets so painful that some nights I wake up with bloody hands from scratching in my sleep. The medics run out of salve and it rains so hard for two days solid that we don't get any birds in. On the day that the rain lets up enough to fly, they come in constantly. Work parties, like ants, form an unbroken line from the landing pad. Ammo comes in; C-rations come; dry clothes and medical supplies; and finally mail.

■■■■■■■■■■

IT IS ABOUT THE MIDDLE OF THE AFTERNOON, AND IT HAS just begun to rain a little harder. Everybody is tired from humping ammo crates and cases of C's uphill through the mud, and some guys have begun to disappear into their hooches so that what was once an unbroken line gets to be a kind of dotted line, with gaps in between bunches of guys. I am walking downhill for a fresh load, with my Boonie hat on and a piece of a poncho liner on my shoulder as a pad, when I see the Shithook come out of the rain clouds in the valley to the west. There's only been one Shithook all day, and it brought a sling of ammo crates, so the sight of another one this late in the day distresses me. I am tired and hungry, and the smell of burning shit that crosses over the landing pad from the shitters has started to make me nauseous.

'Hooks fly differently from Slicks, because they're six

to eight times as big and have twin rotors. 'Hooks remind me of two grasshoppers fucking in midair. The front is controlled by the front blades, and the rear has its own set of blades, so sometimes 'Hooks settle down like they were segmented—they seem to lope across the air currents. Because of the way they fly when they are coming in and slowing down, a sling beneath them has the tendency to swing like a pendulum, and the great weight of a sling full of ammo or artillery pieces usually swings so much that the pilots have to overcorrect, which means they descend very, very slowly. This grasshopper-looking helicopter chugs out of the valley clouds and comes at us smoothly and steadily so long that I wonder if he intends to even drop his load. The sling hangs down slightly behind perpendicular from the bottom of the 'Hook until the pilot cuts its power; then the sling rocks forward and the pilot holds the bird still until it has finished rocking. By that time I, and about everybody around me, can see that it isn't ammo in the net—the net is full of cases of beer.

By the time the sling hits the ground there are a hundred men around the pad. There is a ring of lifers around the sling; then a detail from Commo comes down the hill with rifles. It's crazy, this doughnut of GIs with rifles holding back other GIs, but it makes sense because I would have snarfed as much beer as I could have carried and taken it back for our squad, and since there must be a hundred guys thinking the same thing, the army-within-the-Army is necessary. But the irony of it isn't lost on us guys bunched together staring at the guys from Commo staring at us, shit grins on their faces, like, "What the fuck am I going to do if they charge, shoot?" But nobody charges. The lifers take over and divvy the beer out by company, so that each squad gets a case.

The coolest place in our area is the hole full of water in the corner of our hooch, so we dump most of the case in there and each sit down with one. We are all there except Prophet.

"Wish I had half a bottle of whiskey to go with this," Callme says.

"A coupla shots and a coupla beers, yeah, that might do me right," Pea adds.

"A coupla shots, a coupla beers, a coupla redheads," Murphy says. His eyes get purposely big and he chugs away on his beer as if to emphasize his daydream.

"Couple shots, couple beers, couple women, couple lines of coke," Omar almost shouts, and closes one nostril with his knuckle.

My turn: "Couple shots, couple beers, couple women, couple lines, and a couple weeks."

We get drunk on a beer apiece. Not stumbling drunk, not sloppy, but goddamn happy. The war ceases to exist, as impossible as it seems. The rain seems warm and clean. The dope we smoke and the tape recorder going all help, not to mention the other cases of beer Prophet has stolen and brings now, hidden in a bundle of sandbags. The party goes on, fast at first, then slower and slower as the dope takes over. At times I feel lonely, homesick for Pops and Bull and Chickenfeed. When we get hungry we open five cans of C's and empty them into a helmet, then rapid-fire it with C-4. I am surprised that it is anything but warm, which would have been good enough, but it actually tastes good. After I finish eating, as though I am at home in Mom's living room, I have to take the first shit I've had to take in three days.

Outside, it is as dark as a goddamn empty movie theater. Out of habit, I take my rifle with me and head down the hill with my two packs of toilet paper under my armpit. The shitter is a lot farther away at night, with me half-drunk and Artillery shooting Night Fire from some other Z, than it is during the raining daytime, but I know the way, following the water canal that threads down the hill. Of course I take a couple missteps and get my right foot wet-ter, but I hardly notice, except to be sure I don't drop my toilet paper. The shitter is a three-sided outhouse, of sorts. The three sides are sandbags stacked five feet high, the shit can is a sawed-off fuel drum, and the toilet seat is an ammo crate with one board missing, so that it is only through practice and knowledge that I am able to sit down in the dark without sitting on my balls. In a stroke of insight, it comes to me why real toilet seats are shaped like teardrops, and when I hear my log splash in whatever kind of liquid is below me the feeling is like backing a car perfectly into a parking place—such perfect coordination. In fact, I hate to be done so quick. It is pleasant there, alone. The Z is not as dark as it seemed when I first came out from the candle-lit hooch. There are small light leaks that look fuzzy through the now-soft rain, and everybody is partying. I imagine Charlie knows it, but he couldn't do shit against this hill unless he had the helicopters that we have, or great big guns to bring big rounds in on us from a long ways off. I feel like writing home.

Prophet spoils the party, at least for me. Standing in the center of the hooch, straddling the candle and empty helmet-turned-cookpot with his arms spread out like a plastic Jesus, he mentions that he will be leaving the field the day after tomorrow. It occurs to me, looking at him in the candlelight, that he is standing almost exactly the same way he was standing when I first met him. Then he was bracing himself on the rafters of a hooch roof; now he has one hand planted in the muddy wall of the hooch and holds onto a flimsy board made from ammo-crate lumber that gives the poncho enough of a pitch to run the water off. I think back to how awful he smelled the first time; now all I can smell is incense from sticks stuck in the liner band of the helmet between his feet, the smoke curling up his crotch.

I was afraid of Prophet then. Now I'm seven months

from DEROS and I'm afraid of his being gone. And Peacock will leave in another month or less. When Peacock leaves I will have been in Nam longer than anybody else in the squad except Callmeblack.

"Prophet, what you going to do when you get home?"

"Goddamn if I know," he says, swinging his hands down and planting them in his pockets. He looks like he needs room to pace, but there isn't any. "I guess..." He pauses when the cassette comes to the end of the reel and brings a silence that seems loud after the ribaldry that came with the beer. "I guess," he starts again, "that I'll spend some of my money on a truck or a van or something and just travel around. I want to visit Pops and Chickenfeed, a couple other people. It's gonna be weird, y'know it? I mean being free, being back in the great big World, with pussy and TV, being able to get myself a beer anytime I want, seeing the trees change color, watching it snow. These last couple days I've been thinking of all kinds of shit that I miss. I *guess* I miss it. Like the sound of traffic and the way all the houses in my neighborhood light up at night. I can't wait to see my dog."

He takes his hands out of his pockets and puts them behind his head, then turns around on one toe, then turns again in the opposite direction. He finishes his beer and crushes the can, gets another one out of the sump hole. Only Omar and I are awake now. I can see the bottom of Omar's face in the light from the candle. When Prophet stands up again after getting the beer, all I can see of him is from his waist down; his filthy, wet, torn jungle utes, the envelope pockets bulging, remind me of two cactus plants.

There is a steady dripping behind where Omar sits. The way the poncho is rigged runs the water to that side of the hole, and it drips steadily into a gutter that we dug to help collect it into the sump hole. Omar gets up and bails water out of the sump with an ammo can.

"How long does it rain, dude?" he asks Prophet.

"It'll rain like this—days and nights—for maybe four months."

"Jesus."

"Be glad, Effengee, be glad. You guys will start humping again as soon as it starts to let up. Last year they moved us during the middle of the monsoon season, and if you think this is a bitch you should've been in on that one. The dumb fuckers moved us onto flat ground. The goddamn mud was knee-deep, and we dug down the first foot with our helmets. You couldn't keep the shit on a shovel, so we had to scoop our holes out. We worked shifts for four straight days before we got down to dry ground. They brought in big rolls of plastic and we built one solid roof, as long as a street-car. That goddamn plastic was a perfect zero-scope for the dinks' mortars and they brought it in on us every fucking night. We slept in shallow slit trenches and, when you could get to sleep, the next morning the sides of the trenches would be washed in; it was like sleeping in brown toothpaste. I was an Effengee then; Jesus, that seems like a long time ago. I had this dream one night, that I rolled out of the trench somehow and was rolling downhill, even though there wasn't hardly any hill, and then I saw this Indian with a bow and arrow and he shot me. The next night I was up to go out on LP and we got two mortar rounds and an RPG. I took some of the shrap from the RPG and got my nickname."

I've been watching Omar all the time Prophet is telling the story. Because of the way the light is flickering, watching his face makes me think of seeing one of those old newsreels they used to have at the movies. Omar's eyelids seem to work very slowly, and as he blinks his lids close and open together like a butterfly's wings.

"Dig it," I say. "Omar is an Effengee and I've got just about twice as much time as you had when I came over, Prophet."

"During the heavy-duty wet season it's boring, but time

disappears. Like, don't it seem like the time has gone fast now, even though you thought it was dragging, Chieu Hoi?"

"Abso-fuckin'-lutely. I can remember me and Callmeblack breaking three hundred days, and then two hundred fifty days, and it blows my fucking mind."

Omar's butterfly eyelids stay closed now. He is asleep sitting up, with his head tucked into a corner of the mud walls where no water drips. Prophet must notice he is asleep about the same time I do because he takes the can of beer out of his hand. Then, Prophet puts a chunk of mud into Omar's hand and tickles Omar's face with the end of a shoestring. Smith swipes at the spot and leaves a hunk of the red mud on the tip of his nose. Then he begins to snore.

"I remember when you came, Chieu Hoi." He has squatted down alongside where Omar sits snoring, with the splash of mud on his nose that looks orange in the candlelight now.

"You and another guy, right?"

"Ass: Albert Steven Saxon."

"Boy, was I nuts right about then. I didn't give a shit about you guys or anything else. In fact, I didn't like you."

This sends a quick chill through me, and I think just as quickly how I feel about Smith.

"It all makes some kind of sense, though. You know it? I mean, you've been here what, five and a half months? And now the whole squad has changed and when Peacock leaves you'll be a light squad again so you'll get some other Effengee and it's tough to break those guys in, ain't it? The other day, when the lifers came around about the fragging, I was worried. I mean, hell, man, I don't feel a bit bad about fucking with that asshole Billingham, but I'll be goddamn if I want to stay in LBJ. I'd kill somebody. And all the time the lifers were here I kept thinking they were going to get something out of one of these new guys that might give us away, and I kept thinking I'd end up killing the one they got it out of. Ain't that the shits?"

"Dig it. I was thinking like that too. I wasn't thinking about killing anybody, but I was worried about the lifers getting to one of them."

"That's part of the difference, see what I mean? If Pops had still been here he couldn't have even been as formal or courteous as I was; he would have told 'em to go fuck themselves. And I was thinking of killing somebody, and you were aware of all this shit, but you weren't thinking in terms of killing. I swear it has to do with how long you've been here, because right fucking now they would have to torture me to get me to say 'sir' to them. I'm so short I almost want something to happen, because nobody can touch me. I'm done. I've done what I came here to do— get home again."

"When I first came, when you didn't like me, I was scared of you. I thought you were a gung-ho muthafucker. Even Peacock and Pops and Bull all seemed kind of afraid of you, and still they seemed like they were gung-ho too. Even though I liked being in this squad, I had the feeling that we were all gonna get killed. Ass, his getting it the first night . . . well, I don't know. It seemed like you guys all just accepted it so matter-of-factly. I mean, fuck, man, he was the only guy I knew, except for Callme, and he fuckin' gets killed the first night out here. And you guys . . . goddamn, I just can't say what I mean to."

"I'm sitting here tripping, Chieu Hoi, because you're saying things, whether you can dig it or not, that I want to say, or I want to hear, something like that. I'm gonna be back in The World in three fuckin' days, think of that. And maybe I'm gonna be sitting in a bar in a week and think back to this very fuckin' moment. How am I gonna deal with it? What am I gonna say to the guy sitting next to me? What am I gonna say to *chicks*, man?"

Goddamn, he's crying. This fucking dude who I was so

afraid of a few months ago, the dude who everybody trusted with their lives when I came, the same Prophet who has been hit three fucking times and probably has a Silver Star coming, is crying now. The candlelight seems awfully bright when I look at him; then I realize it is getting light outside. He is sitting on a helmet with his knees drawn up and has streaks running through the mud on his face. I'd stay here another week if I could have a picture of what I see: Omar Smith, his face the color of a new paintbrush's bristles, his head cocked back and to the side toward Prophet, the orange mud dabbed on his nose and the white of his upper teeth showing; Prophet has his Boonie hat on and he is covered solid with the mud; his knees both show through his jungle utes and his arms are tucked in between them, a beer in his hands. As if to give me the feeling that I just snapped the picture with a flash, the candle gives one last burst and dies slowly. During the burst of light, their faces both shine and everything else seems dull: the mud behind them with streaks of water running through it, the ring of a grenade Prophet has for some reason hung round his neck, and those perfectly straight streaks down Prophet's cheeks.

The light now is soft and seems green. I hear somebody get up and something falls or rolls around in the hole next door and I'm going to close my eyes for just a minute. If I could have that picture I'd get it blown up and I would title it. I would call it . . .

● ● ● ● ● ● ● ● ● ● ●

I'M DEPRESSED WHEN I WAKE UP. MAYBE I'M HUNG OVER. I figure I fell asleep sitting up, but I wake up on my back, sort of covered by my field jacket. I'm so fucking miserable. I just want to get clean, for chrissakes. I'm the only one in the hole. I look in my field jacket for a dry pack of cigarettes but the cigarette pocket is empty. In one of the bottom pockets is a pack of Camels. This isn't my jacket.

In the other big pocket is a wad of shoestrings. It's Prophet's jacket. That is why I am so depressed. I'll bet I spent most of the night thinking about Prophet leaving. I try to remember my dream. Nothing. The Camel is stronger than dope and I spend a few minutes blowing smoke rings, easy to do with Camels. I don't get many good ones, but just as the heat begins to burn my fingers I get a beauty that starts out parallel with the side of the hole. It dances in slow motion and finally turns on its side, still round, ghost-colored, until it reaches the plane of the ground, when a wind takes its shape away and it dissolves into the hard rain.

I don't want to get up. I don't want to leave the hole. I don't want to go out for overhead. I want to turn my head to the corner and cry. I wish I was a kid and in my mother's kitchen, able to cry. Prophet has been my mother; he covered me up last night with his field jacket, but I won't cry to him.

Murphy drops down into the hole.

"Hey."

"Hey."

Part of his F.N.G. look is gone. His clothes are all muddy, but they are still crisp. He has his helmet on and the helmet cover is a dead giveaway because there's nothing written on it except *Murphy*. Seeing him helps hide my depression from me for a bit. I have noticed that I switch into a different role around the new guys. It isn't consciously pulling rank, but I always feel like I used to feel when I was the oldest kid on the baseball team.

"Peacock's sick as hell," Murphy says.

"Say what?"

"They think he's got malaria. He's out of his mind. Sometimes he knows where he is and sometimes he thinks he's home."

"Where's he at?"

"Up the hill, in a medic's hooch."

The goddamn rain is torrential. It moves mud down the hill in sloppy wedges as big as the hood of a car. Walking uphill through the mud is like walking through big snowdrifts with heavy boots on, and the rain comes like a billion cold-water faucets. When the drops hit the ground it sounds like dropping a rock in a pond and—because looking down is the only way I can see anything—it fascinates me for a minute to see the rain come down and pick up mud, then scurry downhill. The holes my boots make disappear almost as fast as I can pull my foot out.

Prophet is standing outside the medic's hooch like it isn't raining where he's standing, like he is out behind a church smoking a cigarette, like he isn't waiting to leave the field tomorrow.

"What's the word?"

"He's delirious. A minute ago he was saying something about his roller skates being different colors."

"Are they going to dust him off?"

"Can't get a bird in here now," he says sharply.

I'm only three feet away from him and I can barely make out his blue eyes and those sharp cheekbones because there is so much water falling between us. At the same time I think of the story of Noah's Ark, and it dawns on me that I haven't seen Peacock reading the Bible for a long time. He isn't religious about it or anything, he reads it because of the stories, he says. Still, for no reason I could explain, I turn back downhill. I have to dig my heels in with all the force I can to keep from sliding chin-first to the hooch. I go to Peacock's ruck and open the top flap just enough to get my hand in and feel around until I find it. I tuck it into my pants, then hunch back up the hill and go straight into the hooch without saying anything to Prophet. There is an electric light inside and maybe four or five inches of water on the bottom of the hole. There are skids down, but they are floating, and when I step on one corner it sinks into the mud underneath. Along one side of the hooch is a shelf made from ammo-crate lumber with all kinds of bottles and pastic bags on it. The hooch is wide and long but not very deep. The roof is made out of the metal shit they put down for landing pads, with holes in it about three inches in diameter, and the sandbags on top of it are soaked and leaking. There is a prop on each end of the aisle that keeps the roof from sagging any more than it is now. On one side of the aisle is a medic, in a tee shirt and clean utes. He nods at me, then looks back down at whatever he is reading or thumbing through. It looks like some kind of reference book.

Peacock is lying on the stretcher across the aisle from him. He is lying quiet with his eyes open in a profound version of the thousand-meter stare. He's looking straight up at the ceiling, and even though he is covered with dry blankets he's shivering a little.

"Pea?"

"Forget it, man," the medic tells me. "He's junked up. There's nothing we can do except try to keep his temperature down." He leans over enough to pull the blanket back, and I see that Pea is covered with plastic bags of water with melting ice floating up near the top. Pea doesn't react. It scares me. I know that malaria causes fever, and if your fever gets too high it can cause permanent brain damage. Callmeblack pokes his head through the poncho that covered the door, then disappears again. I'm still standing on the corner of the skid and the other end is sticking up out of the water in the middle of the aisle. The medic steps on it and looks at me.

"Fuck it. I just brought him this."

I hold the Bible out.

"I can't understand books unless they've got graphs and charts," he says.

I feel like a clown, not for any particular reason, but I'm ready to leave, so I stick the Bible underneath the blankets near Pca's feet and go outside. Prophet is gone. Nobody is in sight. I stand where Prophet was standing, long enough to get a cigarette lit underneath my hood and take a couple of drags. Then I put the cigarette in my mouth and look up. I drag with all my might to get as hot a fire on its end as I possibly can, and I keep dragging on it, blowing the smoke out all at the same time. I'm fighting the rain, and it finally wins. When the cigarette is half ash it falls apart in the middle. Fuck this rain. They oughta make a helicopter that can fly through this, but if it could it would be able to fly under water.

Back at our hooch, everybody is sitting in a huddle. There's water a foot deep near the sump hole and three or more inches everywhere else. Everything has been stacked on ammo crates and covered with an extra poncho.

"Chieu Hoi, Callme, you guys better take your squad out and get a coupla logs," Prophet says. It stuns me, the way he says *your* squad, but it also dawns on me that Callme and I are the oldest guys now, all things considered. I wouldn't expect Prophet to go out with us, but I know damn well he would if Peacock wasn't sick. Ever since I've been in Nam I've been fascinated by the way things go on. I'm not about to break it down.

"Let's go."

So down the hill. The perimeter isn't very far away from our hole, but there are only two guys sitting on the other side of the pile of concertina, smoking a bowl and trying to stay covered up with a poncho. Since there is one roll of the wire half stretched out, I figure they must be on detail, probably supposed to be stretching the wire. I'm walking first.

It seems a little strange to be going out into the Bush again after being on the Z for such a long time. There is almost no chance of hitting any shit, because everybody from our side of the hill who's gone out for overhead goes out this way. In fact, we see another group not too far away working with an ax on a tree that looks too big to carry.

Callme is walking last and carrying the radio, and it strikes me that this is the first time outside of the wire for the F.N.G.s. I glance back at Smith and see about what I expect: he looks tense and he is moving his head back and forth. I wait for him to catch up to me.

"Hey, man, we're not going to hit any shit out here today."

"Fuckin'-A, Jack. How do you *know* we're not gonna hit anything?"

"Well, true, dude, I don't know. But I doubt it. Anyway, what I wanted to tell you was that if we were on a hump you wouldn't be watching both sides of the trail and behind you, like you are. Just watch your left side."

I signal for Murphy to come up and tell him to watch the right side.

"Yeah," Callme says, "let's play war. It's been a long time since we been in any shit and I kinda miss it."

He is joking, but those guys don't know that. He looks huge. He has on a poncho and the radio is underneath it, with its aerial coming out the hood. I love the guy.

As soon as I have to start hacking with my machete I begin looking for a tree that will make a big enough log. It's going to be tough enough getting the log back up the hill without having to go through this extra thick shit. Either the rain has slowed a little or the canopy is holding it out. We pick out a tree about ten inches in diameter and start whaling on it with the ax, one guy at a time, the other three on a half-ass lookout. We picked some kind of hard tree. Its leaves are shaped like the bill of a hat and we'll be able to get two logs out of this one tree. I wonder if two of us can carry a log or if we'll all have to come back for the second one. Finally the tree comes down and its branches hang it up off the ground a couple feet. We hack the trunk off at about ten feet and test the weight. It is heavy, but we think two of us can carry it, so we skin the branches off the top and chop off another log about the same length.

It takes almost an hour to get back to the wire. It isn't nearly as far from there to our hole, but the mud makes it impossible to carry the logs. We end up trying to roll one log uphill, which works for a while; then we stick the ax in the top end and two guys pull on it and two guys push. I'm on the pushing end, and by the time we reach the hole I'm solid mud from my fatigue pockets on down. Callme uses the spade to clean me off, peeling off chunks like old paint that is two inches thick.

They're bringing in a Dustoff for Peacock. As always, we hear it before we see it; this time the reason we can't see it is that the clouds and rain are too thick. It's a funny kind of feeling to stand a little distance away when they load Pea onto the bird, like a funeral—not because he is dead and we won't see him anymore—but, since he's doped up and delirious, he couldn't talk back even if we talked to him. So, seeing the medics load him up is sad. The rain washing around in the helicopter's propeller looks like sweat coming off a boxer's face, but silken, more like ice and snow flying behind a snow tire.

■■■■■■■■■■

WE GET THE LOG OVER THE HOOCH, STRETCH THE PONCHO over it, and weight the ends down with sandbags, so it's almost like a real roof. Even though there is probably only a couple hours until dark, we decide to go back after the other log and all five of us go out. When we get out there our whole mood changes for some reason. Prophet is ecstatic. I've never seen him act so crazy. He radios in for permission, then heaves a couple frags as high into the trees as he can. We are a little high, and it is a show to see the frag burst and blow miniature fountains in every direction; then the leaves and sticks come down like rain themselves.

Omar is holding a frag, tossing it into the air and catching it over and over. I can tell he is itching to heave it.

"Throw it," I tell him.

"I always wanted to wheel one of these fuckers when we were working out with 'em in Basic, but of course the asshole DIs wouldn't let me."

"Go ahead, bigstuff," Prophet says. "I don't believe you're any better than I am, or even Chieu Hoi. Chieu Hoi has had a lot of practice at lobbing these fuckers, and I've got five dollars American that says he can match you."

All five of us are crouched behind the log and passing the bowl back and forth. I stand up and throw a frag at a spot on a tree about ten meters away. The spot isn't very big; in fact, the fucking tree isn't very big. The frag barely makes it to the tree on the roll. There is a kind of natural alleyway in the direction we're looking, where the target tree is. We stay behind the fallen tree when we throw in case one of the pins comes out during the flight or bounces out somehow when the frags hit. Mine doesn't hit hard enough to even bend the pin, let alone loosen it. Omar stands up. His face takes on a different look, pure concentration, and he throws three straight strikes, one of which is a direct hit on the spot. And he *wings* the muthafuckers. Before this, I didn't actually believe he was good enough to try out for the Bigs, but I know different now.

If I hadn't seen this happen, I wouldn't believe it: Prophet starts throwing grounders to Omar—pinned frags —and Omar fields them perfectly, three or four times in a row. I am sitting on the log watching. Callmeblack is watching too, calling the runners out. Then Omar tells Prophet to pull the pin on one and throw him a grounder.

"Say fuckin' what?"

"Give me a live one. I can field that fucker and wing it so fast that if Charlie was running to that tree down there he'd be out in time to turn a double play."

"Smith, you're out o' your fuckin' mind, man. Sure as hell, you'd fumble one, and we'd all be dead. You dumb bastard."

"Don't call me a dumb bastard."

"You are dumb, goddamn it!"

"And you've never fucked around over here, huh? You've never done anything out of the ordinary. You're in for a Star; tell me what you did was not dumb."

"There's a difference, Effengee." Prophet looks upset. I mean, he looks confused. His breathing is very fast. He is trying to outstare Smith, but Omar isn't backing down. I don't think Smith is afraid of him, although he might be. I don't know what to think. Then, all of a sudden, Prophet's old self seems to come back. His eyes narrow but his face relaxes.

"You throw me one first," he says.

Now it is Smith's turn to be confused. There are probably six grenades lying around the base of the tree and, maybe to buy time to think, he walks down to get them.

"Let's get the fuck out of here," I say.

"I'm all for that," Murphy says.

"Old Smith is out to prove somefuckinthing," Callme says.

"He's gonna prove five of us can die in one burst," Prophet says.

"He might come back here and throw you one, like you told him," Callme says.

"Ain't no goddamn way," Prophet says. "I just called his bluff. If he wants to play, he's the one who's gonna be the fielder. I'm pitching, then I'm diving the fuck behind that log."

"Voices travel out here," Smith says, back now with an armload of frags.

"What the hell can this prove?"

"I don't want to lose my concentration over here. Throw me one." He sets the rest of them down and tosses one to Prophet.

"Well, goddamn it, the way I see it, I can sure as hell get behind that log before it goes off, so if it goes you're the dead one; and if you do it—well, muthafucker, that's one more story for me to take back to The World with me."

"Throw it."

The three of us move up toward the other end of the log. I still don't believe it's going to happen. I wonder how I could tell anybody about this if Prophet really does pull the pin and Smith really does field it like it is a ground ball and, if it goes off, blows himself—at least him—all to shit, trying to prove something. I know he's only trying to prove it to himself. I can tell by the look on his face that he is in a different world. Even if he does do it, I'll be thinking about it every time we're together for the next few months. The two of them are standing maybe fifteen meters away. We three have gotten out of range and can duck behind the log. Prophet and Smith are staring at each other. Then Prophet throws the frag, still pinned. Smith doesn't go for it. Prophet spits and looks back at us. He looks at the log, and over it, behind it. He looks at Smith and pulls a pin. I see it all in slow motion. Like it is a routine, Smith goes down on it, scoops it up, *hesitates*— and whistles it side-armed at the tree. There is nothing slow-motion about the burst. The sound seems exactly as loud as it should be. It echoes twice. I look first at Murphy, who is blank-eyed and sweating, the scar around his right eye looking like the mark a windshield-wiper arm leaves on a windshield when the blade is worn out.

Callme is headed toward the other two. He slaps five to both of them at the same time. I understand now that he had something invested in this, more than I did, as much as Prophet did, because Smith is black and Callme shares the pride of the accomplishment. We all slap our hands together.

"Time for me to go the fuck home," Prophet says. "My reflexes are shot. Once I rolled that sonofabitch I couldn't move."

"You missed the tree," Murphy says.

WE GET THE LOG BACK UP TO THE HOOCH AND WORK FOR three hours in the dark that is full of rain. Now all five of us can sleep, curled up like puppies, under the roof, and we do.

By morning the rain has slowed. There will be birds coming in. Prophet makes a fast round around the Z saying good-bye; then we sit in our hooch and wait. We listen to Armed Forces Radio: Chickenman. We smoke some. We probably all hear the first bird at the same time, the sound of it cutting through pockets of wet air, the changing sound when it comes closer. Prophet shoulders his ruck and shakes our hands. There are tears in my eyes, so I can't tell if there are any in his. I don't want to look at him anyway.

"You guys keep your fuckin' heads down."

The bird brought in supplies, and the padmen and a detail unload the supplies while Prophet stands waiting, his ruck up high on his back, his rifle in one hand. He has his Boonie hat on and has to hold it down. He shakes the padman's hand and the padman goes to his radio set to talk to the pilots. Prophet gets in and sits on the floor of the helicopter with his feet on the landing struts. The bird goes straight up and hovers momentarily, then crosses over the Z on the other side. When it comes back over us, the pilot has it on its side and Prophet has popped a smoke grenade. The red smoke fans out, and when the pilot banks hard and sends the bird up fast, Prophet pops a yellow smoke. The bird climbs, then levels off and hesitates, floats, dips down once more and rolls to its other side, and banks on a plane parallel with the side of our mountain. It gives me chills. Probably fifty guys on the Z are outside to watch it, and forty-nine cheer and raise their arms in salute to the pilot and to Prophet. I raise both my arms, the chill of my back between them, but I can't overcome the lump in my throat to cheer. The feeling seems familiar but I never figure out why.

PEACOCK'S BIRD

IN A LITTLE OVER A WEEK, ORDERS COME DOWN AND I AM a squad leader. I get a promotion. Callmeblack gets a promotion too. So now Two Squad is my squad, and I feel different. I don't know how I feel, except different. I've got Callme and Omar and Chas Murphy. And Peacock is still in Two; he outranks me, but he is too short to be made squad leader. He has come back and lies around the hooch all day long. He almost never comes outside. He reads and washes his face with peroxide.

"Jesus, I'm going home in a week, boys," he says one night, "and my mother is going to see this goddamn tattoo." He's been taking his malaria medicine and drinking cough syrup for a solid week, and nowadays when he looks at you there is a dullness there that is new. I feel sad for him, but I can't say why. Sometimes I think he's mostly homesick. He could be homesick for home and he could be homesick for the old Two Squad. He just stays fucked up all the time and we leave him alone. We're busy enough waterproofing the roofs. We steal a tarpaulin from near the helicopter pad and stretch that over the first two layers of sandbags, then put another layer on top of it. It works for a couple days but somehow it begins to leak, so the floor of the hooch is constantly muddy. It keeps on raining like hell and there isn't any activity except for Artillery shooting

Night Fires every night. They use up a lot of ammo, and every fairly clear day a Shithook slings a fresh load in and we hump it up the hill. We build everything we need out of empty artillery-round boxes. We eventually have four bunks with hammocks slung above them. Pea helps us build things like the bunks and a writing table that fits into the back wall of the hooch, but he doesn't go outside except to resupply himself with cough medicine. I don't know where he gets it, but I know he takes far more than he's registered for. He's always mellow-high. Omar doesn't like to be around him and sleeps in the other hole. Chas likes him and listens to him tell war stories. I like to hear them too. Pea tells some of the same ones Prophet told. He tells us Prophet was balls-out when he first came, that he really does deserve a Silver Star, that he went through a period where he could do no wrong.

"I fuckin' love Prophet," he says. "And I loved Chickenfeed, and I love you guys too. There is something far beyond the ken of the human mind at work in this mud," he says. Then, because he knows he just said something the rest of us will have to think about, he lies back on his bunk and blows smoke toward the roof. He's got fours days left.

When somebody leaves, it always takes a few days before anything seems normal. I remember when Pops left: Prophet was weirded out for the next week. I don't know how to think about it. I am glad they are going home, for goddamn sure, but thinking about going home can only mean thinking about *me* going home. It's hard for me to think of Peacock back in The World. Over here, he's been a strange bird. He's the best read of anyone I've met over here, and it seems like he might have been a little punkish before he got here—although I don't have any way to know that—yet here he's been as valuable as anyone. He always pulled his load and I look at him now and think of all the times I saw him walking down the trails with the

Sixty over his shoulder, or out in front of him like he was a janitor in a basement, come to wash down the jungle and the Sixty was his mop. It's up to me now to say who carries what. I can't imagine a better gunner than Callme, but I wouldn't want to tell him to be a gunner, I'd want to ask him.

It just keeps on raining. All day long. Every bit of the whole top of the world is emptying into our laps, into our hooches. I have to scrub my rifle every day because it rusts right through the WD-40. The rust on my gun, the rot on my body, these crazy blow-a-hole-in-the-jungle LZs the Army builds, the planes and bombs and dynamite bits that pierce the air over this country . . . all these things seem like they're part of the same cancer. This war seems too small and far away, looking at it from The World, and we aren't men, we're scabs that will go away.

It keeps on raining all night; even the raindrops seem hot. It is too hot to sleep, and the humidity makes condensation form on the low points of the hooch roof, and these drops are hot too. I try lying in my bunk until the sweat that runs down the sides of my face begins to drive me nuts and makes me think there is something crawling all over me. Pea is awake, reading and smoking. He has glasses on but they don't go over his ears; they're stuck to the side of his head. Whatever he is reading looks like it has awfully small print, and the light is only something like seven watts. My mom would warn him against reading without a better light; she'd tell him he'll go blind later in life and by that time it's too late to do anything. I mop the sweat off me as best I can with my poncho liner. The liner is made of some kind of slick material and it isn't very absorbent, so it's like using a squeegee on my face.

Smith is sleeping in this hooch tonight, and I think he's asleep. Two nights ago I woke him up for guard, except he wasn't asleep, he was turned toward the wall crying. I felt sorry for him. I asked him if he wanted to rap and he said no, but he thanked me. The more I'm around him, the more I like him, even though we never say much to each other. It's weird being cooped up on the LZ. I miss going outside the wire, and I didn't ever think I'd think that way. I wouldn't want to go out to hit any shit, but hanging around this goddamn hill for three weeks has begun to make me realize that time went a lot faster when we were outside some of the time. We spend most of the days changing things around little by little. We have bunker walls built between our section and the ones above us and below us. I wonder if there are ten thousand sandbags on this hill yet. Some of the walls are nothing more than dikes to channel the water: short and stubby and thicker on the bottom than on the top. All of a sudden—I don't go to sleep or anything—I'm back home. I'm back at Grandaddy's farm, what is left of it. There are sixty fenced-off acres. He used to keep milk cows, but when Grandma died he quit. He cares mostly about his orchard. The orchard probably has twenty trees in it and is surrounded by a fence made out of round stones that he brought in from the fields he used to plow. Every Sunday he walks around the stone fence and rearranges part of it. Sometimes he will knock some of it apart and restack the boulders, and sometimes he'll only kick the bottom rock in tighter. Blue racers live in the rocks and sun themselves on the berry bushes that grow in one corner. Grandaddy is not the least bit afraid of those snakes. He says they guard his orchard from moles.

I am walking with him, no taller than the fences and only strong enough to lift the little rocks that are on top of the wall. He lets me move any of the top ones I want to. He says he likes to arrange them according to the color, but to me they all look almost the same color except for the dark gray ones he calls niggerheads. When I see him leaning in the fork of an apple tree and trimming off the peeling of an apple I know what Omar was crying about. One of the first places I want to go when I get home is to the

241

orchard. It is a small hill across the creek from what was the farmhouse, grown over with weeds the last time I was there. I'm old enough to lift the big ones now, and I might want to kick some of the bottom—

Fwooomp, fwooomp, fwoomp.

You're shitting me.

It's definitely the sound of rounds leaving mortar tubes. I straighten up and bump my head on the roof. Peacock pulls the light off the battery, and I can hear him move but I can't tell where he goes. Then the rounds hit, not too far away. There are three more times that we can hear the rounds leave, then hit. The barrage walks right past us. It is probably hitting down the hill.

"Smith, incoming," Peacock says. His voice isn't out of control but there is a trace of something in it. Panic, maybe. As he finishes, we hear the next three rounds leave their tubes. By now there is a Sixty working out and then I can hear a grenade launcher go to work, then two more. The origination of the sounds is about 90 degrees one direction from our door, so they are shooting over the Z and the Z is returning fire from the direction of Charlie Company.

"Oh, muthafucker," Peacock wails. "Why tonight? How long are those goddamn dinks gonna fuck with me? Are they gonna fight all goddamn night? Chieu Hoi, you're awake, for chrissakes, aren't you?

"Yeah. I'm going." I'm down off my bunk now, feeling in my ruck for my flashlight since I loaned the other one to Callme.

"Going where, asshole?"

I find the light and grab my rifle. I flip the light toward the side that the other two are on. Peacock is sitting on his bunk against the mud corners of the hooch, now without his glasses. Smith is fumbling with his helmet. I beam the light directly on his rifle to see if I can tell if the safety is on, but I can't and I go to the door. I don't want to be up and moving until I get the rhythm of the mortars down.

"Smith."

"Yeah."

"Stay close behind me. We're going next door first."

Everything is slippery. I put my bandolier around my neck, and while I'm trying to crawl out of the hole the bandolier trips me up and gets tangled around one knee, so I jerk it loose and drag it along by the torn end. We stay low to the ground. There are illumination flares up now and the Sixty is pouring a solid burst on a straight line. There are grenade launchers working too, but no 16's. All the noise is on that one side of the Z. I figure it's just a small squad that sneaked close enough to get off a dozen rounds and *didi-mau*. I know, though, that it means we'll be pulling extra guard. And I know too that the chance of sappers coming at the hill from our section has increased.

"Callme, Murphy."

"We're up, come on in."

This hole is bigger than ours and it is easy to post a guard at the door and still leave room for the others. I have Smith hang at the door and then go down. Since we aren't on the perimeter, our Sixty can't be set up and it is hung between two of the roof supports. Callme has the M-79 broken down and is just now putting it back together. No more rounds have landed since Smith and I made our move. There is a constant popping of our mortars, then the sound of the illumination rounds snapping their parachutes open, and the light that comes in the door is like the light from a movie projector: that color, and flickering. Smith gets silhouetted against the light. He is crouched and has his rifle pointing out. I can tell at a glance that his helmet is crammed so tight onto his head it should hurt. There is nothing for us to do except be sure our weapons are all ready. Murphy and I break our rifles down and shoot them up with WD-40. It takes us about a minute apiece. I count nine grenades, about half of what we should have. Then I think of Peacock by himself in the other hooch. On my way back across the wall, sliding on my ass, it strikes me as incredible that I feel like the protector, that I can even conceive of protecting, or at least feeling protective of, him. It's the total opposite of what used to be.

"Pea, where ya at?" I don't wait for the answer. I slide right through the door. He has his light hooked up again and his glasses on, but I notice he's got his 16, and it's locked and loaded and on rock and roll.

"I'm trying to not be an asshole, man, but do me a favor and flip your safety on, will ya?"

"No. I'm going to disobey a direct order; it seems like a short-timer's prerogative to disobey a direct order, and if you're as high up as I can get one from to disobey, then I'll have to settle for it, but I'm keeping mama wide open all night long, Chieu Hoi."

Partly because everything seems totally fucked up anyway, and partly because it half pisses me off and even scares me, I grab his rifle and lock the safety on. His face is full of surprise, and mine probably is too. It was an action I hadn't thought of ahead of time, just something that I did, and even while I was doing it it seemed absurd. It seems just as absurd when I hand it back to him and even more so when he looks at me and flips it back off.

"Jesus, man, it's not that I don't trust you. You know that. It's just that I've heard too many stories about short-timers fucking themselves up."

Without saying anything, very slowly and with poignant accuracy, he points it at my nuts. My nuts pull into my lungs and shut down my breathing. I pull my shoulders up and start trembling. I expect him to pull the fucking trigger. And if I had shut my eyes he would have pulled it as soon as the barrel got to his neck but I kick at him, at wherever my foot happens to be as I swing my leg, and I am perfectly lucky because I kick it out of his hands and it never goes off. For ten seconds he has the cough-syrup blankness in his face; then his mouth begins to quiver and he closes his eyes. By this time I have hold of his forestock and he isn't even holding on. So I am leaning over him, prepared to do whatever I have to, and he is melting like his face is paraffin. He has his eyes closed so tight that the tops of his skinny cheeks meet his eyebrows and his mouth keeps on moving like a goldfish's does against a glass bowl. It goes on for another minute, me braced against the top bunk and pinning his rifle against the muddy wall, him never changing until I expect something to force its way out: a tear or a scream or a glob of spit or a sigh, one of the pimples on his forehead to burst—something. The flickering of the illumination rounds continues and makes everything that can cast a shadow perform muddy dances. The smell of gunpowder has drifted in too, but as soon as I smell that I realize it is nothing compared to the stench of our collective sweat, and as soon as I realize that I realize, for the first time, that my other hand is around Peacock's neck. I don't know if I have been squeezing hard or not, but as soon as I see it—I see it before I feel it—I pull it off, horrified. I fall back onto his knees, still pinning his rifle against the wall. I look to it as though it might be the only possible connection to reality. It is there in my hand in all its ugly dull black shame.

Peacock still has his eyes cinched shut, but now he is breathing hard and most of the colors in his huge tattoo fight each other in the flickering light. I use the hand that a minute ago had him by the throat to wipe the sweat off my forehead; then I trace the outline of the tattoo on his chest and finally rub him as though I was in The World and on top of a girl. Without opening his eyes, he stops my hand and holds it. I still expect to see something squeeze out of those eyes, but we sit there as though the mud had turned us to clay.

Callme comes in. I can see the confusion in his face by

the little light from Peacock's reading bulb, and I try to signal him with my eyes but he probably can't see my face.

"What the fuck, homes?"

"I . . . we . . . it . . ." I don't know what to say.

"C'mon in, bro," Pea says. "If I've got any more explaining to do I'll do it in the morning, but, simply stated, your squad leader just saved my life."

Callme is still confused, but he sits down on the step and just looks at us, one at a time. I still don't have anything to say when Callme, his voice as deep as the mud, says, "I've seen a lot of that over here. I've seen more lives get saved than I've seen get took, and my black ass is one of them too." Then he pauses, just long enough to take one deep breath and smile, before he says, "You guys go on holding hands. I'm gonna go fight the war with these Effengees in the next hole."

The war is over for the night but I never go to sleep, and I see the morning sneak into the hooch: first light is as red as the mud, then it turns toward yellow, then the rain starts and the light is no color at all, and I fall asleep.

I expect to get sent outside the wire, to recon. I don't expect Peacock to go along. I don't want him along, but when I tell him that I can't think of any argument against what he says.

"Chieu Hoi, it's my only chance to leave this fucking country with any balls. I am not trying to prove a goddamn thing to you. I am going to prove to myself that the first time I pick up a gun in The World I'll know what end I want to look at."

So we go out, Callme walks point. Omar is second, then Murphy with the radio, and Peacock is last, behind me, with the Sixty. We're not very far out before we find where they set up their tubes. The imprint in the ground that the base of the mortars leaves is about half a foot deep. So these poor fuckers were out here pulling their tubes apart when the base was firing back, and from the looks of the hole that the baseplate left, that wouldn't have been a quick job. There is a blood trail too. It's not much of a trail to start with, and just about the time we find it it starts to rain again, so we not only lose the trail, we can't follow the steps very far either.

The stuff we're going through is pretty thin because it is still close enough to the Z that the details that went out to get overhead for the hooches have matted the shit down pretty much. We move plenty slow because since the trails are so well worn it is muddy. Besides, we don't want to go out very far. It feels like playing ball again after not playing for some time. Everything strikes me as a little uncoordinated and sloppy. We bunch up on each other too often, and even though the stuff we're going through isn't all that thick and is pretty easy to see through, we stay closer together than we should most of the time. I sense a kind of tension in Peacock when I look back at him, even though he raises his prescription sunglasses and gives me the thumb. Murphy is all over the trail, trying to keep watching his side and shifting the weight of the radio first toward one side, then toward the other. When Callme stops us we're just beginning to get into some thicker stuff. Murphy strips out of the radio and starts adjusting the straps. His face is red and full-blown and determined-looking all at the same time.

When I pass Omar I'm surprised that he looks as good as he does. He not only doesn't look tired, he also doesn't look especially apprehensive, not as uptight as I expected him to. I slap him on the shoulder and then, as an afterthought, I give his neck a few squeezes the way Pops used to do.

Callme has his helmet pushed way up on his forehead and is staring ahead of us. The rainwater drips off the back of his helmet in brown drops. He is carrying his M-79, and I notice he has an extra bunch of canister rounds in his ruck harness.

"It's weird out here, ain't it, man?" I tell him.

"I'm hip. We got us a different squad."

"Smith OK, or have you been looking back at him?"

"Seems all right, but he doesn't watch me close enough. I had to stop him twice. No big deal."

"Which side's he taking?"

Callme says right but points left. I just look at him until he realizes what he's doing, then he shrugs.

"You wanna get hold of Higher?"

"Yeah, maybe they'll pull us back in."

"Fine with my tired ass. I'm out of shape."

But instead of calling us back they want us to change direction by 90 degrees, which means getting off the trail. I switch Peacock and Smith and saddle up. The rain seems hard, the ruck seems heavy, and the Bush seems thick. We're walking on an incline now, and a lot of the feeling I have about this being an easy safe hump leaves me. This is my first time out as squad leader, and we've got two F.N.G.s. I tell everyone that we should cut down the distance between us and move even slower.

The hump ends up being like a training exercise. We spend that day and that night outside, never seeing shit after we found the blood trail, and once we're out there I get a different kind of fix or feeling or something for the new guys. Peacock seems back closer to his old self, except I sense an apprehension when we find out we're going to stay out for the night. The most important feeling I get is a lot like what I had when I coached kids, but it's a feeling far vaster: kids can only get beat at baseball—a squad gets wiped out in a war. Still, being outside on this mission that doesn't mean much is a good way to break in as a rookie squad leader, and—it's an ace in the hole—I've got a guy out here with me who has to go home tomorrow, so they can't keep us out.

When we contact Higher-higher and they tell us to head back to the Z, we shoot the straightest azimuth we can and

Callme cuts us a trail so direct it'd take a chalkline to mark it.

When we're back in sight of the hill we stop to call in and everybody looks happy in the rain, which comes now at a different angle, mostly out of the north. We pull up and smoke, joke, bullshit, and two things come to me at once when I pick up the radio mike: I'll never see Peacock cradling that Sixty again, and soon I'll begin dealing with lifers and officers because I'm head of this bunch. Peacock looks like he has so many times; slumped against a set of vines, his glasses crooked across his face like a broken line on a weather map; the Sixty its own kind of monument to him somehow as he cleans its mech with the same pink toothbrush I've seen him use for months. He sniffles—not quick sniffles, but somewhere in between a snot-sucker-upper and a breath that bubbles—and strokes the tooth-brush into the mechanism, turns it like he is listening to tumblers fall, then pulls it out with his patented flair. A squad has to trust that fucking gun. We trust if for the confidence it gives us, mostly at night. So if you have to trust the gun you have to trust the gunner, and though I trust Callme the most I need him to be able to rotate positions and it's gotta be either me or him on point for a while. So I decide to try Smith on the Sixty, and I decide to try to explain why to him, and why he has to be good.

■■■■■■■■■■■

I EXPECT PEACOCK'S EXIT TO BE LOW-KEY. I EXPECT HIM to stay stoned all night and all the time until the bird comes, then almost sneak away. But Pea is the epicure of the company, and he proves it by conning somebody out of a canned ham and before the sky even gets dark we are having a party. There's a bottle of whiskey and Omar gets tight with the guy who has it. Murphy and Omar stay pretty close together, so Murphy gets his own self cooked and is holding a small court half an hour after some of

Peacock's invited guests start showing up. Three Squad comes in pairs as their guard gets relieved. I haven't seen much of them since we met right after the ambush, and by the time they get there I am cooked and just want to sit against the sandbags and watch. It isn't raining very hard, and I am under a poncho that makes a lean-to with the sandbag wall, so I just sit back.

An hour into the party, about ten rounds hit on the other side of the Z. I don't know if I am so fucked up and tired I can't react, or whether I somehow know it is only incoming a hill away, but I don't even move. Peacock does, though. He makes it into the hooch, and when I finally get up to go to bed I find him sound asleep with his glasses in his hand. He left his reading light on and an open book is on his chest. I know it's not his Bible but I don't know what it is. I put the light out and crawl up into my bunk. The rain barely makes any noise through the three layers of sandbags, but the sound it does make reminds me of a kitten purring.

■■■■■■■■■■■

A CQ RUNNER COMES AROUND TO FETCH ME FOR MY FIRST meeting as squad leader. The rain is pretty slow, and even before I leave I know I won't get a chance to talk to Pea before he leaves. He is disbursing his souvenirs, and I get to stay around long enough to see him perform his version of good-bye: he sets his Issue glasses on a sandbag that Murphy has leaned against the only standing vegetation on the edge of the perimeter, some kind of bush shaped like a crutch, and he borrows a canister round from Callme, takes aim, and blows the sandbag and the glasses all to hell. He gets a cheer from all of us, and he'll probably lose a stripe for it. He could give a shit. There's a bunch of guys around him but I butt in. Just as I do I hear the first bird coming.

"Hey," he says, "I never say good-bye. You know that."

"Hey, OK."

"Hey, keep your fuckin' head down, Sarge." Without his Issue glasses his eyes look bigger, which doesn't make sense. Maybe I wouldn't have noticed it, except he winks at me real slow and it looks like a garage door going down.

The meeting is held in the TOC conex. TOC stands for Tactical Operations Center, I think. Here I am, squad leader of Two Squad, Echo Company, and I'm not even positive I know what TOC stands for. I feel a bit like an F.N.G. I wonder if I ought to have a pencil and paper. I don't have any idea what this meeting is about, and I can't tell when I get inside the conex if I'm early or on time or late. Two of the other squad leaders are the only other NCOs there except for the First Shirt, who's talking to an officer without a hat on.

I guess I expected to be introduced or something, but here's what happens: almost nothing. The officer the first sergeant was talking to is the Battalion Executive Officer, and XOs have a reputation for being something like a sow's hind tit—just a part of something bigger. This guy might have been one of the officers that came around when the investigation team checked us out, I don't remember. He's like that, unrememberable, unremarkable. While he is talking I notice that his nose seems a little off to the left of his face. He tells us Echo Company will be pulling periodic patrols, and that there should be two men available from each squad all the time to pull details, and that we'll pull guard every other night. He tells us the weather report is rain. He tells us there is a concentration of Charlie—he calls him "enemy personnel"—in the valley we're in, but, because the weather keeps our surveillance craft grounded, we don't know where they are exactly.

I know there was a squad of them not too far outside the wire last night, dropping mortar rounds inside. He tells us our casualties from incoming are negligible. I wonder if any of the guys who might have picked up shrap would completely agree. I'm glad I didn't bother to bring a pencil and paper and when I leave I suddenly remember that I used to hate the Army. I remember why I hate it, and I start hating it again. I hate it more when I get back to our hooches and Peacock is sure-enough gone. I am totally depressed. I wish I could go home, but I am so depressed I don't want to think about home. I don't want to think about anything. I want to sleep, but the mosquitoes keep me awake. I lacquer myself up and they don't land, but even their buzzing keeps me awake and my bunk is hard so I lie there and stare and know the tears should come but won't. I wish I had my dad's pistol so I could shoot the mosquitoes out of the air.

THE DONUT HOLES

I'M A DOUBLE-DIGIT MIDGET: I DROP TO NINETY-NINE days on the first day that it doesn't rain, and Callmeblack goes to Thailand on R&R that same day. I stretch my poncho liner and mosquito netting out in the sun, and the three of us lay ourselves on top of the hooch and listen to music. By now my rot probably covers a third of my body. One patch that started under my arms has spread across my chest and across my back and hurts so bad some nights that I can't sleep any way but almost sitting up. There's more around my balls and down the insides of my legs, and my feet are both covered with it too. So I use most of a can of some new kind of salve on it and stretch out in the sun like a dog. It isn't hot but the sun makes every pimple I have feel neglected and proud of itself. Somebody is shooting at the rats around the dump. There's a big game of Frisbee football down along the concertina and most of the guys are barefooted. A couple of them are nude.

I wanted to go on R&R with Callme but Higher-higher wouldn't let me because the squad is light anyway. We're supposed to get at least one F.N.G. real soon. Omar got three baseballs in the mail a couple months after he came, and he is constantly either juggling them or throwing them against the side of a hooch. His mother sent them to him and they were white when they got here, but now they're

the color of a brown egg even though he takes good care of
them. It's easy to see that he is the best baseball player I've
ever been around. Sometimes he counts the stitches on
their covers and puts his fingers at exactly so many stitches
apart. The only thing he ever seems to get tired of is having
to retrieve his pitches, and he is always bargaining away
C-rats to someone for throwing the balls back to him or
standing in front of the wall like a batter would. Somebody
from another company had a mitt but the dampness ruined
it. Smith tried to repair it with shoestrings but the first time
he threw a ball to Murphy it took half the rotten leather
away. Right now he is sitting with his legs dangling over
the hooch roof, juggling the balls with one hand. Murphy
has sunglasses on and his hand down his pants.

Ninety-nine days.

The distant river looks real wide and is leather-colored.
All day long there are little puffs of clouds up high, but it
never rains. I work on a letter off and on. I write that it
somehow reminded me of spring when the rain quit, but I
don't know why it does. The jungle is all the same color
and it hasn't changed since I came in-country, although it
seemed kind of brown from underneath the canopy when
we were in the other valley. I guess it is simply the fact that
we can be outside without getting wet. Off and on all day I
keep thinking back to other springs, when it would get
warm enough to start painting. I never realized I would
miss the smells, but I do. I try to remember what Latex
smells like but it just teases me because you can't remember a smell, or at least can't make it come through.
All I can smell is aviation fuel and the shit burning in the
cans set along the perimeter, smoking like four rubber-tire
fires. Shit doesn't smell any better when it is burning than
it does when it isn't.

And at the end of this first rainless day I am sitting by
myself between our section and the dike wall that defines
Artillery's territory above us. I am looking west, and the

sun comes right at me and feels warm, warm, warm and makes the small sores of my rot burn like turpentine in a day-old cut. I can see a pretty big card game on a hooch roof below me and hear the yells of the Frisbee football game. The smell of the shit burning is strong; the sandbag that I am sitting on is still wet and soaks through to my ass but that doesn't bother me. I am sucking on a cigarette and sipping on my canteen of water like it was whiskey. Above me, the artillerymen are playing horseshoes with shoes they have fashioned out of the ends of empty canisters: the clanks that the shoes make against their aluminum aiming stakes remind me of someone hitting a chisel with a soft mallet.

I am a double-digit midget. Callme has gone. I start crying. Not really sobbing, but I bow my head onto my knees and let myself shake with soundless heaves that start in my stomach and come at regular intervals to my lungs, where they pause for inspection, then jump out of my throat, one gulp at a time. I am lonely. I am so lonely that the crying is like scribbling on a tablet, making something that will get colored in later, so I feel at once like a child again—like I did when I struck out at my last turn at bat —and a man so charged with loneliness and fear he cannot put it into words, but needs to. I leave my eyes open and I look at my bare feet when the tears splash into the red dust that covers them and runs in streaks that seem too small for all the mist that covers my eyeballs. I would like to go on crying for ninety-nine days, maybe even more than that. I miss Prophet and Pops and Peacock, and I weep for Ass, Eltee Williams, Bull and Chickenfeed and for the guys I never knew but had to see die, and I bawl for an emptiness that only makes me think of a telephone that will not ring. I miss girls and my mother and the taste of Grandaddy's apples. I cry because I don't love Omar or Chas very much yet and because I know it is totally futile to ask God to get me home. I remember Lonesome telling me more than two hundred and fifty days ago that there is nothing between this day and the day ninety-nine from now except luck, unluck, and whatever it is between the two, and I have no say in the matter. Every round that comes in now is going to seem louder and closer; every patrol we go out on from now on is going to stitch my nuts to my stomach with loops of mad fear. I have come through the winter of this long year, and the sun is showing me dirty windows between the here and the there. The there. The there. I say it, I think it; it makes me quit crying.

Somehow I can't make the change to being the squad leader. I guess I have held Pops and Prophet up to the light and looked into them and not been able to find what I know is inside me, a rent like Grandaddy's sinkhole that never gets filled to the top with anything solid. He hated that sinkhole. His dumbest cows strayed into it and tore their udders on junk tar pails and scraps of bailing wire too tangled to ever use again. Spring after spring the road crews left gravel in a pile for him in trade for bushels of apples, and I would go with him, and load the gravel into the wagon, and then go to the sinkhole and fight the hole with a shovelful or a bucketful at a time. Grandaddy would look it over and be sure he saw the cause, the disease of his pasture, that had been sinking as long as some of the apple trees had been growing. But every spring the cause he had found had returned or moved and we would bandage the ground again. Even then, even when I was no taller than the scoop shovel I used, I knew the sinkhole would probably always win. And there is something inside of me like that sinkhole that my mother and brothers have always helped me stem, but now I am in a make-believe world where everybody is a brother and they don't know how or why to border the hole, even if it will sink again. I wish I believed in God, but if I did I would be in jail instead of here.

I am getting a short-timer's attitude. I am too superstitious to trust it.

The whole ten days that Callme is gone I am in the same kind of mood. Once, Murphy catches me sitting in my niche with a poncho over me to keep the mist from soaking my shoulders. He knocks on the sandbags as if they formed a door to a space that I own.

"Chas, if you weaken my wall I'll have you carrying the radio *and* the Sixty. Come. Sit."

"Thanks, Chieu Hoi. Uh, what's up?" His hair is the color of dry coffee mostly, but there is an unusual streak that surrounds his face, and this streak is darker, looks wet all the time, makes me think of the drying edge of paint when you try to start too early in the morning.

"Nothing up that they've told me anything about."

"What I mean, man, is that me and Omar are feeling left out, or like we're leaving you out, or something." He picks at the calluses on his hand while he talks, but he fastens those dark eyes on me.

"Jesus, I've been doing a lot of thinking, but I never thought of it that way, man. It's my fault that you guys see it that way, but it isn't serious as long as we're sitting here on this Z. The thing is, man—and I had this explained to me when I was in-country as long as you guys, by guys who had been here as long as I have, and I still don't understand all of it—something happens when you start getting short. Like, you know, when you can't stop thinking about some chick when you don't even really like her, or you know she's some other dude's chick. You know? I ain't the same kind of scared that I was when I got here, but I'm scared, and I can't kick it; I can't quit thinking about home and how bad I wanna get back there."

I've got a cigarette going and I am moving my hands around trying to help myself explain and the cigarette scoots out of my fingers. It lands in the only dinky puddle under the poncho and sizzles itself dead.

"Shit, Sarge"—he smiles at me—"I just came to say we ain't trying to ignore you. Just—" I give him time to go on, but he doesn't.

"Well, let's us have a squad meeting tonight and see what we can find out about all this, get our spirit back. I ain't avoiding you guys either, I'm just into some kind of thinking stage, and what I'm thinking is older than I am."

"Fuck, I thought when Professor Peacock left, people would talk normal and I'd be able to understand what the fuck they were talking about," he says, kind of out the side of his mouth.

"Yeah, you and me too. I thought I'd always be able to understand what it is that *I'm* saying, but I ain't sure I understand what I just said. Pea must have left a jinx around here to make us talk over our head."

"When y'spose they'll start us back on patrols? Not before Callme gets back, will they?"

"I doubt it, unless they team us up with another light squad. You know this fucking Army, man, they just do things, they don't show you why."

The morale of the troops on the LZ is past its low point. For the next few days it usually rains about half the time instead of all day long, and there is plenty of sun. We keep after our rot and mine starts to clear up a little, which is enough to make me feel better. The sores turn to scabs and the salve keeps the scabs soft. It's hard to keep from picking at the scabs, but the skin underneath where they come off is very pink, even on Omar. The instructions on the cans of salve say to keep applying it after the scabs come off in order to avoid scars, but there isn't enough salve for everybody to do this. Beside, it doesn't all disappear. There are sores where I keep salving but it keeps spreading, only not as fast. The medicine dries white, and every time the sun is out guys are sunning themselves with white shit all over. It makes me think of some memory from a long time ago, something to do with a kid's birthday party, I think, but I can never quite remember it exactly.

Callme's R&R is up but I don't expect him to get back for another three or four days. It's a standard procedure for transients to sham as long as they can in base camp.

One morning, just when we think we've got it beat, this cold rain comes down and puts out the fires of hope we've all been having that the 'soons are over. The three of us are sitting around inside the deep hooch, bitching because the roof has a new leak and we don't even feel like going outside to try to fix it. Omar is stretched out with his back against the wall and his feet up on the pallet that I'm sitting on. Murphy is sitting on the top bunk on Omar's side, hunched over with his elbows on his knees, swinging his feet back and forth. I'm in a kind of daze. I'm depressed by the rain, which seems different this morning. It is the middle of the day and it hasn't quit. All the time it's been raining I've never heard thunder and never seen lightning. It rains without thunder and lightning, and I'm curious about how much rain has fallen during the season. I know an inch has fallen in the night and during the morning, because I left my canteen cup outside. Another inch falls the next night and day, and another one falls before Callme comes back on the first bird that comes in when it is clear the day after that. He looks different.

"Hey, man," I say, "did you get a tan while you were over there, or what? You look different."

"I *am* different, dude. I had me a ton of fun. I mean, dig it, I fucked for three straight days. Bought me a whore as soon as I got there, traded her in after a day, then traded that one in the next day. Then I got a cute l'il thing that wanted more dick than I had left in me."

"Didja leave me any holes I won't fall in if I go to Bangkok on R & R?" Omar says.

"Homes, they might move the whole fuckin' country by the time you get yours."

He has a Polaroid and takes my picture, then one of all of us together. Then Smith takes one of me and Callmeblack. At first I can't believe what the picture shows because I haven't seen myself from head to toe in over nine months, and I am skinny. I've never been skinnier than I am now. I knew I was losing weight because I'm never hungry, but it shocks me a little to see a picture of myself. Callme also has a stack of pictures that he took in Bangkok, and we smoke some dope and go through the stack one at a time while he tells us about each one. Most of them are pictures of his whores: small girls who are probably not more than sixteen years old. They look a lot different than the Vietnamese. They wear dresses and heels and extra-heavy makeup around their eyes, which makes the eyes look bigger but still not round. Their teeth are all even and white and I can feel the latest hardon slip from one side of my barndoor buttons to the other while Callme is telling us about his week in Thailand, then his four-day sham in the Rear, where he fucked a laundry girl and thinks he might have gotten the clap from her. If he had discovered the clap before he left the Rear he might have gotten to stay back there another couple days, but he just started dripping today. He digs into his ruck. It's a different ruck than the one he had been carrying but it isn't new, just cleaner. He gives us each a small pipe made from bamboo and some kind of a shell shaped like an acorn.

"And, Chieu Hoi," he says, "I brought you these so you'll rattle more out there in the Bush." It is a beautiful set of beads, black and white beads carved in random shapes. Callme said the Thai who sold them to him explained that each shape had a different meaning, but Callme couldn't remember any of them except the shape that is sort of like a pitcher or a long-necked bird. There are five of that kind on the string and they are all very very close in shape. That bead is for good luck.

"Say, brother, I got me five more pieces of good luck

now. That oughta get me outa here safe and sound." I put the beads on over the string that Ass gave me so long ago now and I like the feeling I get, but it is not a feeling that fits into words. I slap Callme five and say thanks. We blow another bowl and go through the pictures by ourselves. I keep staring at the picture of me and Callme. Callme looks great and I look like shit, except for the smile on my face. Callme is clean and I am still filthy, and that bothers me too. For all the time I've been over here I've been wishing I had a camera, and I still don't have one. Callme brought a bottle of whiskey back with him, and we debate whether to save it for later or not. The debate lasts about a minute. He draws a line on the label and says that is how much of it we'll drink this time, and we start in, sipping from C-rat tins. We keep the bottle down in the hooch and go outside to sit on top. We're drunk when the Z begins to buzz.

It starts down by the pad. Guys are hollering and slapping high fives all around. We don't know what it is all about, but whatever it is will soon get to us because we can see it travel up the hill as one guy passes it on to another, then little groups scatter into every direction and the hollering keeps going. A fairly fat guy from Artillery who has on pure black sunglasses yells "Donut Holes!" He makes a circle with two fingers and finger-fucks it. The thumb on his right hand is missing.

A rush goes through me: excitement. The Red Cross has volunteers, women who go everywhere the military goes. In the Rear, they man USO clubs, and I saw some of them walking around base camp when we were shipping out. They were dressed in light blue dresses and none of them seemed very good-looking. But that was then. I haven't seen a round-eyed woman for over nine months.

"Say, fuckin' hey," Omar shouts. "I gotta get my black ass tight." He disappears into the other hooch. Chas is sitting on the wall, and he straightens up and begins a Charles Atlas routine.

"Tell me," he says, "do I look like I'm a war hero them girls are gonna want a piece of?"

"You look like Popeye the sailor man, man."

Chas almost spits the pipe out of his mouth and starts laughing.

"I'm gonna get a controlled buzz on," Callme says. "Want another can of booze before I hide it?"

"Hell, yes." I pump what's left in my tin and hand it to him. The whole Z is alive with action. About every hooch has at least a couple guys shaving out of their helmets, and there is music coming from everywhere. I wonder what the girls are going to do and how long they're going to stay. They've got to have their share of courage to come out here; even though it's safe to us, I'd think they would be scared.

Callme comes back to the top without his shirt on. His rot is not as bad as it was before he left on R&R but there are scabs as big as pocket watches on both sides of his chest. I wonder if rot is contagious, and since it is so wicked-looking I wonder what his whores thought of it. I wonder what mine will think, and what my mother will say.

A few minutes later we see the birds coming, still far away, over the muddy river. There are three helicopters, and the way one circles above the other two it must be a gunship. So the Army guards its goodies with its best weapons. I wonder how many Donut Holes have been killed over here. The birds stay in that same fluttering formation—the Cobra flying circles around the Slicks—and as they come closer it makes me think of how a little bird will chase a big, slow buzzard. When they get closer to the pad, the Cobra becomes the buzzard and circles slowly very high. The two Slicks come bobbling onto the pad, which is surrounded by a couple dozen guys. Some of them have on white tee shirts. The lifers sent word around that we were all supposed to get into our flak jackets, but almost nobody has one on.

By now there is a general cheer coming from all over the Z, like the beginning of a ball game. About everybody is standing on hooch roofs, in pairs or in groups as big as squads. A few hooches away there is a guy who hits each of his armpits with half-minute doses of aerosol deodorant. I had forgotten deodorant even came like that, and he begins spraying under the arms of all his buddies too, with plenty of flair.

When the first bird lands, the cheer from the pad is almost as loud as the sound of the bird's rotors. One guy takes off his white tee shirt and lays it on the sandbags where the first leg steps. It is surely the first leg that isn't rot-infested to step there, ever. It is definitely a woman's. Omar has a set of field glasses and Callme says he's going to pull rank if Omar doesn't give them up soon enough. Smith passes them to Callme, then I get them and zero in on the leg, the girl, the Donut Hole. She is definitely American. There are four of them and they have on the blue outfits. The dresses—ah, dresses—are pretty short, so there's a lot of leg that shows through the parade. The parade is made up of the four girls walking up the hill from the pad. The dude who dropped his white tee is escorting the first one, and as they come up the hill he gets outdone by a big black dude who stretches himself across some mud. The guy with the chick on his arm barely hesitates. He walks right across the guy's back and reaches back to get the girl's hand. She hesitates, though, so the guy reaches back with both hands, and the first girl walks across the dude's back. He lies there until all four of them have walked across him, then stands up and bows to the cheers he gets. The mud that covers him from face to feet looks almost orange against his black belly.

The second bird comes down when the pad is clear and it has supplies in it, stuff that the girls brought. There's never been an easier detail to summon than the detail that carries those boxloads of shit up the hill. One more bird comes in after the second Slick leaves, and it's got F.N.G.s on it. It's the same every time F.N.G.s get here: they get out of the bird and stand and everybody knows they're new because of their clothes but nobody does anything for them. It's a sort of initiation. We got dropped into a hole the squad had to cut out of the Bush for us because it was still a rough Z. Even then, even though there wasn't the organization there is here, it was as though us F.N.G.s were invisible for a while. There are six of them standing down on the pad now, not getting any attention and not knowing what the hell to do. What they really don't know is that this isn't an ordinary day.

The girls walk right by the dike that separates our hooch from Artillery's parapets, and by now they have mud splattered on the blue dresses. One is a blonde with short hair and glasses the shade of her salmon fingernails. There are two black chicks. One is short and heavy and the other one is tall and good-looking, sexy, with teeth like tiny white toilets. Callme moans when she goes by, and I try to give him a look that says he doesn't have any soul claim. Then I moan as the redhead comes, last, with legs showing to the thighs, legs that need pantyhose as much as I need a rubber. My dick unfolds. Maybe we're downwind, if there's a wind; maybe they've overdone it; maybe I'm sniffing more than my share of air, but I smell perfume and it is the sweetest thing I've ever smelled in my life. I can actually feel my mouth water when they go by, and as though I am isolated I can pick out the tones of their voices from the noise of the GIs like I'm doing a documentary and they are wearing microphones. Maybe the whiskey and that little bit of pot has *me* wired, but for an uncountable minute I am completely gone from here, yet here too. All the maddening reality recedes and all I am aware of is these chicks setting their boxes all around the biggest parapet, and I feel like I'm at a movie or a play and that I'll be able to leave when it's over.

GIs come up the hill from every direction and they're all carrying something and they all give me the impression they're as mesmerized as I am, and everybody is trying to look a little different than he did an hour ago. A lot of the dudes sitting across the parapet from us look almost clean and I've never noticed how many tattoos there are. A couple guys have cigars.

They are unpacking the boxes, and the redhead stands up on an empty one and waits while the whistles and shouts die down. I'm close enough to see that she has freckles.

"As most of you know, we are Red Cross volunteers. And the Red Cross designates us as Red Cross Donut Dollies. And, as we all know, you guys don't call us dollies, you call us Donut Holes. It's not what you call us that we care about. It is how you like our being here that counts." There's plenty of applause, and it is strangely polite, like we'd just as soon listen to her and the rest of them as hoot and holler. The others are done unpacking now and they've all moved out from the center. The lucky guys with cameras are burning up film. I'd take a few of the girls, but I'd take some of the dudes because I like seeing everybody looking happy. Callme is dashing back with two C-tins of whiskey. His face looks like the guy in his R&R pictures, but his fatigues are dirty already. He doesn't have a shirt on but he found a flak jacket somewhere and he's wearing that, open down the front with grenade rings woven into the zipper. He's got one part of a pair of sunglasses woven through the grenade rings. When he hands me my whiskey either the flak jacket or his armpits smell like fish worms.

The girls have a tape deck and a small amp. They brought three speakers, and a guy from the other side of the parapet digs up a speaker from somewhere, so within a few minutes, while the dude from Commo is hooking all the shit into Artillery's generator, a chant begins. It starts around a few guys from Three Squad who are all wearing hats they made out of sandbags and vines. They all have sunglasses on and get up on top of the parapet wall and form a chorus line. All four of them start clapping, then leaning toward the rest of us as if this were all rehearsed, like they are part of the show, and quick as hell everybody around the parapet is clapping his hands. The clapping starts out slowly at first, everybody starting to clap every time the chorus-line dudes kick their legs. Then the music comes on.

"God damn the pusher man . . ."

I hope that somewhere on the nearest hill there's a dink with a good set of binoculars. They're only used to Psy-Ops helicopters passing over with propaganda messages blaring into the jungle, but right now there is a speaker aimed in every direction and there are a hundred GIs singing along. *Charlie, this is the enemy, these black and white guys singing "Goddamn, ol' Uncle Sam."* And these girls have done this before; they have their routine down pat. After a couple minutes of us clapping for ourselves and whistling, some guys waving their hats in the air, the chorus line doing too many bows, the girls huddled near the tape deck looking in every direction and clapping along with us, they start the music up again without saying anything. It is a song I don't know, something funky, and the fat black chick takes over. She bumps and grinds and flows with the steady *boom-boom-boom* of the beat. She soon has fifty dancing partners standing on the parapet. I'm not one of them, but Callme and Chas are up there. Part of the time they're dancing with the Donut Holes and part of the time they get their own twosome going. *Jesus, for a camera.* Six-foot-plus Callme, with his flak jacket on, probably mostly to cover his rot, over a pair of shoulders like a roll of cold tar, and squatty Chas, as Irish-looking as a leprechaun, doing a boogie with each other.

The girls are digging back into their boxes and dragging out some stuff while the music switches to some instrumental, something jazzy. When Callme and Murphy jump down off the wall, I hand Callme his whiskey back.

"You niggers sure got rhythm," I say.

"You honky muthafuckers sure know how to get high." He's probably saying that because Murphy comes up with a bowl and we duck down below the parapet long enough to blow about half of it. Omar comes back from wherever he's been and takes the bowl to finish it. He's got blue shades on, a tee shirt that was yellow once, and a shit-eating grin on his face. So here's Two Squad, *may we all make it*.

The Donut Holes hook the amp into a mike and turn the volume way down. Then a resupply Slick comes in and we all give the pilots the finger and a hearty boo, and the chicks turn the volume back up. The bird is hovering over the landing pad and we can't hear what the chick is saying. She stands there with the mike in her hand and her hand on her hip. *Goddammit, I'd have a picture of that too, show how war is hell*. I keep flashing on how the spirit has changed so much. Round-eyed women, amplified jams; it's American, *more American than a covey of lifers sitting around a peace table in Paris*, and a spirit like this could do a lot for the war effort if it could be made to go beyond when the chicks leave. A guy vaults over the parapet. He's got his helmet liner on and is probably wearing six sets of beads. His whole chest is covered with beads, and the beads swing ahead of him constantly because he jives along the inside of the parapet wall with his head way forward. He is walking around with his fist in the air and shouting something to the dudes he goes past, but I can't hear him. He goes about halfway around before he takes a shortcut to the middle where the blonde and the black beauty are shouting into each other's ears. They have put the microphone down on a stack of sandbags between them because nobody can hear anything until the Slick takes off. The dude with all the beads picks the microphone up and the dude working the amp turns on the amp. Like he is Jesus with a shitload of fish, this guy starts in on the amp with a harmonica, and little by little we can hear it better and better. He blows some quick blues.

"Hey," he shouts, "let's sing that fuckin' helicopter an old Army Hymn."

"Yeah," we shout all at once, like a chorus.

Then with the mike and the amp and about a hundred GIs singing, we almost drown out the sound of the bird with the hymn—

Him

Him

Fuck him

—and we do it again and all point at the pad. The girls evidently haven't heard the Army Hymn and they laugh through the first verse and help with the second time through. The ringleading dude is between the redhead and the big black chick, and they and probably all of us point at the bird and sing it once more—

HIM, HIM, F-U-U-U-CK HIM

—and the bird, that has never come closer than ten feet to the ground, does something I've never seen one do before: it climbs mostly straight up but a little backwards too. It keeps on climbing and climbing until it is higher than Slicks usually fly, and it swings way up there like the pair of girls' underpants that Prophet tied to the end of his kite when he came back from R&R.

Then the girls divide us into two teams and two girls lead each team in a game of charades that lasts about half an hour. Then they set up ten sandbags in the parapet and choose ten guys to play musical chairs. It seems pretty ridiculous at first, but it gets interesting because it has to be the roughest game of musical chairs ever. When there are only four sandbags left, the five dudes in the circle fight like hell for a seat and one guy gets knocked cold. The Donut Dollies think he is faking it at first but pretty soon a medic turns him over and she gasps. Like this is some kind of school play, when the chick gasps the guy starts coming to and finally gets some applause when he gets back to his feet. The medic is escorting him out, but when he comes to the only puddle in the parapet he scoops up two handfuls of mud and slings it at the dudes sitting on the sandbags. When there is only one sandbag left and two guys walking around it the chicks let the music go on a long time. These two guys are stalking around the sandbag like two kittens. They swat at each other and try to shove each other away. When the music stops the little guy dives head first onto the bag and the other guy tries once to get him off but can't. The winner gets a pair of boxer shorts, still in the package. He tears the package open and pulls them on over the cutoffs he's wearing.

The last song on the tape is by the Animals, "We Gotta Get Out of This Place." It's always been a popular song, but it has never been sung by as many guys at once. The Donut Holes blow us kisses good-bye after they pass out Red Cross packs and give pocket Bibles to anybody who wants one. When the group goes by us this time, I get the feeling the chicks are tired and that their smiles are almost used up. I'm tired too and I focus on the redhead's neck, covered with freckles. I'm not the least surprised by the hardon and I must be lost in a daydream, because it surprises me when I hear somebody calling my name.

"Sergeant Sauers?" It's one of the new guys who came in when the Holes did.

"You might say that," I say.

"Huh?"

"It's been a long time since anybody called me Sauers, and I can only think of one other time when anybody called me Sergeant."

"My name's Bostick," the guy says. He's about my height and has blond curly hair and glasses. He keeps sniffling. The other guy's name is Roosevelt Wilson. They follow me down the hill, and when the Donut Holes' bird takes off, my hardon leaves with it. So here I am with two more F.N.G.s, two guys who've barely been in the Bush, Callme, and me. That makes Two Squad full.

When I lie down to go to sleep I can't drop off. I get the feeling that the vacation is over. The 'soons seemed like hell when they were heavy, but now they're almost over and that will mean we start humping again, and probably moving. I'm nervous and wornout both. I'm high and depressed. I'm scared and I'm the one who dares not be. I've got a guard slot with Roosevelt Wilson in about three hours and I feel like calling in sick. I honest-to-God feel like telling them I'm sick. I think the first thing I'm going to tell Wilson is that being a short-timer ain't all it's cracked up to be. Shit, it isn't his fault, but he couldn't understand *where* the fuck I'd be coming from. I must lullaby myself to sleep singing along with the Donut Holes. "We gotta get out of this place, if it's the last thing we ever do. . . ."

THE YELLOW
BRICK ROAD

A SPECIAL SQUAD LEADERS' MEETING IS HELD TO TELL US we will be going on the offensive. Three companies are going to have patrols out constantly, and it is our intention to "initiate contact." After that meeting Echo Company has its own meeting. The CO is sitting under a tent flap with two platoon lieutenants. A map covered with plastic is propped up against the tent wall; it's marked "classified," and before the meeting begins each of the squad leaders gets a map too. I can tell in a glance mine isn't the same map as the one propped up there. What my map shows, it turns out, is a blowup of the middle of the big map. There's a wide blue line running across the top with smaller lines feeding into it. I guess that the big one is the river we can see in the distance.

"Men," the CO begins, "we've been laying around for over two months now and the enemy has been busy. Our intelligence shows there is a high concentration of personnel throughout this area, NVA regulars. We believe the NVA is using this area as a staging area to move troops down south. It is our job to discover this concentration of enemy, to engage them in battle, and to destroy their mission before they can get grouped with the other forces to mount an offensive."

The CO is a captain who came right at the beginning of the monsoons. He speaks in precise words. He doesn't move his hands at all when he speaks, but his eyes are constantly roaming over our group. It makes me a little uncomfortable when his eyes and mine meet; I don't like what he is saying.

"We will have small patrols out there all the time. Always more than one. It is expected that the enemy will be in platoon-size or smaller groups, but because we intend to have ground forces out all the time, there will only be an initial air offensive, and whatever support you guys need will have to be called in precisely."

My mouth is going dry. I keep listening but he mostly repeats himself. The map I have is made on thick paper and should fold into the big ute pocket with maybe three creases. I wonder how soon we're going out. I'm nervous with all the new guys. It's going to be me and Callme all alone for a while. It's like driving through fog at night, too fast for your eyes to keep up with your headlights, except compared to this that is Mickey Mouse. I hope I've got at least a couple days out there before we get so far out we're into Charlie's land. Even that, Charlie's place, is something I have to be able to explain to these guys. My fucking ass depends on it. The CO says Alpha Company will start the patrols and that Echo will be pulling security around the Z while they're out. Then we'll go out and Bravo Company will be on the Z.

It isn't dark yet when we gather on top of the big hooch. There is a slow breeze blowing out of the south. It isn't exactly cold, but it feels good to wear a shirt. Artillery is firing over our heads and we can see the traces of the rounds hitting, maybe five or six kliks out. They must be firing support for somebody because they're putting plenty of shit out there. It's a nicer show when we get loaded. The

F.N.G. effect takes over. Omar and Murphy keep up with the dope, but the two new guys are out of their fucking minds after a couple rounds. Wilson just begins giggling in a high-pitched tone that climbs a few octaves, then falls back down into his throat and starts over again. It's contagious, and I start giggling myself. Callmeblack winks at me.

"Hey, little brother, how about one more shotgun?"

Wilson about chokes. Bostick was giggling a minute ago, but now he's sober-looking, probably paranoid.

"Good dope, we got here, eh?"

"Jesus Fuckin' Christ, man, how long am I gonna be high?"

"Probably a year."

"Short," Callmc says. It's the first time I've heard him say it. "We have eighty-six days left."

"So short we need a stepladder to take a piss, can you dig it?"

This is a familiar ritual now. New guys. Old guys. Old guys talking about getting short. Even though I'm short I can remember painfully how it felt to be on the other end of this conversation, to hear other guys talking about *days* left when I had a *year*. Man, I've seen a lot of guys come and go. No one ever writes back. I think it's because once you leave it seems like the only guys left here are F.N.G.s, even though they aren't really.

The first week is our week of security, and it helps. We take three-manners outside the wire to the edge of the thick stuff and set up. The guards keep changing every three hours, and sometimes we get relieved, then have to go a quarter of the way around the Z and set up again. So the F.N.G.s at least get used to carrying a ruck, and since sometimes we go out into the Bush we get into a formation when we do: point man, radio, back man. I switch us all around, from one position to the other, so they get to cut a trail and hump the radio too. Callme is doing the same thing when those three guys go out. We pull almost five straight days of the short humps and spend all those nights outside the wire. That's good too, because we don't smoke on guard and one night we even dig a slit trench, even though I don't expect any shit to fall.

Our radio batteries start to get weak on the fifth day. It's my fault; I should have been sure we had the extra set but I didn't expect to be outside all the time. When the radio starts getting flaky I'm ready to get our ass back to the wire. It has started to get humid too. It's hard to believe that after it rained like hell for so long the ground can begin to dry out in the high spots, but it does. Part of the time we'll be walking through mud halfway up our boots, then we'll come up on a spot that is solid. By now my boots are almost worn through on the sides. A lot of the canvas is rotted out and the eyelets are half gone. I keep the boots on by wrapping my laces around and around my feet and ankles. Wilson is taking his new boots off to get to his aching feet. It's the first time I notice he's got both dog tags around his neck still.

"Hey, Rosey baby, you gotta separate those dog tags."

"Why?"

"So they won't rattle in the Bush. Put one through one of your bootlaces for now."

It hits me as one of those small things that piss me off, when there's no reason to get pissed off about it. I think I'm pissed off at myself but I'm not sure why.

We are to spend the next two nights on the Z, then we're going out. The squads that have been out this week hit some shit and there is something new to worry about. Usually, it is the Viet Cong that sets booby traps, and since most of the VC are down south or around the big cities, we've never had to worry much about those kinds of tactics. But the patrols from Bravo Company hit three booby traps within the week. The NVA used some of the monsoon time to rig the trails with traps. The battalion even calls in a special group of guys who are trained to defuse mines. These guys stay on the Z because so far none of the patrols has come upon a mine that they saw before they blew it. The mines are planted in the trails and are big enough to blow away two or three guys when they go. One squad had a guy get blown in half and two other guys in the patrol caught shrap. A guy from another patrol dropped his ruck on the ground and then sat on it, which set the mine off, and the ruck absorbed most of the shock but the concussion blew the dude off the ground and into the trees. I was on the pad picking up some C's when that patrol got CA'd back, and the dude was still in shock: white and trembling, his eyes roaming around like ball bearings out of their race, his pants bloody and torn from his ass to the back of his knees. He was talking but his sentences didn't make sense; his fucking mind was blown as surely as that booby trap. It scares me. It didn't take long to forget worrying about the shit that can happen when we were sitting in the hooch getting high and listening to it rain, but now it all comes back. For the first time in a hundred days the sight of Chickenfeed comes back to haunt me, and I am shaking when I get back to our area with the C's.

Callmeblack is still out with Murphy and Bostick. They should be back within a couple of hours. I try to pick them up on the radio but they don't answer. I feel like a mother, worrying the way I do, and I am plenty relieved when I see that big black sonofabitch come out of the Bush and push toward the wire. I meet him at the concertina and he's got a shit-eating grin on his face. When I see the other two guys I know why because they look like they've been run hard and put away wet. Callme force-marched them the last two kliks and it is all they can do to even stand up under the weight of their rucks when they hit the wire.

"You get these guys in shape, did you?"

"Man, they ain't nothin' but a coupla white pussies. I don't know if they're going to work out or not."

"Hey, asshole," Murphy pants, "I was just beginning to hit my stride."

"You'll get your chance," Callme says. He goes behind Murphy and takes the weight of Murphy's ruck and Murphy slides out of it and squats down to bury his sweat-wet face in a towel. His face is as red as an artilleryman's flashlight. Bostick is some other color—somewhere between yellow and white. He doesn't sit down but paces in a wide circle with his hands on his hips like a runner who's just finished a race. These guys will be all right.

●●●●●●●●●●●

BECAUSE WE'LL BE GOING OUT THE NEXT DAY WE DON'T have any guard tonight, but I can't get to sleep for a long time. I get briefed at a squad leaders' meeting and get our tentative route. It is into some heavy stuff that none of the other patrols have crossed yet, going toward the top of my map, toward the Blue Line, which is for sure the big river we can see from the hill. The map shows a speed trail going part of the way and then a bunch of smaller trails taking off in about every direction. That's not a good territory to be the first into. Not many of the squads that have been out have seen many NVA, but a lot of them have hit two- or three-man squads who didn't stop to fight. The casualties for the last week are two dead and eight wounded, which isn't all that high, considering how many guys have been out there. The theory is that the dinks are set up just beyond the range of the loops the patrols have been making. Now it is Echo Company's turn to hump and we are going to be making longer humps, bigger circles.

I can't go to sleep until I can imagine the squad out there and imagine the lineup. Since I am the squad leader I'm not supposed to walk point but I'm going to start out on point anyway. I am worried about booby traps because I don't know what to look for, even though the lifers tell us to look ahead for any signs where the ground has been turned. With the transition between the 'soons and the dry season, every fucking foot of ground looks disturbed. I'm just gonna watch for footprints and stay off the trails when we can. I have a lot more faith in Smith than I used to, so I want him in the middle with the radio, and I'll put Bostick between him and me with the M-79. Rosey Wilson has gotten the nickname Rosehips because he's constantly grinding with any music he hears. Rosehips will be grinding his way along between Bostick and Murphy, then Callmeblack at the rear. I know I'm going to rotate point man but I don't know when. I figure I'll know the right time, and I'll put Callme there.

As if it's exactly what I need before I can drop off to sleep, I get up to go take a piss. I am surprised by the moon; it is waiting on me like a piece of Styrofoam bobbing along some clouds the color of asphalt. The piss is good and if I had brought a cigarette I'd stay up with the moon awhile.

"Chieu Hoi." Callme is awake too, smoking on top of the hooch.

"Jesus Fuckin' Christ. I'm sure alert, ain't I?"

"Can't sleep either?"

"Not even."

"This is weird, ain't it, bro? Here we are, muthafucker, the top cats without no top hats."

"I'm hip."

"All we can do is gut it out and hope them lucky beads of yours keeps the odds even."

"You high, man?"

"High on nuthin'."

"Wanna get fucked up?"

"I could dig it."

When I get back with the dope and my cigarettes, Callme says, "Sure is shitty to have to start thinking about getting killed again, say?"

I don't answer him. He doesn't expect one. The moon

floats onto the top of Callme's head after the bowl, and it makes him look like he's wearing a halo. The only thing I can hear is the whirling of TOC's generator and some radio from the same direction that must be on Artillery's push. The night is warm and seems like it rubs against my face, soft somehow."

"If I knew what date it is," Callmeblack says, "I'd know if it is exactly my brother's birthday or not. I know it's close. He'll be nineteen. For all I know they could've drafted him by now."

"They can't send him over as long as you're here, but by the time he's prepared to come here you'll be gone. They just keep on filling up the pool, with guys like Rosehips and Bostick and your brother and probably mine too."

There are some bugs or frogs or something talking. Way off over the ridge that shows up in the moonlight like a wrinkle in a black dropcloth is the sound of the base camp. I listen for a while because everything is so quiet, but I'm not sure if I can hear anything or not. If fact, after I come out of my reverie I'm not sure if that's even the right direction for base camp. But somewhere there is a low rumbling sound that I don't know, something like a branch blowing a limb against a roof.

"You hear something, Callme?"

"No, why?"

"I hear some noise that sounds familiar. Listen. It's a plane, I think."

Then we see some fighter planes that look like silver bullets pass across the moon. Then the sound comes. Like somebody clearing his throat a floor above you.

"Whattaya think, dude? We got us a squad?"

"I feel better about them than I did last week, but I'd just as soon not hit any shit. Not only because of them. I mean, before, we used to kinda depend on Prophet and those guys, dig it, and now it's us. You and me are the guys those guys are depending on—"

"It works both ways too."

"I know, but what I'm saying is that I miss being able to slack off a little. This is some thing different, it—"

"It's first-string shit. Does Bostick seem gung-ho to you?"

"Never thought of it, really, but yeah, kind of."

"Thing is, I don't know if I'm glad of that or not. I mean, let him go out there and see if his confidence remains if we hit any shit."

And a minute after that I know what the planes were doing because we can see an arc light reflect off the clouds, then hear the sound. The sound is quicker than it ought to be. It is something big, so big-sounding, without being extra loud, that it seems like there will be a wave of concussion coming too.

"Goddamn, arc lights. Maybe this is the year they wanna kick ol' Charlie's ass back into China or wherever the fuck he came from."

"It's like spring training, ain't it? Fuckers lay low all during the rain, which is fine by me, then start bringing pee, get ourselves back in the race."

"Meanwhile the dinks are working all through the wet season, in their dinky-ass way. They're checking things twice by now. I'll bet that fuckin' Bush out there is loaded with firecrackers. Why don't the lifers bring in the bomb squads? Those guys sitting down there in the hooches are just dudes who know how to detonate booby traps and shit, but what good are they if we don't find 'em before we blow 'em?"

"Whattaya think? Think we can get lucky? I mean, hell, man, the only time I ever saw a fucking booby trap was in Basic Training. They showed us shit like punji stakes and those poison gates that get one guy at a time."

"I remember seeing a typical buried mine. Fuck, what's typical about a whole goddamn range of mountains full of jungle? Them mines were easy to find in Georgia paydirt, but when I think about what's out there I know goddamn well the dinks can fool this ol' ass."

"I figure maybe our best bet is to stay off the trails."

"Who's walking point?"

"Me."

"Good. I mean, either me or you."

"Good your ownfuckinself, because when I can't take it anymore you're the one to take over. I keep thinking back to the first time I was up there, on point, y'know? I was one scared sonofabitch, and I wasn't *even* goddamn thinking about booby traps."

"This whole fuckin' thing changes around mighty-ass fast. Seems kinda like we've fought a couple different kinds of war already, and this one'll be different too."

"You know, brother, I can't get this out of my mind. Maybe I'm infected with some kind of leftover Prophetism, but I ain't looking forward to going out there. Dig it? It's fear; I'm afraid, but there's something else running around my brain. I'd sure as hell keep from going out if I could, if I weren't a short-timer. Now listen to me. Don't think I'm being an asshole. I mean . . . I'm not sure what I wanna say here. I got the shitty feeling that we weren't lucky enough to have seen the last of our shit."

"Take an R & R, homes."

"It's a little bit like I can't. It'd hurt me worse if I left and you guys hit the bad shit without me. I'd feel guilty for the rest of my life. Fuck, I don't know what I mean, but I know what I feel, and it doesn't have much to do with them lifers telling us there's a bunch of dinks out there. I've been thinking about my brother a lot too. I wish he'd come visit me, then I'd send him home. And I'd like to see my mom too in, say, Hawaii or something. Fuck it, this is just another way of walking around saying I'm scared, but there ain't shit we can do about it."

We stay quiet, as if by mutual consent. We've been sitting here for an easy hour. We can hear the guards change out on the concertina. A pair of dudes walk pretty nearby us on their way to the coffeepot at the top of the hill.

"Man," Callme says. He drags the word out a long time in that bottom-of-the-world voice. Then he doesn't say anything. He takes a big breath and leans forward a little bit to light one of those rare cigarettes he smokes. He lights it with all the practice of a pro: one quick spark. The orange glow from behind his hand makes his face look really long and thin and some color like looking through a nylon stocking. "Man," he says again, "if we both make it home, let's promise each other something. Let's promise we're gonna get together and drink us some real whiskey, talk us some shit, can do?"

"Can do."

He chuckles to himself.

"Dude, I wanna see you in East Louis."

"Say what?"

"Say, I wanna see you come see me at home. Back there, white dudes don't come around except to push dope or buy pussy, or somehow otherwise fuck over us niggers."

"That stings, Callme. I'll come. Don't you fret that black ass of yours, I'll come. What am I gonna be, *afraid*?"

The moon-gone-halo has ducked behind the clouds now, but I can still see Callme plain as day. Maybe it's because I'm so used to looking at him. We put our hands in the air at the same time and make fists, then—like the moon said to—slam our fists together, and slam them together again. It hurts.

■■■■■■■■■■■

I FEEL LIKE I'VE SLEPT GOOD WHEN I WAKE UP TO THE sound of somebody pounding on something pretty close by, up the hill. It must be Artillery moving an aiming stake. They sight in their guns or something every morning. All I know is they've got red and white stakes that the guns use somehow to sight in. It sounds like a sheetmetal man shaping a heat duct. I'd like to stay here awhile. Bostick is sleeping on the bunk on the other side. His snores are out of cadence with the hammering metal. I wonder what time it is and why a runner hasn't come around to get me to a meeting. Then I remember there was something different about talking to Callme last night, like we were men talking about when we were boys.

For months now I've been swinging myself out of my bunk by getting hold of one of our rafters and helicoptering my legs down to the aisle. There are holes where my boots hit every morning. Bostick's knees jerk when I hit the ground. The shaft of sun that comes through the doorway strikes his blond hair and makes him look like a dandelion, the way his arms look like leaves and the way he has his chin buried so all I can see is his curly hair. One boot is cocked on his foot like he tried to get it off but fell asleep before he could. Omar is outside shaving. He gets some kind of special cream from home that looks like tub caulk. He keeps himself clean.

"Big O."

"Chieu Hoi. When we leaving?"

"You anxious?"

"Can't wait."

"I'm gonna talk to my joint, then I'll talk to the lifers. Maybe Charlie quit last night."

●●●●●●●●●●●

WE'RE TWO KLIKS OUT WHEN WE KNOW CHARLIE DIDN'T quit. It has been thick walking for the past hour or so. I am keeping us off the trail and cutting point with the machete. The fucking bugs are as thick as anything else. Every time I whack some of the bush away, the bugs fall on me and scatter like echoes in a funeral parlor. We stay maybe fifteen meters off the trail and I am one worn-out GI after an hour of cutting. My arms feel like I've been trying to hit

Omar's fastballs for two days. The machete is sharp and slices everything with a single swing, but I have to cut a trail big enough to crawl through. I begin to consider switching with Callme and even making time on the trail when I hear the crack.

It is an AK; it sounds like a piece of lumber breaking. It is followed by two more cracks and Murphy's cry. A sniper has hit Murphy, and we all go down and start crawling. The sniper isn't very close. The sound comes from about ten o'clock, probably from the other side of the trail. It sounds like he is in a tree or up on some high ground. He is accurate, but the round Murphy takes barely scratches him. His helmet liner has a crease *on the inside*. The round traveled between his helmet liner and his head. After the first five rounds—it all happens so fast—we are all splayed out in a circle on the ground, everybody looking a different way but everybody damn sure which direction the sniping is coming from. He keeps putting a round into the vines above us. Every minute or so he fires, and the closest one goes barely over me. I see it hit a bush about two feet off the ground, maybe five feet away from me. I can't tell if he can see us or just knows where we are, but my heart is beating like a goddamn ninety-pound air hammer. Murphy is lying on his back and rubbing his helmet liner like it is part of his head, in shock. Callme crawls toward me on his elbows until I halt him. The others are all spoked out in the circle and they all seem to be looking at me. Another crack but I can't tell where the round goes.

"Callme, can you get a grenade round out there?"

"I'll be goddamned if I know. This shit is too thick, I think. I might bust the round on a vine so close it would spray us."

"Roger that."

Bostick has the radio.

If he looked like a dandelion when he was asleep this morning he looks like a green pencil with a yellow eraser now because he is stretched out so fucking stiff. He is on his stomach and looks like he wants to crawl up into his helmet. Maybe he looks like that because I feel like that. The sniper busts another cap, then two quick ones, and some leaves ten feet away squirt in every direction. It seems like it takes a solid minute for the flakes to quit falling.

We are pinned down. Even though we can't get any support in this close, I take the hand mike off Bostick's back.

"Lima Zulu, Lima Zulu. Echo Two, over." I forget our code name but I could give a fuck; they'll know who we are.

No answer. For a minute I flash that the batteries could be weak again, but I know we put fresh ones in. I break squelch a couple times and its sound seems as loud as the next crack that comes, but I don't see where it hits. I know we have to do somefuckingthing before Charlie gets some help. I figure that there must only be one guy or one gun or they'd be on our ass by now. But him popping those rounds means that we can't be too far away from more of them. I try the push again.

"Lima, Lima, come back. Over."

The transmission is weak but I can hear them answer. I reach over to turn the volume up and another round rebounds just above us, so either he is able to see us or it is coincidence.

"Lima, Roderick, we're in some shit. I repeat. Pinned down. Sniper. Too close for support. Over."

"Roderick, Lima. Roger. Can you give your approximate papa, over?"

"Wait one."

I locate the grids and send them back.

"Roger that. Be advised. Air support on the way, over."

I want to tell them that air support ain't going to do any good, but I know it's a ridiculous thing to say. Support is support, whether it's in the goddamn clouds and can't shoot anyway, or whether it's an HE round we have to call in on ourselves. *Jesus*. It's times like this when squads call the shit right in on top of themselves. All of a sudden I pity the poor fuckers that would have to call the rounds in on top of himself. That ain't no choice; that is dying, simple as that. I won't do it. What the fuck good would it do to wipe your own fucking squad out to get one dink? Of course there is more than one dink out there, somewhere close, or he wouldn't be taking the chance he is, but the guy who calls The World in has got to live with that. And if he calls The World in he'll live maybe five minutes, which must be a hell of a long time to live with the fact that you give up, you're calling rounds as big as wastebaskets in on yourself and your squad. Fuck that. We'll die one at a time first.

I can't even tell how long I've been out of touch with the ground I'm lying on, but it's like my mind won't snap back to the real thing. Instead, I'm thinking this heavy-duty shit that probably doesn't have a thing to do with anything. But I come back a little—*not that much, though* —when Charlie slams three deliberate rounds into the bush. The rounds are all off target by maybe ten feet so now I wonder if he doesn't know what he's shooting at. *He's just keeping us pinned down. There are more guys coming and he's just keeping our heads down until they get here and can overrun us.* Like it is a goddamn holy revelation, it comes that fast and I'm so sure of it.

The spokes of our defensive position have given way. Everybody is pretty much facing the direction that the rounds are coming from now. That ain't cool, so I look at Rosehips, who looks back at me just like I didn't want him to, like a scared dog, and I motion him to turn around enough to be facing in another direction. There's no reason to think Charlie isn't coming from the opposite direction the sniper is in. I have to slap Omar to get his attention and turn him around, but we at least have four directions covered. I catch the look on Callme's face and I know it must be the same as mine: fear and determination, like being counted on to get a sneak hit with a man on base, something dumb and long-ago like that. His one arm still cradles the M-79 but his other one keeps pushing his helmet liner up, then straightening it down onto his forehead. Like it is predestined, we both look at Murphy. He is as gray as a newspaper and still fucked up from the shock, but he is quiet. His eyes have the glassy look, that look like he is seeing something half a foot in front of him that we can't see. I can see powder burns on the top part of his cheek; it looks like he has been working in a dirty attic all morning and only rubbed himself once.

This is weird. I ought to be doing something, maybe shaking in my boots or shitting in my pants, but I ought to be reacting. Instead I keep on feeling like King Shit, like whatever happens will happen, and I can't do anything about it. And after one more set of rounds that pump off like a whipping stick, so unimportant that I don't count them this time, it comes to me that there's only one thing I *can* do, and that is to charge this sonofabitch. Or I can send somebody else out. I'm the fucking squad leader. Which is about like saying it's my basketball and everybody knows I won't take it and go home. But I'm the dude, *dude*. So I tell them the plan as fast as I think of it.

"Listen up. I'm gonna start crawling that way. I'm gonna be heaving frags the first time that muthafucker squeezes one in this direction. Omar, you follow me by the count of ten. After you can't see me anymore, you count to ten and then come out winging them grenades like they was baseballs. Don't worry about throwing over me, because Murphy is gonna be right behind you, throwing his own damn self." And when I look at Murphy I know I can't count on him. Of course, if it gets to him there isn't anything left of me to count on anyway, but I know it isn't practical to send him third. Deep in my gut I want to keep Callme last, but that's stupid too. Fuck it.

"Callme, you come after Omar, OK?"

"Okay."

"Say what?"

"I'm the one oughta go first. You're the squad leader, homes."

Callmeblack sometimes has a hard-ass look that I think I remember from the first time in the barracks when we had just gotten in-country. It's a look that is scary all by itself, like his head comes off and just floats in front of your face, defiant-like. He has that look now. The sonofabitch.

"It's my choice, fucker."

"Don't treat me like that, Chieu Hoi. Either one guy gets hit, nobody gets hit, or we all eat our shorts right here. I know that."

So somehow a few minutes pass and Callme is crawling out of our setup on his elbows. I at least trade him weapons. We do it silently and like none of the rest of them are even around, but I give him my Sixteen and take the grenade launcher, which feels like a sledgehammer. The last thing I do before he starts crawling is probably the smartest thing I've done since we got sniped: I give him the double clip Prophet gave me when he left, the special-welded set of back-to-back clips that puts out thirty-some rounds at the twist of his wrist. Omar counts to ten exactly as fast as I do because when I get to eleven he starts out with his helmet liner foremost like he is going to ramrod the sniper if he has to.

And I don't give much of a fuck about Wilson and Bostick when I start out after Smith, my goddamn heart beating as slow as a flat tire. If us three get it those three are going to too, and I'm not so sure Murphy is gonna pull out of whatever zone he is in anyway.

Whatever else that sniper is, he's got to be surprised when he pulls a couple rounds off and gets a burst of Sixteen back, then a frag, then another frag. I wonder if Callme threw them both or whether Smith threw one too but I raise up onto my knees for a minute so that I can crawl faster and I can hear the footsteps go away like rubber bands popping. I can hear the muthafucker running away! And Callmeblack, probably with a version of the stare on his face, throws another flag after the rubber-band footsteps that patter out of our hearing now.

So it's over.

I want to jump square in Bostick's shit because he almost yells. He tells us, close-to-too-soon, that the LZ has a gunship up above us. Like we need it now. Smith and Callme are hugging each other and I'm a step behind them. And Bostick, the goddamn talking broom, yells at us that we've got air support. We pick up fourteen shell casings, their brass as bright on the green floor as a set of connect-the-dots in a puzzle book. It seems so amazing that we're all still alive and just chased Charlie away that when Callme backs a few steps away from us and sets the mine off, the sound like a pillow dropped off a bed and the smoke that comes from his legs burning streaks a feeling from the back of my neck to my knees as stiff as re-bar, a feeling that I know isn't going to go away as fast as the bird that we've got to get down here now to stop Callme from screaming, to shut that mouth that wants to shut itself but can't quit crying, "My knees, my legs, my fucking balls man I can't feel nothing Chieu Hoi come put me back together Chieu Hoi tell me you bastard tell me it didn't happen tell me I can wake up, homes, tell me, Chieu Hoi please please please Chieu Hoi tell me I ain't gonna die man."

And I'm yelling at Bostick. I hear myself yell even after I did it. I hear like I'm Bostick. I hear me say to get on the bird push and get a Dustoff out here. And next thing I know I am halfway up a tree whacking away at all the branches as though the machete was no heavier than a swizzle stick and I see the branches fall toward the rest of the squad who are doing what they can to keep up with me and pretty soon I see the hole that is the sky that is where the goddamn bird better show up awful fast to stop Callme from screaming and as soon as he's on that bird I want to take the whole fucking squad after that goddamn sniper.

The Dustoff comes and drops a medic down on a chair that looks like a fucking baby's high chair and the bird looks like a toy up there so fucking small through the hole I cut all by myself. The medic is way too tall to be a medic. He has a big black mustache and he ties Callme's legs off but the blood still squirts out like rusty, cuss-worthy water boils out of a solder joint that ain't tight. When we lift Callme's stretcher on to the high-chair-looking-thing the medic gets hold of its bottom with his left hand. The bird sounds like a valve-out compressor and the litter and the dangling medic disappear through the hole like the sky is a hole itself. Then I know I'm in more shock than Murphy, who got greased alongside his temple an hour ago, and I wonder if I'm ever coming back down to earth or whether Two Squad is going to be chiseled on my gravestone.

OLD FOLKS' HOME

I DON'T KNOW WHERE I AM. I MUST STILL BE IN THE FIELD instead of in the Rear because I'm inside a tent and there are other people around. I am a little bit awake but I am as much asleep, and it seems like I go in and out for a couple hours. I want to talk. I want to find out what is going on, but every time I get awake enough to talk I just want to go to sleep again. *Either I want to or I just do.* I'm doped up, I know that, and I'm in some kind of hospital or something. I'm too drugged to even turn my head, but out of the corner of my eye I can see people moving. Like the curtain blowing around an open window, somebody is moving around on my right side. When I try to roll my head that way I fall asleep again.

I wonder if it has been hours or days since I last woke up. I see, or feel, that I'm connected to some kind of bottles. Nothing hurts. I can't tell how much of my body is down there but nothing hurts. I am so occupied with trying to figure out what is going on that when I start to drift back to some other time, *Mom walking in and out of the room, the curtains blowing around my window like brown ghosts,* I want to·yank my mind back to wherever the fuck I am. Nothing hurts. Callme stepped on a mine and we dusted him off. I am still in my jungle utes. *Nothing hurts.*

"Sauers, can you hear me, Sarge?"

There is a heavy guy standing over me with no shirt on and his dog tags are dangling ahead of him. This time, waking up is like opening one eye at a time. First his face comes into focus like a TV tuning in, his dog tags swinging between us like they are determined to hypnotize me back to sleep; but then, like my other eyelid comes unglued so I can see more, the hair on his chest and the red streaks in his eyes come in too, and I think I can feel my hand. I try to talk to him but my voice is glued to my throat.

"Yeah" is all I manage.

"You've been down the yellow brick road," he says. He makes a motion through the air like a roller-coaster track.

I don't know what he's talking about but I don't much care, because I am beginning to realize I can feel little sections of my body. I can move my fingers and wiggle my toes. *I have felt like this before.* It is like coming to after getting knocked out, except it ought to come back faster.

This guy is a stranger. He has hold of my wrist, and he peels my eyelids back with two other fingers and his thumb on my nose, and shines a little flashlight in my eyes. I get an image, or a memory, of a welder flipping his safety glasses down and using the air lever to begin a burn into steel.

It turns out that my nerves are what burned the hole. The medic's name is Wagner. Wagner doesn't know all the details, but they brought me in at night and I was flipped out. He doesn't know where they got me, and I don't either. He doesn't know anything about Callme but says he will try to find out. He tells me I'm doped up, that's all, and that in another twelve hours my muscles will work again.

"How could I flip out?" I ask him next time I'm awake.

"You can call it battle fatigue."

This time he has a shirt on and there is another medic walking behind him. There's a generator whirring and I hear choppers not too far away. There are two other guys in the tent. I watch one of them drag on a cigarette.

"What do *you* call it?"

"What do *I* call it? Hmmm," he said, "I call it battle fatigue. Yeah, that's what I call it, but just because everybody else does. You guys who come in here like this seem plain fucking tired to me. Whipped. You sleep for days at a time—of course you're doped up so you *can* sleep—and, hell, man, I never thought about its name. I guess maybe that's a diagnosis instead of a name, as far as we're concerned. I've never been in combat. . . ."

I can't concentrate on what he's saying. I *feel* plain-ass tired and there's something hanging on my mind like Spanish moss. That's the thing that keeps coming back to me: Spanish moss. Every time I review what happened it is all clear, up until Callme's bird goes and I am looking up into the trees; then I see some other trees somewhere, full of Spanish moss. Trying to remember anything after Callme's bird is like trying to dial in a radio station that keeps getting overridden by a more powerful one.

It's ungoddamnly hot and the sweat stands in the crevices between my eyelids and the bottom of my forehead, then rolls out and down the sides of my face, like tears.

Callme is screaming, screaming, and the voice is more like a puppy's prayer than the voice of a big man, even though that voice is recorded in English on the vines and trees of that spot of jungle.

Tears roll down like the sweat, so that when I turn my head enough to empty my eyes there are small red puddles on my shoulder and on the cot.

I think.

I fade in and out. One time when I'm halfway between sleep and waking I think the medics are going to shoot me up again but it is a dream.

I think.

I am naked except for a wristband and my beads. There

is mosquito netting above my cot and I put in a lot of time staring at it.

My sense of time is all fucked up. I constantly go to sleep, then wake up, and I always try to tell whether it is night or day, but sometimes I can't even stay awake long enough to decide that. At one time I was connected to a bottle that is still hanging up above the mosquito net. I'm surprised to discover that I can move my arms and legs, although when I first try them it is the same as being completely stoned. I have to watch the way my elbows bend and the way my knees work to be sure they're going in the direction I mean for them to. I'm no more coordinated than if I were all tangled up in the mosquito net.

It is dark beyond the tent flap. There is no sound anywhere and it is so hot that the fabric on my cot feels like scorching beach sand.

I think.

I'm not sure of anything.

One time when I wake up I hear something that ought to be familiar. It is daytime because there is a shadow around the tent flap. That tent flap is always closed. I think I'm waiting on myself to fall asleep again but I don't. Now I recognize the sound—guns somewhere, way the fuck far away. Maybe thunder, except there is air coming at me through a rip between the tent's floor and its side, and the air feels like it's coming out a defroster vent in an old truck.

I sure would like to be riding in an old truck, a kind of cold day, hauling Grandaddy to town for his check, about opening day of rabbit season with a transparent frost on the briars, except I'm here and until I burn part of this fucking year out of my memory I don't want to see Grandaddy, or home, or a rabbit.

I don't think.

I feel like an old man when I start getting up off the cot, half a leg at a time. I sit on it. There is no one else in the tent. The ghosts of my boots are on my feet. After wearing them for a month straight, it feels like I've still got them on. But I don't have anything on. My dick is shriveled up. My feet look like my ankles are wrapped in tape, where the hair on my legs stops. They are the whitest thing in the light that comes from the three yellow bulbs hung onto a piece of an ammo crate. There are bugs—moths, I think— flying drunk-like around the lights.

I am totally spastic pulling my pants on, and I don't have a good sense of balance, so I sit on the edge of the cot and slip them up over each leg one joint at a time. *A little kid dressing myself.* I wonder how many days it has been since I walked. My boots are under the cot, tied together with a piece of black string. Either that black string or the meager glint of the dog tag chills me. I think that to have my boots pulled off and tied together is pure helplessness, and I think Callme or Prophet or Chickenfeed or Ass would know more about that than me. *Callme's boots could probably get peeled off if there is anything left to peel them off of.*

My feet slide across the bottom of the tent like two mops. Just when I reach the flap a medic who isn't Wagner comes in. I am startled and I can see him look at me like he is afraid for a minute.

"Hey, Sarge, you're up and about, huh?"

"How long have I been here? And where am I?" I think the anxiety must show in my voice. I'm not really sure what I'm afraid of, but getting off that cot feels like escaping from something.

"Let's see. . . ."

I expect him to start looking through some of the papers he has in his hand but he doesn't. He rolls the papers up and sticks them under his left arm and puts his chin in his left hand. Now I notice he is an officer, a first lieutenant.

"You came in the day before yesterday."

"You mean I've been doped up for more than two days?"

"Yeah," he says, looking right at me, smiling, "you can put it that way, doped up."

He runs one finger around the rim of his watch.

"You've had three shots and each shot lasts about twelve hours. If you can sleep tonight you don't need any more; if you, uh, have trouble, we'll give you something because you need to rest. Your mind needs the rest whether your body does or not. Do you have any soreness, Sarge?"

When I was feeling myself up for pain I wasn't looking for soreness, I was looking for wounds, and now that he asks me I realize that my ankles are sore and that either my back or chest hurts too. It dawns on me without him saying anything that I was strapped down. He is looking at me now, looking right into my face like he is trying to see something there, and all I feel is astounded.

"Sir, do you know any more about what happened than Wagner does?"

"Son, I truthfully don't know what happened out there. You're in a field evac unit, and out there is totally different from here. Understand that. I *could* read the reports to you, but these reports never do anybody any good when it comes to understanding what has happened. They just tell me and my staff the circumstances, so we can treat you to the best of our knowledge and with the best of our limited resources."

"Would I want to hear the report, doc? I mean, would it embarrass me, would it make me cry, doc, sir?" I'm starting; the tears are sneaking around from behind my eyeballs and I expect them to fall out any time now. *If I start crying and . . .fuck it.*

He is about my height, and first he puts his hand on my shoulder and then he squeezes the back of my neck with his thumb and another finger. It makes me think of Pops. It allows the first relaxed breath to come in, and it makes me feel more secure on my feet, now beginning to get covered with red dust.

■■■■■■■■■■■

AFTER SO MUCH TIME IN THE FIELD IT IS HARD TO REALIZE that this place is part of the war. I mean, it is surprisingly small, and there aren't very many GIs. It's like a leper colony must be. There is only a single roll of concertina going around the perimeter and there are three guard towers and two APCs. It has been almost a year since I've seen anything with wheels. The APCs are the size of a small dump truck and remind me of an enormous bug. They aren't tanks, because they have rubber tires that are probably five feet tall. There is a 50-caliber mounted on top and a place for the gunner to sit that's surrounded by short walls. The guys who man these things all have their own thing hanging out, a flag, a signature. One of them has its name, *Lifesaver*, painted in white letters, and it has a drawing of a roll of LifeSavers.

The end of the LifeSaver package is a body bag instead of tin foil. The bag has a zipper half open and there are three faces of Charlie looking out of the zipper. Even painted, the faces are frightening. Two of them have small pointed beards like Ho Chi Minh wears, and they're all being held by their hair by a hand that has three white fingers and two black ones and is as big as the three faces combined. The painting reminds me that I don't have a camera and don't have any pictures except some that different guys have given me, and all of a sudden I realize that I don't even have my ruck. There is a guy sitting on top of the turret, cleaning his fingernails with a bayonet.

"Hey, dude," he says when he sees me looking at the painting.

"What is it?"

"It's nineteen more days. You?"

"More than that."

"Where'd you come in from?"

"Echo, First and Twelfth."

"Bad shit?"

"Fucked my day up."

"That can happen."

"Been out there?"

He turns his back toward me and points at his shoulder, which looks like a mirror does when it needs resilvering. The wound is the color of a faded bandanna and there are still stitches in it, like they have to operate on it every so often. The thread that comes out of his back looks like a line that's been in the bottom of a tackle box for five years. Some of his back is smeared with ointment that has trapped gnats and other bugs. Even now I can see flies land, then pull off like they have to lift one leg at a time out of jelly.

"Where'd you buy it, a Halloween shop?"

"Charlie was running a special, three for the asking."

He means two other guys got hit, I guess.

"You a grunt?"

"A gunner, Second and the Eighth, mech."

"Working around here?"

"Nah, not then. We were south and east, near Qui Nhon."

"What kind of joint is this place?"

"It's a field evac unit for short-timers."

"No shit?"

"No shit. Most of these guys are in for fatigue."

"No shit?"

"No shit. You're in an old folks' home. When you leave here you probably won't have to go back out to the Bush. They'll get you a job in the back. Maybe you'll even stay here like me. You can fire one of these Fifties, can't you?"

"I could sure pick it up in a hurry."

"Doesn't matter anyway, we only fire during mad minutes. The dinks never fuck with this place. No use. And

Camp Enari is just over Signal Hill—those hills. You ever been there?"

I've never been there but I know it's an awfully big place, base camp for the whole division. This guy is telling me I'm probably done in the Bush, so I'm going to disappear from out there just like Bull Durham did, so long ago.

"Listen, don't get your hopes way the fuck up high, in case they change something, but everybody who I've seen go through here ends up sticking close to mama."

"I'm ready, man. I'll quit. I've seen my share of shit and not gotten hit. But about everybody else has."

"You won't get a Heart, but you've been hit."

"Say what?"

"The war got you between the eyes, dude."

"You some kind of authority?"

"I've been pulling this duty for two months, and getting this scar drained twice a week. I've had this conversation before, homes. Guys like you come in every few days."

"What do you mean, guys like me?"

"I don't know."

"C'mon, dude."

I think that if I'd never been out there that maybe I wouldn't be able to think like this, but I have, and I've been in a lot of shit and I've been hit. . . .

He shifts around on the turret and rubs his hand across the belt of ammo that feeds the Fifty. He has on a ring and when he runs it across the rounds it makes me think of scraping a steel fence to paint.

"Man, man. I'm tired, y'know? I'm fuckin' tired of everything. And I'm tired of this conversation—"

"Hey, fucker—"

"Hey fucker, nuthin'. Let me explain myself. It ain't tired of talking to you that I'm tired of. And I don't know what it is exactly, but I'm tired, so tired."

It dawns on me that this guy—I don't even know his name—is here for the same reason I am. I was thinking that he was here because of his wound, but now I don't think so.

"What I'm trying to say is something like this: even though it's over for me, and for you, and for everybody here, something ain't right. I'm tired of us kind of guys sitting around talking, because the talk doesn't seem to mean anything anymore. There are still guys out there and there are gonna be more guys come back here because they're tired. Fatigue. Fuck, I was more fatigued when we were pulling road duty in paddies for three straight weeks and only sleeping maybe four hours a night. But this shit, this fatigue"—he spits "—it's always right here around my neck, something I can't wash off; it's like a tattoo, man. Like a goddamn tattoo. You know those Jews who have their prison-camp numbers tattooed on their wrists? It's like I've got one too. Once in a while when I get completely fucked up and can go to sleep, I wake up thinking it's over, that I'm clean. But that's rare. Most of the time I can't go to sleep in the first place, and when I get to sleep I just go through the shit from six months ago again. You'll notice that one of the most common sounds here at night is screaming. Think of it. So fucking many guys screaming at night and they are all real private screams, from private dreams, man, that ain't nobody can get into. The only guys who know what the guys is screaming about are all probably dead or getting wheeled around a corridor in Japan."

Then he starts sobbing, and when I climb up on the track I feel like a clumsy fat kid getting onto monkey bars for the first time. I try stepping on the rim of the big wheel and swinging myself up, but it isn't smooth and I end up crawling along the side of the APC as if it were a scaffold plank two stories high. Now that I am up here I just squat in front of him and watch. The cry doesn't last very long. I wink at him when he quits and he looks at me. He gives me the peace sign and shoots a hawker out one side of his nose. It makes a sound when it lands on the side of the APC, a *ping* almost, is honey-colored, shaped like an elm leaf.

●●●●●●●●●●●

NOBODY HASSLES ME. I WALK AROUND THE PERIMETER but stay far enough inside so that I don't have to talk to anybody. All there is to this place is a ring of APCs and five big tents set up inside the ring. There is a regular-looking outhouse with rocks leading up to its door on one side of the hill. Two guys are sitting in the shade of the outhouse, painting the rocks white.

There is something so strange about all this that it scares me to think about it. The war seems over—a month ago, a year maybe, like it never happened—and I want to fight off the feeling that comes when I am lying on the cot, staring, the feeling that the tanker said was like a tattoo. I feel branded, awkward, very alone. Once more, I feel like writing home. What would I say? *Dear Mom, Grandaddy, all, I am through. I can't come home yet but don't worry about me but don't bother sending any more letters but don't expect me home any sooner but when I get there I think I'll want to be by myself because I need to feel sorry for some guys maybe sorry for myself because I am full of something too big for my skin too big for the farmhouse too big for the pasture too big for the town. I want to be done killing but that's a stupid thing to say. I just want to tell you I am OK and that's a stupider thing to say.*

I expect somebody to come to the tent and tell me something, order me to do something, explain something to me. I can't stay awake very long yet. The flies are thick and make too much noise. They stay near the ridge of the tent —screaming, buzzing, bumping around the rigging poles —until I sit up on the cot; then they come down a few at a time and swarm around me and land on my face.

It is hot. I strip off all my utes and stand up, naked. Most of my skin is awful to look at. Half my skin above my waist and all of it below my knees is covered with leftover scabs and dried blood that could be Callme's, rashes where my utes rub, cuts that have been infected and turned black, scars that are as white as chalk, scars that I don't even remember getting. I am so skinny my ribs look like the shank of an old screw jack. I hate looking at myself so I wring the sweat out of my utes and pull them back on. The scabs rip open again.

There are flies between my pants and my legs. I can't so much feel them on my legs as I can hear their trapped buzzes and sense their frantic wing-beating dance. If I tie my pants legs off they might suffocate and I will have to pick their carcasses out of the hair on my legs. I scrub the back of my teeth with a clean section of the poncho liner and lie down, knowing I am going to roll over and crush some of the flies still busy under my pants legs.

I am held to a tree by a leather strap a foot wide. Two Squad is below me and there is a dink on the other side of a small hill but I can't yell at the squad. The dink watches the squad and ever so slowly pumps a round at them, then another one. I can see he only has a couple dozen rounds. Callme is beginning to crawl toward the dink and the dink can't see him. Callme heaves a frag and the dink lets it explode against the bottom of a green tree. The tree opens up in slow motion until its pith looks like a bone, then it falls. There is another frag but the dink is a dozen steps ahead of it, running downhill lickety-split. I sigh and the sigh makes me shrink enough that I am sliding out of the leather strap and down the rough tree trunk when Callme steps back and his legs—slow motion—rip open from knee to foot, to the white bone. And I can yell now: "I'LL KILL YOU YOU YELLOW FUCKING DINK YOU LITTLE BAS-TARD YOU YOU ANY OF YOU. CHIEU HOI YOU COCKSUCKER YOU" and I can't tell by looking behind the medic if it is night or day but I know it isn't raining, hasn't rained in a month. The medic stands away from me.

We are afraid of each other. I know I was dreaming and screaming and I know I'm awake now and I know it is going to take all I've got to keep from screaming again. The flies are asleep and the moths are curlicueing through the yellow light. The medic's hair is matted and the sweat on his face is plastic-looking.

"I was dreaming, doc."

"A dream? A nightmare maybe."

"Ne-ne-neither, doc, th-th-that was real real, m-m-man." So I stutter instead of scream.

"There are a couple other guys awake. They're playing cards in the tent on top of the hill. Why don't you go up there?"

"It's ni-ni-nighttime, huh?"

"Yeah."

"Doc, do you know how hard it is to be-believe it's night and there aren't any g-g—any big big guns firing? It's been eleven months, man, e-e-e-eleven months, man, since I was awake at night and couldn't hear any guns. Does-doesn't the base camp fire at night?"

"A lot of nights, yeah. I guess I don't much notice it."

"What's my-my program, doc? Am I going back out to the B-B-Bush, or what?"

"You think it's easier to sleep out there, with the guns firing?"

"I feel like I'm on some kind of island here. I don't feel like there's anything else around here. Like the neighbors m-moved away. You don't know what I mean, d-do you?"

"Sort of. You need rest, dude."

"I feel like I'm painting a floor and the floor is the bottom of a cartoon, and even though I know better I got myself painted into a corner of the cartoon floor, and I-I-I gotta wait for the paint to dry."

"That's a great way to put it."

Now it's me who doesn't know what *he* means. And I hardly know what I mean either, but that's the way I feel.

Except maybe the cartoon bit. I'm not too sure I feel like I'm in a cartoon, but I figure it will help explain it. Wagner looks a little like somebody I knew from the Bush, somebody I can't quite place, a guy from another company, another time. His face looks so goddamn brittle now. I wish I could make him laugh. I wish I could laugh. I wish it was a month ago and I was laughing. I ought to be laughing in another month, and I ought to be winging home. I'll laugh then.

I have the dream a lot. I never see the guy who was on the APC again, and I wish I could, because I want to blame him for making me scream at night. No, blame isn't the right word. There seem to be a lot of things that I can't find the right word for. I can't describe how I feel, walking around the perimeter every morning. I prowl. I feel caged in. I wonder what is going on in the Bush.

I've gotten to know a guy named Curtis and another guy called Geek and the three of us smoke dope in the mornings and walk around most of the day or play cards. They're both from my brigade but different battalions. Geek claims he is shamming. It is hard to say. I've seen him go into an act awful fast to get out of pulling a detail, all right, but I've also seen the thousand-meter stare take over his face.

Curtis is healing. He was the only survivor from an ambush. The dinks left him for dead but he was rescued. He's got a long time left in-country but he won't go back out. The ambush was his first share of shit and it blew his mind wide open. A couple times every day he looks at me, or through me, or at Geek, or at a water wagon and says, "They're all dead; God, they're all dead." It gives me the chills every time, it scares me. They dope him up at night and he never wakes up screaming.

The dream isn't always the same. Sometimes it's me crawling along the ground and Callmeblack is up in the tree, but he isn't strapped there; he looks like Jesus on a cross, or an angel. He looks dead. Once Callme gets blown straight up and passes by me with the look on his face that he had when he stepped on the mine.

And morning after morning I realize that the feeling the dude on the APC was talking about shows on my face. One time I am shaving and my face looks totally different. I look like a kid who is trying to keep from crying and I can't shave the look off.

When I've got twenty days left I request to go out to the Bush. My ruck never caught up with me, and I want to go back out there once more to find out exactly what happened. In order to request it I have to go before the ranking officer, and he won't be on the compound for three days. I can't sleep that night, but I feel altogether calm. I wish I had my rifle to clean.

■■■■■■■■■■

THE CO IS A YOUNG MAJOR. HE IS SITTING, WITH HIS LEGS crossed, in his corner of the big tent when I go in and he has on a shirt that looks specially made. It is a lot like our jungle utes except it has an extra row of pockets, and the pockets all have something in them. The major is wearing a .45 in a shoulder holster. He had a big brown mustache and his teeth are yellow but his face is wonderful. I prove to myself that I haven't forgotten everything I ever knew about Army protocol when I report:

"Sir, Sergeant Gabriel Sauers, Echo Company, First Battalion, Twelfth Infantry."

"Sit down, Sergeant."

The only place to sit is on a stack of boxes beside his desk.

"How are you feeling these days, Sauers?"

"You mean, do I feel like I'm nuts, sir, or what?"

"Since you said it, I'd guess you feel like you're nuts, whatever that means, eh?" He raises one eyebrow and smiles. The yellow teeth grind together under the mustache.

"Sir. Hell, I wake up at night screaming. I hit the dirt whenever the base camp guns fire. My hands shake like the end of a fishing pole."

He has long legs and his boots are clean. He keeps his eyes right on mine. The eyeballs move back and forth a little bit, like he is looking into one of my eyes, then the other. He lights a cigarette and shakes one out at me.

"Sergeant, what do you remember about the trauma?"

"Sir?"

I know what he means but I act like I don't. He doesn't fall for it, I guess. He just blows smoke out his nose and looks at me.

"Do you mean, what do I remember about Callme getting hit?"

"Is that the last thing you remember about being in the Bush, then you woke up here?"

"Yes, sir."

"Tell me about it, Sergeant."

So I do. He seems interested all the way through, and I tell him almost matter-of-factly.

"This Callme," he says. "How long did you know him?"

"All the time."

"All? All of what?"

"Man, sir, he and I came in-country together. Me, Callmeblack, and another guy called Ass. We all came together and went to Echo Company."

"The other guy? Ass?"

"He got killed first night we were out there." My voice breaks. I have been expecting it to.

"You've had a rough tour of duty, Sarge."

"Not as rough as them."

"Maybe that remains to be seen. No, I don't mean that. Not *only* that. I mean you've had a lot of loss to deal with.

You don't have to go back to the field, son, so why do you want to? What's out there?"

"The war is out there."

I feel comfortable talking to this man, even though he's an officer. I wonder what he would think of me if he knew about the fragging. When I tell him the war is in the field he first nods his head yes, then he shakes it no, and for the first time in a long time I have a nice thought: he reminds me of a base-path coach passing signs.

"This is more complicated than a simple request, Sergeant. You have suffered some awful traumatic experiences, and you have the option of staying here where the likelihood of those sort of experiences is negligible, yet you seem to honestly want to go back out there. Can you tell me why you want to go back to where the war is?"

He moves his hands like he is scolding me at first, then he gestures with one of them like he is reaching into the air between us and means to get hold of my words and scoop them toward him.

"I don't know if I can or not. It's something like wanting to go back to see the house you were born in. I mean, I was out there for almost three hundred days and, sure, it's where the shit happens. But I'm not afraid of getting hit anymore. I don't want to stay out there very long, believe me, but I want to go back and see a couple guys, and I want to see if I can find my rucksack. It never got shipped back here. And, this place gives me the creeps, sir, the goddamn creeps."

"Like wanting to see the house you born in, eh? Actually, I can understand what you mean by that. I think that's a big part of it, all right. Anything else that you expect if you go back out there?"

"This is hard to say, sir, but I want to go back and see what happened that got me dusted off. Somebody will tell me, and maybe then I can remember some of it. Not being able to remember it is hell, sir, fuckin'-A hell. Can you dig it? I mean, can you understand?"

"I can dig it, troop. And there is something admirable about it. But I have to tell you, I'm not sure it is the right thing to do, for your sake."

We sigh at the same time.

"Let me think about it. Let me see if I can find out any more of the circumstances. If I can find out what occurred, would that satisfy you?"

"Just part of me. Like I said, there's still the going back to where I came from. You say you understand that. And I want a DEROS ride."

It would help cure me, I swear, the DEROS ride. I want to say my good-byes, climb into a bird, buzz the LZ, pop smoke, go out of sight with the glory of a grunt.

The next day is the hottest I've ever seen. The air is thick with the heat. Walking out of the tent and into the sun is like walking into a big clothes dryer that isn't spinning. I pull my Boonie hat out and I suddenly wonder if I was wearing it when they dusted me off. It is so hot that I can feel the little bit of coolness from the hat. So I go to the water buffalo and soak my hat, then my shoulders too, but the water evaporates off my shoulders instantly. It would be a sonofabitch to hump today.

Some little white guy, so white he looks like he's been underneath the ammo crate all the time he's been here, meets me going back from the water trailer and says the CO wants to talk to me.

"Sauers," the Co says, "I talked to your unit and there is a potential problem, but if you still want to go, I'll let you, even though I'm still not sure it is a good idea. In fact, especially now. I'll be going against the advice of people out there. How'd you get the nickname 'Chieu Hoi,' Sergeant?"

"Why, sir?"

"I'll tell you why, if you still wonder, after you tell me

307

how you got the name, and I tell you the account of your actions."

I am puzzled and a little scared of something, but I don't know what.

"In Vietnamese, chieu hoi means 'surrender'—"

"Literally, to the Vietnamese, it means 'with open arms.' I may be back here in the Rear, but we were taught that too. Now, I want you to relax and simply tell me the story."

"Yeah, O-OK." *Why am I stuttering again now?* "My squad hit some shit on an ambush, and at that time Two Squad was a bunch of other guys, guys who'd been here awhile, and I was an Effengee. I don't know if I had even gotten shot at yet. And I-I ended up sc-screaming at two gooks who'd already given up. I was st-standing over these gooks and I-I-I would have killed them if they moved b-b-but there they were. I can still see their faces. They're curled up on the ground and-and-and I-I was scared by all the shit and . . . so the dudes in my squad—"

"—gave you the name."

"That's all there is to it, sir."

His bottom yellow teeth come up on the mustache the way an envelope flap seals itself down after you lick it and he shuts both his eyes, then opens his eyes and his mouth at the same time and tells me this:

"You led your squad back to the LZ after Callme got dusted off and you didn't say anything on the way back, Sergeant, and one of your men was still in traumatic shock and you walked behind him, Sergeant, some of the time with your M-16 in his back, and when you got back to the LZ you began screaming for the company commander to come to the wire and you were repeating, continuously, Sergeant, 'ChieufuckingHoi you whole goddamn army,' and you made some threats on your man's life and on the commander's life.

"Do you remember any of that now?"

I don't know. I can't tell if I do or not. I see the scene but I don't know if I am remembering it or seeing it as he tells me. His voice seems far away and I'm looking right at him—my heart flapping like a flag in a stiff wind—feeling queasy and—

"You made threats of a serious nature, Sergeant, and you cannot be allowed to carry a weapon."

Evidently I faint. The rest of that day, probably all of the night that I am asleep, certainly all the time I lie awake sweating through my pants, I try my goddamnedest to remember it. It seems familiar like a dream seems familiar.

It tortures me.

Thinking about it sometimes makes me shake and sometimes makes me completely still as if I am in a woods waiting for a squirrel to move—that still. One of those times when I'm half between sleep and not-sleep, I have a version of the dream, except I am hunting squirrel. But the squirrel is a dink and I lie still, so very still, and I catch sight of him but I don't have a gun and he hangs around the side of a tree trunk looking at me, scampers down toward the ground and looks at me, goes onto a branch directly over my head and looks at me; he chatter-laughs and it sounds like *ch-ch-ch-chieu hoi chieu hoi, ch-ch-ch-ch-ch-chieu hoi.*

After another boring week I get a jeep ride into the base camp and I get a steel pot from the armorer. Then I catch a Slick out over the big base camp guard towers and over some lowlands, and when the mountains tear into the sky I know I'm getting closer. From a long ways off, the way the Z is cut into the trees and eases down the side of the red hill in irregular driplike shapes, it looks like God spilled blood.

D.E.R.O.S.

THINGS SOUND FUNNY. THE BIRD'S MOTOR SOUNDS LIKE it isn't running right. Four or five guys scramble into the Slick after I get off and I am still standing there on the pad like a dumb-ass, like an F.N.G. I don't have anything except my canteen and steel pot. I don't have a gun. *Is that possible? Am I out here without a gun? Somebody will give me one if I need it.*

The bird lifts off behind me. The CO is walking toward me. The goddamn captain is coming. There's somebody with him. I just barely recognize the CO, but I know it's him. One of his shoulders is lower than the other, like he ought to limp, but he doesn't. I know it is stupid and bad luck to salute when you're in the Bush, but I feel like I should. I just about do when he stops in front of me and stands there with his legs apart and his hands behind him.

"Sir. I just came out to say good-bye, sir."

"To me, Sauers?"

"No. Uh, sir. What about Callmeblack?"

"Riggins?"

Riggins? Justin Riggins. Callmeblack's real name.

I start to answer him but he starts talking at the same time.

"I don't have a report on Riggins, Sauers."

This fucker is cold. He's still fighting the war and the

310

only way he knows how to fight is to be a cold sonofabitch. I'm not sorry if I threatened this prick. My cool
comes back. Maybe it's good that I don't have my rifle, or
a frag. I could get a frag easy. The sweat comes out of the
bottom of my hat and runs down my face, and I feel like
the CO is looking at it. He is barely sweating. Maybe that's
his test. If it is, he wins. If he is waiting for me to apolo-
gize, he loses. I'm not going to bring it up. Everything
around us looks frypan hot. There are heat waves coming
off the empty rubber water blivets stacked on one side of
the pad. There is dust on everything. It's the color of eggplant meat, almost. It is incredible to think how hard it was
raining here two months ago. The hooch roofs are covered
by dust too, and the LZ looks like a bunch of rusty burning
barrels turned upside down.

"Sauers, as long as you're on this LZ you are under my
command. You are no longer the squad leader of Two
Squad, Echo Company."

His head looks like an eggplant too.

The Z hasn't gotten any bigger. There aren't new
hooches, but the firing line has been cleared out beyond the
concertina. There are work parties beyond the wire now. I
know they're out there smoking dope. I wonder if the CO
knows they are. Walking around, I feel like some kind of
jack-off outsider, because I don't have a rifle or a ruck. As
I pass the other companies I look for somebody I recognize
but they all look new. Not new, but different.

It doesn't exactly feel like a homecoming, and it feels
stranger when I get to Two Squad's AO and nobody is
there. Either they're out on a hump or they're on a work
party. When I see their rucks I know they must be out
working.

I stand on top of the big hooch to see if I can spot them
on the perimeter, and I notice the guy who was with the
CO. He's leaning against a parapet higher up on the Z,
with his arms folded, sunglasses on. I get the feeling he is

watching me. Fuck it, what do they want me to do, *explain* something?

I flipped out, you assholes. You're wasting your time watching me.

There is a big flock of birds in the trees, on the edge of the tree line. Evidently they are eating the heads of the plants the work parties cut down. There are probably a hundred birds all sizes and several colors.

Then Artillery blows a battery. I dive from where I was standing to behind a hooch wall; before I even hit the ground and roll over I realize what I've done. I think I even heard the firemaster yell "Fire one!" but it doesn't matter whether I heard it or not, because my reaction is to the sound of the guns. When they fire, the concussion rips along the ground like a wave and my hands tremble when I light a cigarette and sit up. I'm back out where I said I wanted to be.

When the guns go off, the flock of birds flies up and makes a circle over the bottom part of the Z, then settles back down. It looks like somebody scattering broken pieces of different-colored bottles.

Now I don't know what I want to do. I don't feel as much at home here as I thought I would. Do I want to go back to the old folks' home? I feel too much out of place. I don't belong here anymore. You can't be a part of this without a gun, so when they took my gun away from me they took away something more. I wonder if they know that.

The hooch is not much changed, but there are some new shelves that hang from string tied to one of the roof joists. Being in it is as different as everything else has been. Even though I helped build this roof, cut down this very log, dragged it through the wire out there that was mud then and is strictly dust now, and even though I filled my share of these sandbags and could probably find a spade mark that I left somewhere in the dirt, it's all somebody else's now. I recognize Murphy's ruck in one corner.

Did I march him in with my gun in his back?

I go back outside and swing up onto the hooch's roof. I don't want to look, but I want to know if anybody is still watching me. Fuck it. I won't be here long.

In the Bush, a lot can happen in a couple of months. In fact, a lot *has* to happen. The squads have to be left up to something near full number, or the squad can't go out. Since Callmeblack and I are both gone, Two Squad must have some new guys, either F.N.G.s or guys they drew out of another squad somewhere. Neither Murphy nor Smith has been out here long enough to be a squad leader, and Bostick and Wilson are so new somebody should still be holding their hands. Funny that the CO made such a point of telling me I was no longer the squad leader. Doesn't the sonofabitch know I couldn't be if I wanted to? Is he stupid or what?

A Shithook comes in and drops coils of concertina outside the perimeter. It stirs up a huge blood-colored cloud of dust as it descends enough to drop its load. Somebody out there has to climb up on the load to unhook the sling. I remember what a fight it is to see your way through that dust. Even from where I am sitting the dust gets into my mouth, behind my teeth. I don't go inside the hooch because I want to watch. I will always be fascinated by these birds, what they can do, how they do it. This giant seems so slow-moving, so deliberate, like even though it has the whole sky to turn around in, it is cramped for space.

One of the first things I want to do when the squad comes back in is get high. I wonder if I could find any dope in the hooch if I looked. But if I looked, it would be like snooping; this isn't my hooch anymore. Even though two months ago I could have looked through anybody's ruck for anything, if I did it now I'd feel like I was doing something wrong.

It is time to go home. I don't have a home here now; not base camp, not the Bush. Only the old folks' home.

Jesus.

■■■■■■■■■■

I MUST HAVE FALLEN ASLEEP. I WAKE UP ALL AT ONCE. There is a whole shitload of flies buzzing around, landing on one thing at a time, then together swarming away from that thing and onto something else. Their collective sound is loud. *Loud enough to wake me up?* They are hovering around a wadded-up sandbag on the other side of the small wall that goes around the steps down to the doorway. They are a small cloud, the size of a new ruck.

Just about the time I decide to go down into the hooch to see if my ruck is laid away down there, I see the squad come through the wire and start walking toward me. I am nervous. I don't feel like anybody's old friend. I don't know what to expect. I don't know what I did.

Rosehips is first. I barely remember him. He's awfully small. I think his rifle is slung over his shoulder and it looks like he has a machete in his hand. He walks like he is high, cocky-like. Then comes Murphy, small too, wearing a Boonie hat, a pair of cut-off ODs, and his boots. Bostick is third, his hair shorter now, and still more blond than cornsilk. Smith is last and dragging behind, juggling two baseballs in one hand. Murphy sees me first.

"Chieu Hoi, *chieu hoi.*"

"You got me." His blue eyes seem to look at every single bit of me at the same time. He is more tanned, and the little scar alongside his eye has more shape than ever, a quarter moon.

"Man," Wilson says, "we didn't think you'd be back out here."

"Why not?" I can't keep the challenge out of my voice, although I don't feel especially bitter.

"Figured you'd sham away the rest of your time, that's

314

all," Murphy answers, and there is authority in his answer. It makes me think he is probably the squad leader now.

"Well, I came out to get high. Any chance of that?"

"Easy duty," Smith says. He tosses the balls to Murphy. They are beat up now, about half the covers are ragged and they are the color of coffee. Murphy throws them to me. Smith goes inside and comes back with a bowl.

"The lifers might be watching me."

"What're they gonna do, send you to the Bush?"

"They took my rifle away. Maybe this time they'll take my pants away."

"No gun? What the fuck is that?"

"It's a long story, bro, and I don't even know the beginning of it, which is why I'm out here in the first place, to find out. I guess I'm dangerous with a gun in my hand."

"Did you find out anything about Callme? They don't tell us shit." I first flash that Murphy asks me just to change the subject, but then I know better. It is hard to keep remembering how tight we all were. At the same time, it's hard to forget. It is difficult to define our relationship now, and I suspect that these guys feel that too.

"Nothing, except he was sent to Japan. I've been in an old folks' home."

"Say what?"

"I think I've been to the only place in Nam that doesn't have a name. Christ, we name every hill we stay on, but I never heard this place called anything except an evac hospital. It's back near base camp. Evidently it is a nuthouse-like joint."

"Did they lock you in?" Bostick asks.

"They shot me up and tied me down at first."

"Why?"

"That's why I'm out here. I don't know what happened, except they told me I went nuts. You guys tell me."

At first everybody is quiet and I get the hint that they're uncomfortable. I expect Murphy to do the talking, and I look hard at him, ready to hear anything. But Smith starts. He is tossing a ball from one hand to the other and he watches it at first, then he turns to look at me.

"You flipped, man. I guess, anyway. One minute you were OK, and then you were after us."

I take a big hit off the bowl that is coming around and wait for him to go on but I have to urge him.

"After you? After you with what? How?"

"Don't you remember any of this?" Murphy says.

"All I remember is getting Callme's bird in there."

"Well, you just sat down after that. You sat on the ground. None of us knew what to do for a while and we were talking to you but you didn't seem like you heard us. You *looked* all right. I mean, you weren't just staring or anything, but you wouldn't say anything. We couldn't get you to answer us, and we had clearance to come back to the Z and had to get the fuck going."

The first effect of the dope hits. It is like stepping onto an escalator and being taken down one floor, and the hooch seems to grow smaller all of a sudden. We're all inside. I am sitting in the corner farthest from the door. The light around the opening is beginning to change color; evidently the sun is going behind clouds, then coming again, which causes the doorway to look like it is moving.

"Well, I want to know it all. They told me at the old folks' home that I marched you guys back here with my rifle. Is th-th-that true?" Stuttering sneaks up on me.

"You were the closest, Bostick. You tell him," Murphy says.

Murphy and Bostick are sitting on the opposite side of the hooch from me. Rosehips and Omar are on my side. Wilson has his eyes closed but I don't know if he is asleep or not. I get the feeling—it is more than a feeling, I'm sure of this—that these guys have talked about this before. They probably sat right here and reconstructed what went down. But I was a ghost to them then, and I am here now.

Bostick looks nervous as hell. I don't think he ever will grow up. Of all the guys I've met in Nam, except maybe the little white mouse in the old folks' home, Bostick seems the most unlike a GI who belongs in The Nam. I wonder if he'll survive. Now I realize he is afraid of me; I've been staring hard at him, and we never knew each other. It's the familiar Old Guy–F.N.G. confrontation, except this one is loaded with something explosive. I look down between my feet, just to take my eyes off his face. I don't look back up and I tell him to go on.

"You gotta dig this, man," Smith tells me. "The dude only wants to know what happened. Tell him straight up."

I look at Smith, then over at Bostick again. The left half of Bostick's face is in the light from the doorway and the way a certain streak cuts through his hair makes me think of dandelions gone to seed.

"Tell me, dammit."

"You all of a sudden got up off the ground and started cutting point back here, and when we were pretty close you stopped. Then you—you looked crazy then, man, your eyes—you started walking back the other way on the trail we'd just come down and when you got to where I was you stopped. I'll never forget the look on your face, man. You looked scared or something. You said you were gonna make goddamn sure Callme didn't die and you pointed your rifle right in my face. I was shaking like a mutha-fucker because I didn't know if you were gonna shoot me or what and you were calm as hell. You said, '*Chieu hoi,* muthafucker, *chieu hoi.*' I think you flipped out."

I can tell by the way he says it that he doesn't know how much of an understatement it is. *Flipped out? Christ, I guess.* It is scary to listen to this. It is like hearing a story about somebody else who you'd be afraid of if you met, except it is me—or was—that I'm meeting.

"Battle fatigue." Either they all hear me and simply accept the explanation, or nothing I can say would affect them. I am holding the bowl. It is out, and I light it and still hold it. Omar flips two balls and catches them in one hand. He just does it that once. I listen for a minute because I thought I heard a real, live birdcall outside. But there aren't any birds inside an LZ; I imagined it.

"What else?"

"I didn't know what you wanted me to do. I was one scared sonofabitch. So I put my hands up and you told me to walk. I did. Some of the time you were pointing your rifle at me. What would you do?"

"Same fucking thing you did, Bostick. It don't matter who it is with the gun if the gun is pointing at you. I'm sorry I did it. I was nuts. But I want to know all of it."

"When we got back here," Murphy says, looking right at me, his scar the only part of his face that catches the last light, "you knew the guy pulling guard at the wire, and you told him to get on the radio and tell the CO you had a prisoner."

"No shit?"

"No shit. And you told the dude on guard to tell the CO he was a killer. That it wasn't us who were the killers, it was him. Then Smith and Wilson took your gun away and you stood there like your pants were down. We tried to get hold of you but you started swinging. It took four or five of us to get you down. Then a medic shot you up with something and they called a bird. Bostick here, the chickenshit, he started crying."

So now I know.

"I came back to the Bush so's to hear all about it, you know? It was hell not knowing what I did, how I ended up there. I can't say as though I know *why* I did it. It just happened to me. The same way it happened to you guys, it happened to me, except I was the one doing it. I fucking flipped out. I had seen enough, a little too much. A hell of a lot of the guys I've been here with have gotten fucked up, and I just got tired of seeing it."

"Chieu Hoi, we've already figured that out. We don't hold anything against you. You did your time."

"Thanks."

For now, what these guys think is important. It won't be long before I'm back in The World. I don't know what matters there. I'll figure it out. Wilson is snoring.

"What now, dude?"

"Within a couple days I'll leave the field forever, get me a DEROS ride. It's over, Murphy, over as hell. Unless this hooch takes a direct hit while I'm here or my bird falls out of the sky, I'm home."

"Jesus."

"I hear you. It'll happen to you too."

Way up high or way far off is the sound of Nam, the *whump thump-whump* of a helicopter.

● ● ● ● ● ● ● ● ● ● ●

THE NIGHT FIRE WAKES ME EACH AND EVERY TIME FOR THE next three nights. On the fourth morning I am sitting on a parapet when the sun comes. It's a righteous rise: the eastern horizon is a fried egg because there is a round cloud at the bottom of the sky, as yellow as a yolk. The guys who pulled last guard seem to stand up and stretch one at a time as the yolk grows hotter and more orange and the sky gets littered with wispy slices of cloud that I make into orange peels. I hadn't forgotten, but I'm real glad to see such a beauty again. Especially today.

I'll be in The World before that sun comes up ten more times, maybe fewer. A DEROS ride, some time in the Rear. Then, The World: hot baths, cold beer; no bullets, no noise. For a year I've been trying to imagine this sunrise, and now I want *it* to stutter, to hang here. I don't need to cry but I need something like that. I feel emptied. Over

here a guy's friends precede him and the dudes who come
after are something else. It must be a way we protect ourselves, to not love somebody as much when they don't
have as much chance of living as you do.

∎∎▪∎∎∎∎∎∎∎∎

THE SUN ROLLS OUT OF ITS CLOUDY BLANKET AND THE
cloud catches on fire. The line to water begins, a dude at a
time. They come from every direction: over the hill and
down, with a dirty towel around their shoulders, and out
from the holes along the wire, cigarettes stuck in their
faces. And it is the water trailer that gives birth to the
sounds of my last day: a radio hatches Chickenman, a cassette player blows blues into the fiery sky, laughing leaps
out of the final darknesses. It's like I know everybody and
nobody.

I've used enough paint to fill the water trailer, maybe
twice, but I've never had this urge before: I wonder if I can
paint pictures.

I can't remember what a barking dog sounds like. This
time of year the trees are beginning to push leaves out of
their bud sacs. Grandaddy swears you can hear it happen
—he has to have the Reds' game on so loud the radio
vibrates enough to inch across the kitchen counter, but he
can hear the buds break. Maybe I'll go into the woods with
him next week and we'll listen. He'll want me to talk,
though. They'll want to know what the guns sounded like,
and the helicopters. If they want to hear inside my dream
I'm going to lie to them and leave.

There's nothing in my ruck worth saving. When Bostick
waves up I souvenir him the black-and-white good-luck
beads that Callme brought back from R&R. I give them to
him without apologizing for sticking a gun in his back. I
give the rest of them a handshake, a hug, a promise that I'll
write, that broken promise which has always come with

somebody going, and when I get to the pad it is already so hot that my helmet liner skates around my forehead on sweat.

DB101346. The black numbers are on every helicopter the Army flies, but I've never noticed them before. These numbers stand out on the sky like a bare fish hook. My bird.

The padman keeps smoke grenades in a crate. Certain colors mean certain things if he needs that information, and the smoke from the grenade tells the pilot exactly the course of the wind. I need two smokes and I grab one that is yellow and one that is green.

The pilots' helmets look like two walnut shells. Me, maybe ten mermite cans, empty red mail sacks, and a chockful rucksack are the passengers. The ruck probably belongs to somebody who got dusted off. I can tell that it doesn't belong to a grunt—an Arty dude maybe. I sit on the floor and hang my feet out one door. The padman's face appears through the windshield, between the walnut-shell helmets. The padman points back behind the pilots, at me, and one pilot turns partway around. He gives me the peace sign and the bird soon comes up against my ass, hangs there at four feet for a couple seconds, then augers into the sky that no longer had any orange peels in it.

Two Squad is splayed on the hooch roof. The bird climbs and putts toward the shadows. Our shadow is distinct below us. Then the ground comes up like a spread dropcloth, splotches of color and wrinkles of olive drab. I pull the pin on the yellow smoke and we go onto our side —my side—and lie there, a hundred feet above the Z, long enough for the yellow smoke to rise above us. Then the pilot does a jig and I drop the yellow canister into the jungle on the pad side. The pilot circles and dives and climbs once more and I pop the green at the top. The bottom of the bird falls out and we roll left, then right, then left, and hover an instant so I can see the green smoke trail through the air like willows along a crooked river. I drop the canister on the other side of the LZ, so my last look is the bald hill growing two tufts of color out its ears.

There is no sound in the clouds except the crazy dangerous music of the bird: *da-da-da-dum.*

"We can't all be heroes. Somebody has to sit on the curb and clap as they go by."

—Will Rogers

About the Author

Don Bodey is a Vietnam veteran. An itinerant carpenter, he lives in several places with his son, Sky, and Sky's mother, Clare.

MOVING, ACTION-FILLED WAR STORIES OF UNMISTAKABLE AUTHENTICITY